3

环境与景观

environment &
landscape architecture

ela
annals

ela annals 3

Publisher Whee-Young Oh 오휘영
Editor ela Korea Editorial team 환경과조경 편집부
Project manager Sang Baek Park 박상백
Editorial Design Byung Ho Lim 임병호

Address 529-5, Munbal-dong, Paju-si, Gyeonggi-do, South Korea(#413-756)
경기도 파주시 문발동 파주출판도시 529-5 환경과조경사옥
TEL 82-31-955-4966~8 **FAX** 82-31-955-4969
e-mail klam@chol.com **http://www.ela-korea.com**

Published by ela Korea, Jokyung Publishing
환경과조경, 도서출판 조경
First Published April 19, 2013
Fixed price $80

contents

Works of Landscape Architecture

Park
08 Music Park in Seville
20 Almere Mandelapark
32 South Pointe Park
46 Railroad Park
62 The CityDeck
72 Park am Gleisdreieck
83 Toronto Central Waterfront
92 Lincoln Park
100 Uptown Normal Circle

Garden
112 Gardens by the Bay
124 Side Effect
136 Sensational Garden

Plaza
148 Urban Redevelopment of the Plaza del Milenio
160 Erie Street Plaza
168 MediaCityUK Exterior Spaces
178 Plaza Ricard Viñes

Public Space
188 Burbank Water and Power Magnolia Power Plant Campus
202 Gubei Pedestrian Promenade
214 D-Cube City
230 Marina Bay Sands Integrated Resort

2012 ASLA Professional Awards

General Design
246 Qunli Stormwater Park
252 Canada's Sugar Beach
258 Lafayette Greens
264 Quarry Garden in Shanghai Botanical Garden
270 Arizona State University Polytechnic Campusn
276 200 5th Avenue
282 Powell Street Promenade
288 Tudela-Culip (Club Med) Restoration Project
294 Shangri La Botanical Garden
300 Winnipeg Skating Shelters
306 National 9/11 Memorial
312 Sunnylands Center & Gardens

Residential Design
318 Drs. Julian and Raye Richardson Apartments
320 Quaker Smith Point Residence
322 Quattro by Sansiri
324 New Century Garden: A Garden of Water and Light
326 Malinalco Private Residence
328 Maple Hill Residence
330 Reordering Old Quarry
332 Urban Spring

334 **Analysis and Planning**
338 **Communications**
339 **Research**
339 **Landmark Award**

340 **INDEX**

Works of Lan Arc

PARK

Music Park in Seville
Costa Fierros Arquitectos, Seville

Almere Mandelapark
Karres en Brands, Almere

South Pointe Park
Hargreaves Associates, Miami

Railroad Park
Tom Leader Studio, Birmingham

The CityDeck
Stoss Landscape Urbanism, Green Bay

Park am Gleisdreieck
Atelier LOIDL, Berlin

Toronto Central Waterfront
West 8 urban design & landscape architecture, Toronto

Lincoln Park
West 8 urban design & landscape architecture, Miami

Uptown Normal Circle
Hoerr Schaudt Landscape Architects, Normal

GARDEN

Gardens by the Bay
Grant Associates, Singapore

Side Effect
Amir Lotan, Bat Yam

Sensational Garden
Nabito Architects and Partners, Frosinone

PLAZA

Urban Redevelopment of the Plaza del Milenio
EXP ARCHITECTES and DAD ARQUITECTURA, Valladolid

Erie Street Plaza
Stoss Landscape Urbanism, Milwaukee

MediaCityUK Exterior Spaces
Gillespies, Salford

Plaza Ricard Viñes
Benedetta Tagliabue, Lleida

PUBLIC SPACE

Burbank Water and Power Magnolia Power Plant Campus
AHBE Landscape Architects, Burbank

Gubei Pedestrian Promenade
SWA Los Angeles Office, Shanghai

D-Cube City
Oikosdesign landscape + architecture, Seoul

Marina Bay Sands Integrated Resort
PWP Landscape Architecture, Singapore

dscape
hitecture

Music Park in Seville
Almere Mandelapark
South Pointe Park
Railroad Park
The CityDeck

Park

Park am Gleisdreieck
Toronto Central Waterfront
Lincoln Park
Uptown Normal Circle

Music Park in Seville

Costa Fierros Arquitectos

Architects _ Costa Fierros Arquitectos - Sara Tavares Costa, Pablo F. Díaz-Fierros

Collaborators _ David Breva, Paula Ferreira, Pedro Rito Nobre, David Ampe, Elena González, Rosario Alcantarilla, Sergio González, Cristina Rubiño, Alejandro Rodríguez

Landscape _ Erneato Fernández Sanmartín, Sara Tavres Costa

Location _ Barrio de la Música, Seville, Spain

Build surface area _ 32.487㎡

Construction _ 2011. 11

Photograph _ Pablo F. Díaz-Fierros

Text & Material _ Costa Fierros Arquitectos, Pablo Díaz-Fierros, Fotografía de Arquitectura

The Park is located in an existing degraded area, lacking of facilities, and known historically as a land dividing the nearby quarters (Aguilas and Los Prunos neighbourhoods) and isolating their inhabitants
공원은 현재 시설이 부족하고, 역사적으로 주변 구역(아길라스와 로스 프루노스 주변)을 분리하고 주민들을 고립시키는 땅으로 알려진 곳에 위치한다

In the East side, the level difference is solved with retaining walls embracing and protecting the plazas at the surrounding neighbourhoods levels. There is a lift and an escalator next to the station entrance for accessibility

동쪽 면에서는 주변의 높이에 맞춰 광장을 둘러싸고 보호하는 지지벽으로 높이 문제를 해결했다. 역 입구 옆에는 엘리베이터와 에스컬레이터가 있다

세비야의 음악 공원

세비야의 음악 공원은 비세야의 바리오 데 네스트라 세뇨라 델 아길라Barrio de Nuestra Señora del Águila와 바라오 데 라 무지카Barrio de la Música 사이에 위치한다.

공원은 현재 시설이 부족하고, 역사적으로 주변 구역 아길라스와 로스 프루노스 주변을 분리하고 주민들을 고립시키는 땅으로 알려진 곳에 위치한다.

음악 공원은 도시 재생과 세비야의 지하 인프라스트럭처 작업과 연결된 통합의 측면에서 매우 독특한 마스터플랜을 갖는다. 공원 구역은 32,487㎡이고, 공원 중앙에 있는 코체라 역의 접근과 역 양쪽에 위치한 주택들의 연결을 보장한다.

새롭게 조성된 경관은 주변을 산책하거나 공원의 설계된 구역에서 휴식을 즐기는 것을 돕고, 다양한 도시의 여정을 지속시켜 이를 보다 편리하고 모두에게 접근을 용이하게 한다.

여기에는 다시 살아나 내부적으로 잘 연결되는 더욱 화합하는 도시, 그리고 보다 인간적이고 양질의 옥외 공간을 제공하여 주민들에게 보다 나은 삶의 질을 제공한다는 이중의 목적이 있다.

공원은 완만한 경사를 따라 역의 높이에 이르는 남북 산책로를 따라 구성되었다. 다른 횡단 순환로가 주요 산책로와 주변의 거리와 광장을 연결한다.

동쪽 면에서는 주변의 높이에 맞춰 광장을 둘러싸고 보호하는 지지벽으로 높이 문제를 해결했다. 역 입구 옆에는 엘리베이터와 에스컬레이터가 있다.

서쪽 면에서는 지하 터널과 평행하고 커브 자체가 서쪽 중앙 입구를 향하는 램프를 만드는 지지벽으로 레벨 차이를 해결했다. 아길라 마리나와 아길라 데 오로 스트리트의 보행로 사이의 모퉁이에 또 다른 엘리베이터가 있다.

세라믹 타일이나 석회석과 화강암 자갈 같은 최상급의 포장재를 사용하여, 패턴이 반복되어 공원의 여러 구역을 연결하는 기하학을 형성한다. 이러한 패턴은 세비야 알카자르 궁전의 '인형의 정원Patio de Muñecas'에 있는 세라믹 패턴에서 영감을 받았다.

The park is organized along a North-South promenade that reaches the station level with a gentle slope. Other transversal circulations connect the main promenade with the surrounding streets and plazas

공원은 완만한 경사를 따라 역의 높이에 이르는 남북 산책로를 따라 구성되었다. 다른 횡단 순환로가 주요 산책로와 주변의 거리와 광장을 연결한다

The new landscape created helps to enjoy a walk around it or having a rest in the designated areas of the park, and the continuity of the different urban itineraries, making them more convenient and accessible for everybody
새롭게 조성된 경관은 주변을 산책하거나 공원의 설계된 구역에서 휴식을 즐기는 것을 돕고, 다양한 도시의 여정을 지속시켜 이를 보다 편리하고 모두에게 접근을 용이하게 한다

Music Park in Seville

Plot located between Barrio de Nuestra Señora del Águila and Barrio de la Música in Sevilla.

The Park is located in an existing degraded area, lacking of facilities, and known historically as a land dividing the nearby quarters (Aguilas and Los Prunos neighbourhoods) and isolating their inhabitants.

Parque de la Musica is a unique masterplan in terms of urban renovation and integration linked to Sevilla Underground infraestructure works. The Park area is 32.487m^2 and ensures accessibility to Cocheras Station, located at the centre of the Park, and the connectivity between the houses located at both sides of the station.

The new landscape created helps to enjoy a walk around it or having a rest in the designated areas of the park, and the continuity of the different urban itineraries, making them more convenient and accessible for everybody.

There is a dual purpose: a more cohesive city, regenerated and with better internal connections, and providing a more human and better quality outdoor space and therefore better quality of life for their inhabitants.

The park is organized along a North-South promenade that reaches the station level with a gentle slope. Other transversal circulations connect the main promenade with the surrounding streets and plazas.

In the East side, the level difference is solved with retaining walls embracing and protecting the plazas at the surrounding neighbourhoods levels. There is a lift and an escalator next to the station entrance for accessibility.

In the West side, the level difference is resolved with a retaining wall that goes parallel to the underground tunnel and curves itself creating the ramp directing to the main West entrance. There is another lift for access at the corner between the pedestrian street Aguila Marina and Aguila de Oro Street.

First quality pavement materials have been used: ceramic tiles, cobblestone of lime and granite stones. The patterns are repeated creating a geometry that connects all the different areas in the park. This pattern is inspired in an existing ceramic pattern in the Patio de Munecas from the Reales Alcazares in Sevilla.

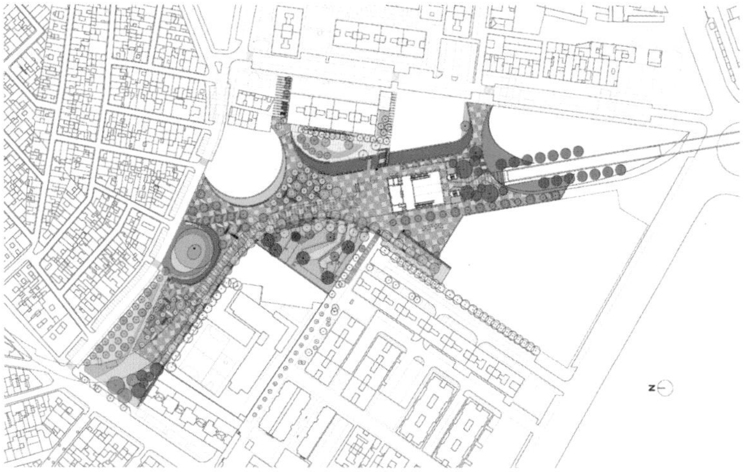

General Plan

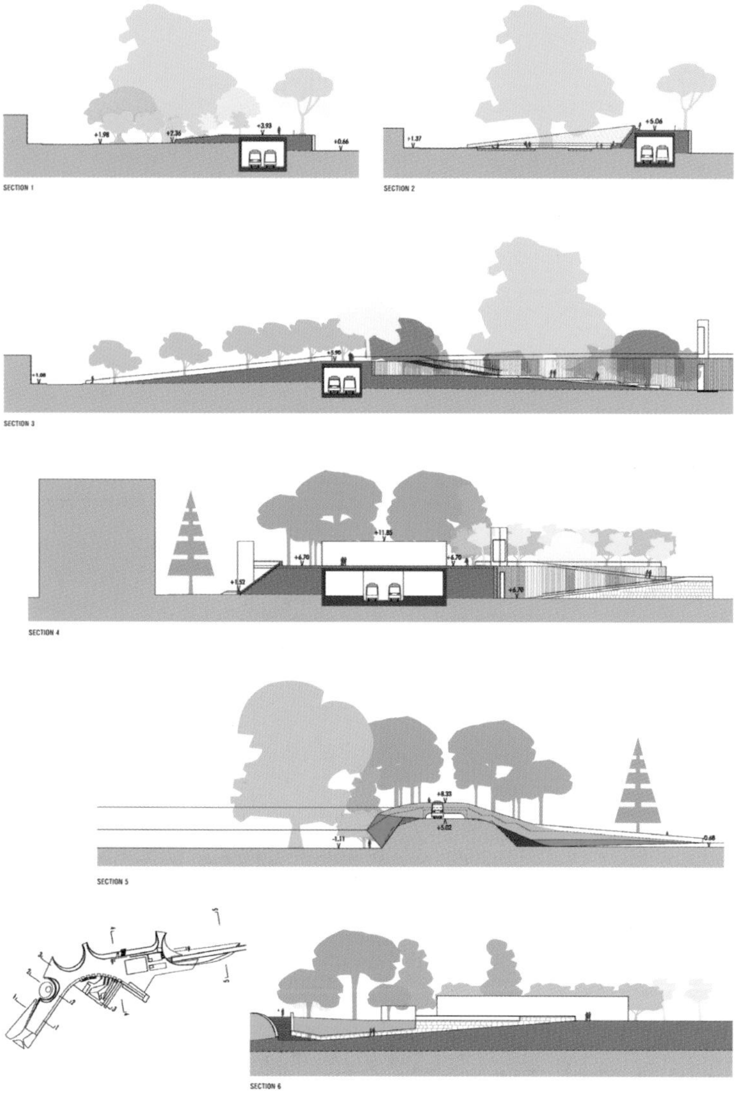

Sections

First quality pavement materials have been used: ceramic tiles, cobblestone of lime and granite stones. The patterns are repeated creating a geometry that connects all the different areas in the park
세라믹 타일이나 석회석과 화강암 자갈 같은 최상급의 포장재를 사용하여, 패턴이 반복되어 공원의 여러 구역을 연결하는 기하학을 형성한다

Parque de la Musica is a unique masterplan in terms of urban renovation and integration linked to Sevilla Underground infraestructure works. The Park area is 32.487m^2 and ensures accessibility to Cocheras Station, located at the centre of the Park, and the connectivity between the houses located at both sides of the station

음악 공원은 도시 재생과 세비야의 지하 인프라스트럭처 작업과 연결된 통합의 측면에서 매우 독특한 마스터플랜을 갖는다. 공원 구역은 32,487㎡이고, 공원 중앙에 있는 코체라 역의 접근과 역 양쪽에 위치한 주택들의 연결을 보장한다

Almere Mandelapark

Karres en Brands

카레스 앤 브랜즈Karres en Brands가 설계한 공원 및 광장이 알미르역 인근의 신규 상업지구에 완공되어 문을 열었다. 이 상업지구에는 투자업체 유로커머스Eurocommerce가 개발한 세 동의 사무용 건물이 자리 잡고 있는데, 그 높이가 120미터로 플레볼란트Flevoland 지방에서는 가장 높은 빌딩의 지위를 차지하고 있다. 공원은 이들 사무용 건물에 부속된 지하주차장 위에, 광장은 빌딩과 역 사이를 연결하는 공간에 위치하고 있다. 이 지역은 네덜란드에서 가장 젊은 도시인 알미르를 위해 렘 콜하스Rem Koolhass가 마련한 마스터플랜 '인스턴트 스카이라인Instant Skyline'의 한 축이기도 하다. 카레스 앤 브랜즈는 이처럼 완벽하게 인공적인 주변 환경을 바탕으로 '인스턴트 아이덴티티Instant Identity'를 구축하고 있다.

공원은 지하 4층 규모 주차장 두 곳의 지붕 위에 건립되었는데, 200미터 길이의 이 공원은 네덜란드 내에서 가장 큰 규모의 옥상공원이다. 분수 및 연못, 잔디밭, 다년생 식물, 그리고 꽃이 피는 관목 등으로 이루어진 이 공원은 극도로 도시화된 주변 환경 속에서 녹색 오아시스로서의 역할을 맡고 있다. 공원을 건물 꼭대기에서 내려다보면 마치 계절에 따라 그 색을 달리하는 녹색 패치워크를 떠올리게 된다. 일렬로 식재된 잘 자란 나무들은 공원이 지닌 시각적, 공간적 특성을 오롯이 드러내고 있다. 공원의 북쪽 언저리를 따라 자리 잡은 200미터 길이의 연못은 공원에 대한 관심을 환기시킨다. 테라조terrazzo 아스팔트로 만들어진 산책로는 끊김없고 매끈한 표면을 자랑한다.

공원과 역 사이에 만들어진 광장은 보행로를 적절히 활용함으로써 이들 두 공간을 적절히 연결해주고 있다. 여러 가지 보도 포장재들을 바코드 패턴으로 결합해 역과 도심에서 볼 수 있는 자연석과 공원에 사용된 테라조 아스팔트 등을 모두 만나볼 수 있게 하였다.

A park and a square designed by Karres en Brands have been completed in the new business district near Almere train station. The new district includes three office towers developed by the investor Eurocommerce, which are the highest in Flevoland at a height of 120 meters. The park is situated above the underground car parking for the office towers, while the square mediates the area between the towers and the train station. This area is part of a masterplan by Rem Koolhaas for Almere, an "Instant Skyline" defines the edge of the youngest city in the Netherlands. Karres and Brands adds an "Instant Identity" in this completely artificial context.

The park is situated on the roof of two four-layered underground parking garages. With its 200 meter length, it's the largest rooftop park in the Netherlands. The park is a green oasis in a highly urban environment, a landscape with water features, grasses, perennials and flowering shrubs. Seen from top of the towers, the park shows itself as a green patchwork that changes color throughout the seasons. An avenue of mature plane trees defines a visual and spatial edge of the park. A 200 meter long pond runs along the northern edge of the park, drawing attention to the scale of the park. The paths are made of terrazzo asphalt, creating a continuous and seamless surface.

The square created between the park and station mediates between these two areas by the treatment of the pavement. Several paving materials are combined in a bar code pattern, bringing together the natural stone of the station and city center and the terrazzo asphalt in the park.

The park is a green oasis in a highly urban environment

이 공원은 극도로 도시화된 주변 환경 속에서 녹색 오아시스로서의 역할을 맡고 있다

Landscape Architects _ Karres en Brands (Bart Brands, Jeroen Marseille, Joost de Natris, Paul Portheine, Uta Krause, Carlie Young, Annalen Grüss)

Architecture _ Dam and Partners, ZZDP, Cie Architects.

Client _ Almere City Council

Location _ Former Mandela Park, Almere, The Netherlands

Area _ 3.3 hectares

Design _ 2006 ~ 2010

Construction _ 2010 ~ 2011

Photograph _ Francois Hendrickx

Text & Meterial _ Karres en Brands

Seen from top of the towers, the park shows itself as a green patchwork that changes color throughout the seasons

건물 꼭대기에서 내려다보면 마치 계절에 따라 그 색을 달리하는 녹색 패치워크가 떠오른다

Master Plan

A 200 meter long pond runs along the northern edge of the park

공원의 북쪽 언저리를 따라 자리 잡은 200미터 길이의 연못

The park is situated on the roof of two four-layered underground parking garages

공원은 지하 4층 규모 주차장 두 곳의 지붕 위에 건립되었다

The paths are made of terrazzo asphalt
테라조 아스팔트로 만들어진 산책로

South Pointe Park creates an animated and ecologically sensitive community park in lively and flamboyant South Beach

사우스 포인트 파크는 활기차고 화려한 사우스 비치에 생기 넘치고 생태적으로 민감한 커뮤니티 공원을 창조하였다

South Pointe Park

Hargreaves Associates

다양한 도시 공원 프로그램과 지역 정원, 회복된 자생 서식지의 통합, 그리고 도심 동선체계와의 연결을 통해, 그동안 잘 이용되지 않던 이 공원은 새롭게 재생되어 주변과 지역의 명소로 변모했다. 도시와 크루즈선의 뱃길과 해변이라는 세 양상을 결합하여 문화적, 프로그램적, 환경적 요구사항을 중첩시키는 해결책을 통해 앞으로 다가올 수십 년 동안 마이애미의 오픈 스페이스 라이프에 기여할 중심지가 되었다.

The revitalization of this underutilized public park transforms it into a neighborhood and regional destination through the integration of diversified urban park programs, regional gardens and restored native habitats, and the connection with urban circulation systems. By unifying its three edges – urban, cruise ship passage and beach – it becomes a center that, through the resolution of overlapping cultural, programmatic and environmental requirements, will contribute to the open space life in Miami for decades to come.

Design _ Hargreaves Associates, Inc.
Local Landscape Architects _ Savino Millmer Design Studio
Architects _ William Lane Architects
Location _ Miami Beach, Florida, USA
Area _ 89,000㎡
Completion _ 2011
Photograph _ Courtesy of Hargreaves Associates
Text & Material _ Hargreaves Associates

사우스 포인트 파크는 활기차고 화려한 사우스 비치South Beach에 생기 넘치고 생태적으로 민감한 커뮤니티 공원을 창조하였다. 공원은 대서양 해안에 있는 비스케인 만으로 들어가는 인공의 작은 만인 가버먼트 컷Government Cut을 따라 현존하는 19에이커 면적의 공원을 재설계한 것이다. 현재 22에이커의 공원은 두 개의 상응하는 길인 서펀틴 워크Serpentine Walk와 컷 워크Cut Walk를 따라 길게 자리 잡고 있어, 중요한 지역적 연결과 가버먼트 컷과 대서양을 향한 경관을 제공한다. 길들은 비스케인 만 해안을 가로지르는 베이 워크Baywalk와 대서양 쪽으로 접근하게 하는 비치 워크Beach Walk와 모두 연결되어 있다. 가버먼트 컷을 따라 놓인 워터프론트 산책로인 1,800피트 길이의 선형의 컷워크Cutwalk는 공원을 길게 가로지르며 공원의 경사보다 12~18도 정도로 솟아올라, 기준선Datum의 역할을 한다. 길의 높이는 여기에 조각 작품과 같은 무게감을 부여하고, 이를 공원의 표면과 분리시킨다. 이를 구성하는 도미니카 산호석화석화된 산호로 만들어진 돌의 물성은 인접한 바다의 자연적 과정을 암시한다. 공원에서 길은 오브제인 동시에 선으로 인식되는 한편, 길 위에서의 경험은 관람자의 느낌을 고양한다. 이러한 길은 산책로의 연극성을 조장하고, 비스케인 만을 오가는 거대한 크루즈 선을 위한 이상적인 조망 플랫폼을 제공한다.

South Pointe Park creates an animated and ecologically sensitive community park in lively and flamboyant South Beach. The park is a redesign of an existing 19 acre park along Government Cut, an artificial inlet to Biscayne Bay at the Atlantic Ocean coast. The now 22 acre park positions two corresponding circulation paths – the Serpentine Walk and the Cut Walk – across its length to provide critical regional connections and views out to Government Cut and the Atlantic Ocean. The paths connect to both the Baywalk that traverses the Biscayne Bay coast, and the Beach Walk which provides access along the Atlantic Ocean. The 1,800 foot long linear Cutwalk, a waterfront promenade along Government Cut, acts as a datum, rising between 12-18° above the grade of the park across its length. The height of the path gives it the heft of a sculptural object and sets it apart from the surface of the park. Constructed from Dominican Keystone, a stone of fossilized coral, the materiality suggests the natural processes of the adjacent sea. From the park, the path is perceived both as object and line, while the experience on the path heightens the sense of spectatorship. This pathway encourages the theater of the promenade, and provides the ideal viewing platform for the massive cruise ships entering and leaving Biscayne Bay.

The park also features three areas of open lawn which support free and flexible program

공원에는 자유롭고 유연한 프로그램을 지원하는 세 개의 야외 풀밭도 있다

A seatwall amphitheater creates an informal staging area and seating overlooking the water playground

계단식 관람석은 물놀이장을 내려다보는 비격식적인 공연 구역과 좌석을 창조한다

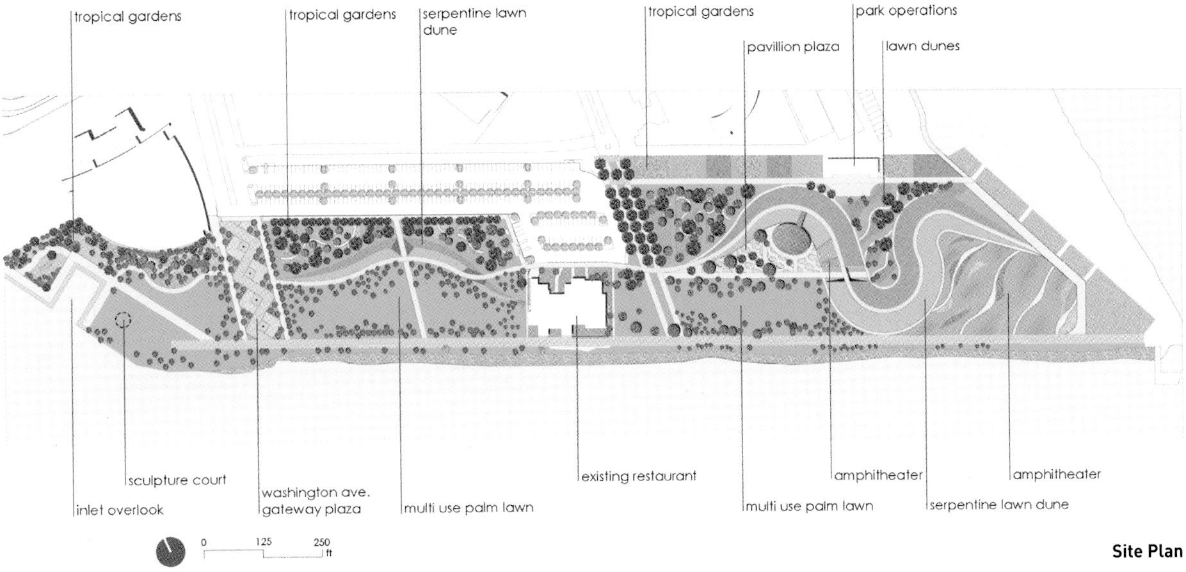
tropical gardens
tropical gardens
serpentine lawn dune
tropical gardens
park operations
pavillion plaza
lawn dunes
sculpture court
inlet overlook
washington ave. gateway plaza
multi use palm lawn
existing restaurant
amphitheater
multi use palm lawn
amphitheater
serpentine lawn dune
0
125
250
ft

Site Plan

컷워크의 강력한 선적 움직임과 대조적으로 한가롭게 굽이진 구불구불한 지형이 대서양 비치 워크에서 시작하여, 대서양을 향한 드라마틱한 경관을 볼 수 있도록 솟아 올라있는데, 이는 파빌리온 구조물의 꼭대기로 접근하고, 베이 워크와 만날 때까지 서쪽으로 이어진다. 지형은 이를 따라가는 활기찬 움직임을 만들고, 끊임없이 변화하는 움직임의 시각적인 경험은 생생하고 매우 재미있다. 지형의 뒤틀림은 작은 정원 구역에서 공원을 관통하는 모티프로 반복된다. 구불구불한 지형의 해안 쪽에 있는 구부러진 띠 형태의 자생 사구 식재는 안쪽 경사지의 추상적인 사구 지형 및 야자수와 대조된다. 자생 지피식물과 야자, 낙엽수로 이루어진 해안가 해먹 식재가 있는 작은 정원 구역의 지형은 구불구불한 길을 반복한다. 하층에 풀과 양치식물이 있는 야자나무 숲은 공원의 북쪽 경계를 따라 도시적 맥락에 대한 완충지를 형성한다. 커다란 하드스케이프 입구 광장을 통해 워싱턴 애비뉴와 오션 드라이브라는 두 주요 가로를 공원으로 연장하는 디자인은 공원을 도시 조직 속으로 통합시킨다.

공원 내에는 카페와 시설이 있는 파빌리온이 휴식 장소를 형성한다. 계단식 관람석은 물놀이장을 내려다보는 비격식적인 공연 구역과 좌석을 창조한다. 또한 공원에는 자유롭고 유연한 프로그램을 지원하는 세 개의 야외 풀밭도 있다. 이 풀밭 구역에는 활발한 활동을 견디며 염분에도 강한 잔디를 심었고, 열대성 폭우 후에 물을 저장하도록 설계되었다. 대상지에 있던 다 자란 나무들은 공사기간 동안 가식되었다가 풀밭에 다시 심어져, 공원 개장과 동시에 즉각적인 시각적 효과를 얻었다. 도시의 계속 진행 중인 공원 관리에 필요한 수익을 제공하는 현재의 레스토랑을 공원과 통합하는 것도 또 다른 디자인 도전이었다. 차량 접근과 레스토랑에 가까운 주차장을 확보하기 위해, 도심 쪽 출입구가 끝부분에 만들어졌다. 또한 공원 내부에 레스토랑 프로그램을 수용하는 한편, 공원의 순환을 강조하는 야외 다이닝 테라스도 컷워크 옆에 마련되었다.

In counterpoint to the strong linear move of the Cutwalk, a serpentine landform with leisurely twists and turns begins at the Atlantic Ocean Beach Walk, rises up to allow dramatic views out to the Atlantic Ocean, and access to the top of the pavilion structure and continues west until it meets the Bay Walk. The landform encourages spirited movement along it, and the heightened experience of an ever-changing visual field of movement is enlivened and enthralling. The twisting of the landform is echoed as a motif throughout the park in smaller garden areas. Sinuous bands of native dune plantings on the ocean side of the serpentine landform are contrasted with abstracted dune landforms and palm trees on the inside slope of the serpentine. A smaller garden area of coastal hammock plantings of native ground covers, palms and deciduous trees echo the twisting path of the landform. A bosque of palms with understory grasses and ferns creates a buffer to the urban context along the northern edge of the park. The design integrates the park into the urban fabric by extending two major streets – Washington Avenue and Ocean Drive – into the park with generous hardscape entry plazas.

At the interior of the park a pavilion with café and facilities creates a point of rest. A seatwall amphitheater creates an informal staging area and seating overlooking the water playground. The park also features three areas of open lawn which support free and flexible program. These areas of lawn are planted with salt tolerant turfgrasses to withstand active use and are engineered to retain water after tropical storm events. Mature trees from the site were stored during construction and then replanted on the lawn, achieving an immediate visual impact at the opening of the park. Another design challenge was to integrate the existing restaurant within the park as it provides revenue for the city''s ongoing maintenance of the park. In order to bring vehicular access and parking close to the restaurant, the design creates an urban entrance edge. Also outdoor dining terraces flank the Cut Walk, emphasizing the circulation of the park while accommodating the restaurant programming within it.

At the interior of the park a pavilion with café and facilities creates a point of rest
공원 내에는 카페와 시설이 있는 파빌리온이 휴식 장소를 형성한다

From the park, the path is perceived both as object and line, while the experience on the path heightens the sense of spectatorship

공원에서 길은 오브제인 동시에 선으로 인식되는 한편, 길 위에서의 경험은 관람자의 느낌을 고양한다

지속가능한 디자인과 재생하는 식재

프로젝트는 민감한 해안 수계에 바로 인접해 있고, 우수를 모아 거두어들이는 통합체계를 포함한다. 22에이커의 대상지에 내리는 빗물의 거의 대부분이 수집되어 대상지에 유입된다. 플로리다 남부의 계절성 아열대 폭우에 대비하기 위해, 비가 조금 내릴 때 부지 내 경사를 활용하여 지표면에 흐르는 빗물을 자생 식물이 식재된 보다 넓은 지역으로 유도하는데, 이는 빗물이 스며들게 하여 전통적 배수구조에 의존하는 것을 최소화한다. 25년 혹은 그 이상 동안, 풀밭 지역은 주입 벽을 통해 깊은 대수층을 다시 채우는 일시적인 저류소의 역할을 하게 되므로 빗물이 대양이나 만, 작은 만으로 바로 유입되는 것을 방지한다.

식재 디자인 컨셉은 공원의 다양한 프로그램 활용을 반영하는 한편, 이러한 공원 공간을 규정하는 단순하면서도 강력한 시각적 언어를 창출한다. 즉각적인 시각적 효과를 얻기 위해, 기존의 450그루 이상의 나무와 야자수가 현장 묘목원에 가식되었다가 주요 공사가 완성된 뒤 다시 옮겨졌다. 공원의 활발한 레크리에이션 구역에는 가뭄과 염분에 내성이 있는 잔디인 씨쇼어 파스팔룸Seashore Paspalum을 심었고, 비정형으로 모아 심은 토종 사발야자Sabal Palms와 코코넛야자Coconut Palms로 둘러싸여 있다. 해안 쪽을 따라, 일련의 인공 사구와 패각암 길이 시 오트Sea Oats와 갯메꽃Railroad Vine, 게일라디아Gaillardia, 고삼Necklace Pod, 유카Yucca 종을 포함한 토종/내건성 해안 식물 군집 사이로 나아간다.

해변으로 가는 북쪽 산책로를 따라 식재된 일련의 숲은 근처의 주택 개발 경관을 가려주고, 보다 비정형으로 식재된 해먹 구역의 토종 서식지를 증가시키도록 설계되었다. 오션 드라이브 프로미네이드Ocean Drive Promenade에는 투종 아메리카 버드나무Green Buttonwoods를 심었고, 사이사이에는 꽃이 피는 토종 지피 식물을 띠 모양으로 번갈아 심었다.

Sinuous bands of native dune plantings on the ocean side of the serpentine landform are contrasted with abstracted dune landforms and palm trees on the inside slope of the serpentine

구불구불한 지형의 해안 쪽에 있는 구부러진 띠 형태의 자생 사구 식재는 안쪽 경사지의 추상적인 사구 지형 및 야자수와 대조를 이룬다

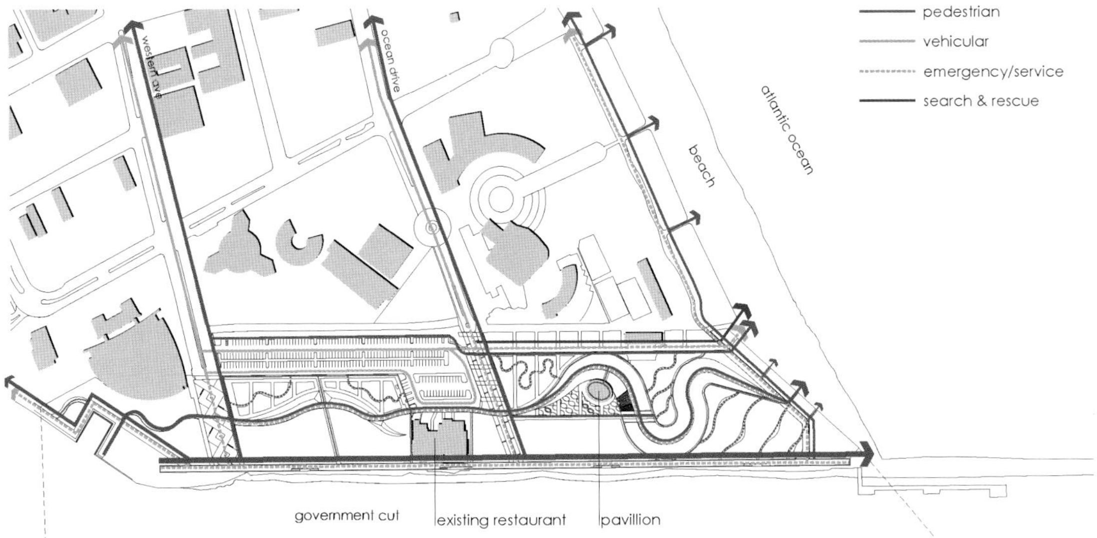

A. Urban Context

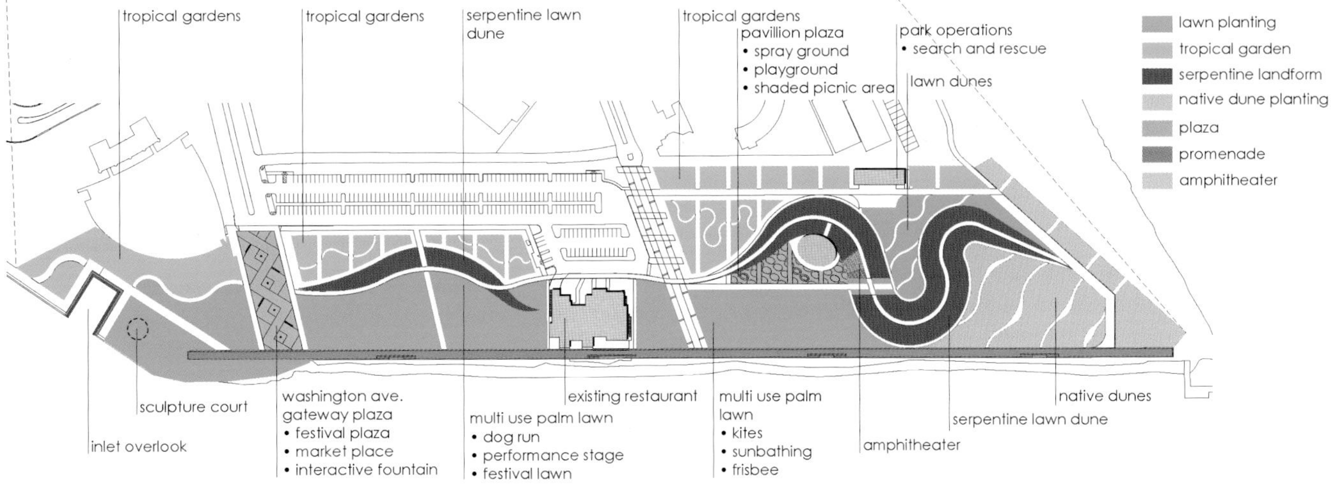

B. Landscape Type & Programs

Sustainability Design & Regenerative Planting

Given the project's immediate adjacency to sensitive coastal hydrology and includes an integrated system of rainwater collection and harvesting. Nearly all the rainwater that falls on the 22-acre site is harvested and retained on site. To address the seasonal sub-tropical rainfalls of south Florida, site grading was utilized to direct surface flow during small rain events into large areas of native plantings, which allow for infiltration and to minimize reliance on traditional drainage structures. During 25-year or greater storm events, lawn areas serve as temporary detention basins that replenish deep aquifers (through injection wells) and thereby prevent stormwater from entering the Ocean, Bay or Inlet.

The planting design concept reflects the park's various program uses while creating a simple and powerful visual language to define these park spaces. To achieve an immediate visual impact, over 450 existing trees and palms were transplanted to an on-site nursery then relocated once major construction was completed. The park's active recreation zones were planted with Seashore Paspalum, a drought and salt tolerant grass, and embraced by an informal massing of native Sabal Palms and Coconut Palms. Along the ocean side, a series of man-made dunes and coquina shell paths lead through masses of native/xeric coastal vegetation, including Sea Oats, Railroad Vine, Gaillardia, Necklace Pod and Yucca species.

Along the north promenade to the Beach, a series of planted bosques buffers the view both to and from the adjacent residential development, and is designed to augment the native habitat of the more informally planted hammock areas. The Ocean Drive Promenade is planted with native Green Buttonwoods, and alternating bands of flowering native groundcovers.

The paths connect to both the Baywalk that traverses the Biscayne Bay coast, and the Beach Walk which provides access along the Atlantic Ocean
길들은 비스케인 만 해안을 가로지르는 베이워크와 대서양 쪽으로 접근하게 하는 비치 워크와 모두 연결되어 있다

Railroad Park

Tom Leader Studio

10년간의 발전

이 공원은 버밍햄시 도시계획과에 의해 세밀하고 전략적인 연구의 혜택을 받았다. 이는 전체 도심에 대한 ULI의 연구에 이은 성장과 개선을 위한 핵심 계획을 규정하는 UDA의 새로운 도심 마스터플랜을 포함한다. 이 대상지의 주요 도심 공원이 도심의 남쪽 절반 부분의 성장과 활성화에 기여할 것이라는 합의가 이 작업에서 생겨났다.

버밍햄은 부유하거나 유력한 도시는 아니다. 사실, 여기는 앨라배마 밖의 사람들에게는 시민 평등권 투쟁의 장으로 가장 잘 알려져 있을 것이다. 이 도시는 다른 많은 도시들이 그러했듯 지난 수십 년 동안 도심의 소매 중심지를 텅 비게 하거나 충분히 사용되지 않게 하는 교외로의 탈출을 경험했다. 이러한 현상들은 중요한 일들을 조직하고 실행하는 능력뿐만 아니라, 역사와 교외 이주의 관점에서도 극복해야 할 것이 많다는 인식을 하게 하였다. 오랫동안 논의된 이 공원의 조성은 그런 생각을 극적으로 뒤집었고, 도시 전체가 이제는 자신들 스스로 재생시켜 나갈 수 있음을 확인시켜 주었다. 레일로드 파크가 개장한 4개월 동안, 웨스트엔드West end에는 마이너리그 야구장 부지가 확보되어 설계되었고 버밍햄 배론스(마이너리그 야구팀)를 교외에서 돌아오게 하였다, 이스트엔드East end에는 '문화 용광로The Cultural Furnace'를 위한 국내 디자인 공모전이 진행 중이다아래 설명 참조. 바비큐를 즐기는 도시에서 피트니스 센터들이 생겨나고, 다락방 개조가 공원 주변으로 우후죽순으로 증가하였으며, 이보다 더욱 중요한 것은, 공원이 도시 전체에서 여러 인종이 통합되고, 가장 많이 사용되는 공간이 되었다는 점이다. 다행히도, 모든 이가 이 공원에서 환영받는다는 기분이 들고 쉽게 새로운 사람들을 만날 수 있다.

Ten Years of Evolution

This park was the beneficiary of a thoughtful and strategic series of studies by the City Planning department. This included a ULI study of the entire downtown followed by a new downtown master plan by UDA identifying key initiatives for growth and improvement. Emerging from this work was a consensus that a major downtown park on this site would help organize and stimulate growth in the southern half of the downtown.

Birmingham is not a rich or powerful city. In fact, it is perhaps best known to those outside Alabama as a civil rights battleground. The city experienced a flight to the suburbs in previous decades similar to many other cities, leaving parts of the downtown retail core vacant or under utilized. These factors contributed to a sense there that there was much to overcome in terms of history and suburban migration as well as the ability to organize and get significant things done. The realization of this long-discussed park has dramatically reversed that thinking. It has deeply inspired the entire city to now believe it can continue to regenerate itself. Within the 4 months since Railroad Park has opened, it has given rise to site acquisition and design of a minor league ballpark, (Retrieving the Birmingham Barons from the suburbs!) at the west end. At the east end, a national design competition for the 'Cultural Furnace' (See below) is underway. In a city of barbeque, fitness center start-ups and loft conversions are sprouting like mushrooms all around the park perimeter. Even more important, the park has become the most racially integrated and heavily-used space in the entire city. Thankfully, every person feels welcome here and prone to meeting new people.

Aerial image of the park with phase II amphitheater by Kennedy Violich Architecture
레일로드 파크의 전경

Design _ Tom Leader Studio

Location _ Birmingham, Alabama, U.S.A

Area _ 76,890㎡

Client _ City of Birmingham

Completion _ 2010

Photograph _ Tom Leader Studio

Text & Material _ Tom Leader Studio

Even more important, the park has become the most racially integrated and heavily-used space in the entire city

무엇보다 중요한 것은, 공원이 도시 전체에서 여러 인종이 통합되고, 가장 많이 사용되는 공간이 되었다는 점이다

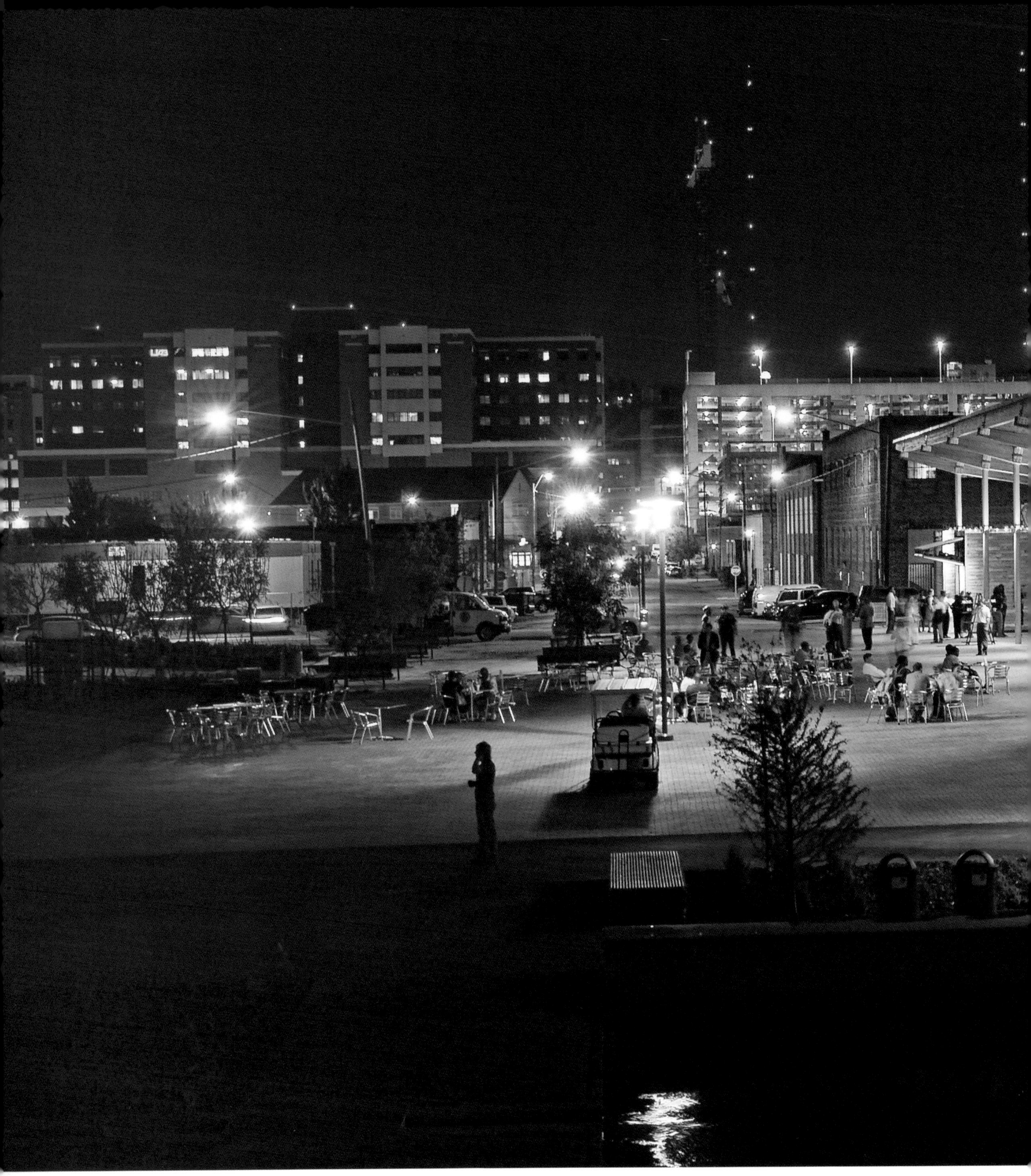

지형과 물

설계상의 문제 뿐만 아니라 불황기의 적은 예산 때문에, 지형이 이를 완수하고 공원을 구성하는 주요 수단이 되었다. 대상지의 남쪽 부지를 파내어 관개 저수지와 유거수를 생태적으로 여과하여 하천 시스템으로 작동하는 새 호수를 만들었고, 북쪽 부지는 전체 대상지를 남쪽으로 기울어지게 하는 일련의 둔덕으로 지어졌다. 대상지의 낮은 고도는 바로 인접한 수변의 물을 저장하고 수해 방지에 적합한 장소를 만든다. 호수는 여름철 관개 수요를 위한 현장의 주요 저수지가 되고, 도심에서 더위를 식히고 레크리에이션을 할 수 있는 카누와 외륜선이 완비된 공간을 제공한다. 주변부에는 넓은 생태 정화 습지가 조성되었다. 호수와 하천체계는 물이 공원을 지나 웨스트엔드에 있는 낮은 지점에 있는 홍수저장소로 흐르면서 물이 유지하고 스며들어 생태적으로 정화되는 구역의 홍수 배수지를 구성한다. 하천이 만나는 각각의 길은 공원의 주위를 부드럽게 흘러내려 골막이와 둑, 습지, 저장소를 형성한다.

Topography and Water

For reasons of a lean recession-era budget as well as design, topography became the central means of accomplishing this and organizing the park. The south side of the site was excavated for a new lake which functions as an irrigation reservoir and a stream system which biofilters runoff and the north side was built up into a series of knolls generally tilt the entire site toward the south. The site's low elevation makes a logical place to store water from the immediate watershed and to provide flood protection. The lake creates a major reservoir on site for summer irrigation needs and brings a cooling, recreational presence to the downtown, complete with canoes and paddleboats. Its fringes are planted with large bio-filtration wetlands. The lake and stream system organizes district storm drainage, detaining, infiltrating, and bio-filtering water as it passes through the park to a flood storage low point at the west end. Each major pathway the stream encounters creates a check dam, weir, and wetland pond storage that gently descend the length of the park.

The lake creates a major reservoir on site for summer irrigation needs and brings a cooling

호수는 여름철 관개 수요를 위한 현장의 주요 저수지가 되고, 더위를 식히는 역할을 한다

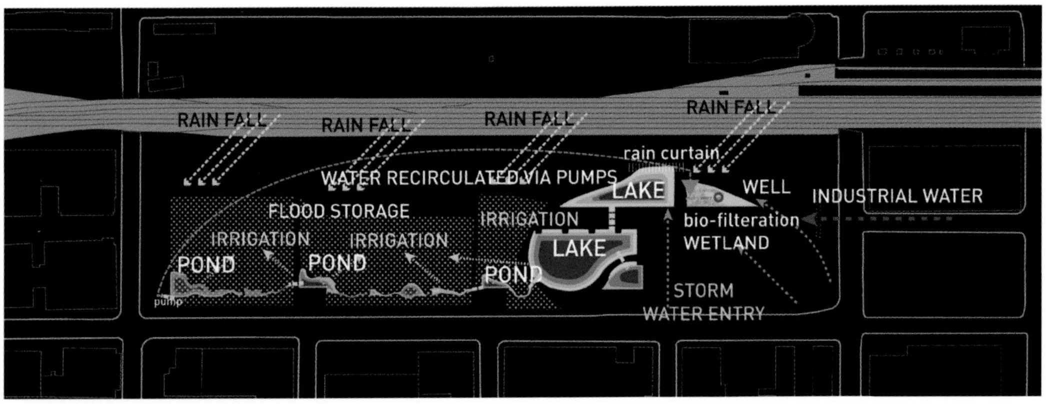

Water topography Diagram 워터 지형 다이어그램

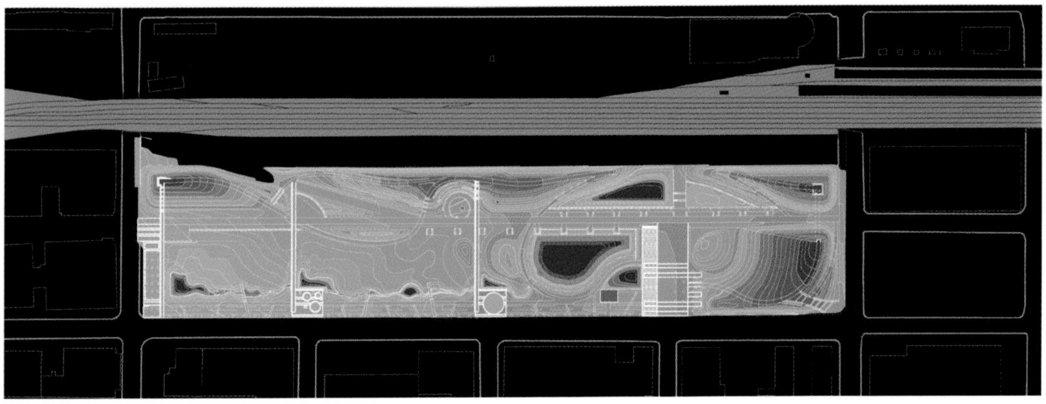

Topography Diagram 지형 다이어그램

Playarea from railtrail 레일트레일의 놀이터

그리드의 연장

높낮이가 있는 지형이 수직적 차원을 구성하는데, 이는 도심의 가로 그리드의 연장 선상에도 놓인다. 사우스 애비뉴 1번가를 따라 놓인 공원의 남쪽 가장자리는 프린스턴 엘름의 그늘진 소로로 보행자들을 모아, 공원 끝에 있는 14번가에서 18번가의 다섯 거리에 해당하는 다섯 개의 다양한 진입광장으로 이들을 이끈다. 각각의 광장은 대상지를 가로질러 북쪽의 레일 트레일과 만나는 목조 보행로에 고정된다. 공원의 주요 입구는 앨라배마 대학 구역으로, 남쪽으로 5블록 연장되어 어린이병원까지 이르는 보행자 통로에서 끝나는 17번가 광장이다. 17번가 광장은 공원으로도 깊이 연장되어 공원의 주요 도착지와 모임 공간을 이룬다. 광장은 이스트게이트 파빌리온Eastgate Pavilion의 활동을 모으고 조직하며, 원형 극장은 도착과 매표소의 역할을 한다. TLS는 음식과 상품 판매구역과 사무실 공간, 화장실을 포함한 4개의 목조 '유개화차지붕이 있는 화물차'를 완전히 덮을 수 있는 이스트게이트 파빌리온도 디자인했다.

Extending the Grid

While undulating topography structures the vertical dimension, it also overlaid by extensions of the urban street grid. The Southern edge of the park along 1st Avenue South is a key pedestrian corridor collecting pedestrians in shady allee of Princeton Elms and delivering them to one of five different entry plazas corresponding to the five streets, 14th through 18th, that end on the park. Each plaza anchors wooden boardwalk that extend across the site to meet the rail trail on the north. The park's primary entry point is the 17th Street plaza which terminates a planned pedestrian corridor extending 5 blocks into the University of Alabama district to the south and reaching Children's Hospital. The 17th street plaza also extends much deeper into the park and forms its main arrival and gathering space. The plaza collects and organizes the activities of the Eastgate event pavilion, and the amphitheater arrival and ticketing. TLS also designed the Eastgate pavilion which creates a simple train shed canopy over 4 wooden 'boxcars' containing food and merchandise concessions, office space, and restrooms.

산책로

구舊거리에 늘어선 주요 시설과 철도 지역권에 의해 동서로 이어지는 주요 산책로는 공원을 동서로 양분한다. 이 선형의 연결 장치는 나무의 '섬'과 대상지를 정리하고 파다가 나온 자재로 속을 채운 돌망태로 구성되는데 이는 그늘을 드리우는 전시 정원으로 이어진다. 산책로는 퍼레이드 장식 차량 기술에 기반을 둔 계절마다 바뀌는 '예술 차량'을 위한 시설로도 계획되었다. 이 차량은 탈 수 있고, 그늘을 제공하고, 하루 종일 산책로를 느린 속도로 왔다 갔다 할 것이다. 이 동일한 동-서 통로는 공원 너머로 연장되어, 현존하는 거리를 따라 동쪽으로 8블록 떨어진 역사적인 슬로스 제련소로 연결될 예정이다.

The Promenade

Running east-west, a major promenade bisects the park east-west as necessitated by major utilities and rail easements in the old street ROW. This linear connector is framed by shade tree 'islands' and display gardens that are structured by gabions filled with recovered material from site clearing and excavation. The Promenade is also planned to be the home for a seasonally changeable 'art vehicle' based on parade float technology. The vehicle will be ride-able, provide shade, and move at slow speeds back and forth on the promenade all day long. This same east-west corridor extends beyond the park to create future connections along this existing ROW to historic Sloss Furnace 8 blocks to the east.

Linear connector is framed by shade tree 'islands' and display gardens that are structured by gabions filled with recovered material from site clearing and excavation

선형의 산책로는 나무의 '섬'과 대상지를 정리하고 파다가 나온 자재로 속을 채운 돌망태로 구성되는데 이는 그늘을 드리우는 전시 정원으로 이어진다

문화 용광로

공원 계획의 핵심적인 미래 계획은 18번가를 가로질러 공원과 마주한 구획을 위한 것이다. 이 전략적인 구획의 북쪽 절반은 현재 곧 사용하지 않게 될 우아한 벽돌의 화력발전소가 차지하고 있다. 남쪽 절반은 시영 주차장이다. 공원 설계자의 끈질긴 재촉으로, 이 구획들은 함께 주요한 창조적이고 문화적인 시설인 '문화 용광로'로 여겨지게 되는데, 이는 강력하게 공원과 맞물리게 될 것이다. TLS가 심사하는 설계 공모전이 현재 진행 중이다.

The Cultural Furnace

A key future initiative of the park planning is for the parcel directly facing the park across 18th Street. The northern half of this strategic parcel is currently occupied by an elegant brick steam plant soon to go out of service. The southern half is a city parking lot. At the persistent urging of the park designer, these joint parcels are together being considered for a major creative and cultural facility – the 'Cultural Furnace' which will powerfully engage the park. A design competition with TLS on its jury is now underway.

Movies are shown at the grass amphitheater where people spread out on blankets and chairs for the evening

저녁에 사람들은 이불과 의자를 가지고 잔디 원형극장에서 영화를 감상한다

The CityDeck

Stoss Landscape Urbanism

시티데크는 그린베이Green Bay의 폭스Fox 강변을 따라 시행되는 다단계 재개발 프로젝트의 핵심이라 할 수 있다. 이 프로젝트의 목적은 강에 대한 접근성을 괄목할 만큼 높이는 것과 더불어 강변에서 펼쳐지는 생태계 및 사회적 활동의 다양성을 증대하는 것이다.

대지 조건과 난관

해당 장소는 대개 50~60피트 너비를 유지하며 남북으로 길게 펼쳐진 2에이커 규모의 토지이며, 그린베이 도심에 위치한 폭스 강변에 자리 잡고 있다. 그 길이는 대략 0.25마일이며, 강을 가로지르는 두 개의 교량 사이에 위치한다. 프로젝트가 시작될 무렵 주변 지역은 대부분 공지로 남아있거나, 방치되어 있었고, 주차장 등으로 사용되고 있었다. 인근에 위치한 건물들은 강변이 아닌, 그 반대 방향을 바라보는 형태로 건축되어 있었다. 당연하게도 이곳에서 사회적 활동이나 시민들의 방문 등을 기대하기란 거의 불가능한 일이었다. 일부러 찾아올 이유가 전혀 없었기 때문이다. 보행자 도로는 강과 뭍을 가로지르는 차단벽 위에 높이 자리하고 있었기 때문에 강으로 직접 접근할 수 있는 방법이 없었고, 배를 타고 가다가 뭍으로 올라올 수도 없는 상황이었다. 기반 시설에 있어서의 제약 요인들을 살펴보자면, 해당 지역은 과거에 철도망의 중심이었으며, 그 정도가 낮은 오염 지역을 여럿 가지고 있었다. 차단벽들은 모두 고유한 개별적 특성을 갖고 있기 때문에 어떤 새로운 디자인이든 어느 정도의 타협이 수반되어야만 한다. 또한 이 지역은 상수면이 높은 편이며, 주요 도시 기반 시설과 맞닿아 있다. 폭스강은 겨울 동안 대개 얼어붙게 되며, 강물 위로는 얼음이 떠다니게 된다. 새로운 개방형 공간 계획과 더불어 해당 장소에는 소방차가 접근할 수 있는 방안이 강구되어야 했는데, 이처럼 좁고 긴 형태의 토지에 이를 실현하는 데에는 상당한 어려움이 따랐다.

디자인 전략

이와 같은 난관들을 돌파하기 위해 디자인팀은 새로운 개방형 공간 및 강변 개발을 위한 보다 광범위한 도시 디자인 전략을 마련하는 데 힘썼다. 재정 및 실용성에 무게를 둔 아이디어들을 통해 약 여섯 개 블록에 이르는 공간을 긍정적인 방향으로 변화시키는 한편, 도심과 새로이 연결시킬 수 있으리라 기대되었다. 디자인팀은 도로들을 연결하고 새로운 개발 지역을 만들어냄으로써, 새롭게 제안된 건물들과 개방형 공간이 공생적 관계를 바탕으로 시너지 효과를 창출하리라 기대했다. 시티데크 프로젝트의 첫 단계는 이와 같은 도시 디자인 연구 및 전략을 바탕으로 수립되었는데, 현재 이 전략은 개방형 공간과 그 궤를 같이하며 발전되어 가고 있다. 폭넓은 대중은 물론, 시정부 관계자 및 다양한 민간, 지역, 주, 그리고 연방 기관들과의 긴밀한 협조 속에 모든 일이 진행되었다.

디자인 특성

시티데크 프로젝트 1단계의 목표는 물리적 · 환경적 복잡성을 지닌 기반 시설 중심의 해당 지역의 경관을 조정하고, 사회 · 경제적 재활성화라는 요구에 부응하는 것이다. 프로젝트를 통해 새로운 도심 워터프론트가 탄생하게 된다. 이 지역에서 가장 소중한 환경적, 경제적 자산인 폭스강으로 연결되는 새로운 관문이 마련되는 것이다.

시작은 강변에 단순한 형태의 보드워크를 설치하는 것부터이다. 촘촘하게 연결된 목재 보드워크는 기술적/실용적 문제에 적절히 부응하면서 마치 파도가 넘실대는 듯한 구불구불한 모습을 자아낸다. 이처럼 보드워크가 구부러지는 곳에는 다양한 의자, 벤치, 그리고 편안한 긴 의자 등이 설치되는데, 일부는 강과 가까운 장소에, 또 다른 일부는 조금 멀리 떨어져 강을 내려다보는 곳에 위치하게 된다. 사람들이 자신들의 기분, 취향, 조명, 그리고 그날의 날씨 등에 따라 다양한 앉을 자리를 선택할 수 있도록 하는 것이 이 아이디어의 핵심이다.

목재 보드워크는 해당 지역의 북쪽 끝에 자리한 차단벽 위에 설치되어 강을 지나는 바지선이나 작은 레저용 선박 등을 내려다볼 수 있는 환상적인 공간을 만들어낸다.

도시와 맞닿은 곳에 이르러 보드워크는 다시 안쪽으로 휘어져 홍수 피해로부터 인근 건물들을 보호하는 한편, 상업 및 외식, 그리고 휴식 등의 용도로 사용될 수 있는 강변 테라스 공간을 제공한다. 별도로 마련된 광장은 축제나, 노점, 그리고 다양한 활동을 위한 자유로운 공간으로 활용되고, 공연 등이 있을 때에는 그 크기가 두배로 늘어

In the fall, the Gingkos, Kentucky coffee trees, and Liberty elms all turn bright yellow. In combination with the custom green pavers, they subtly mark football season with the green and gold of the Green Bay Packers ©Stoss Landscape Urbanism

나 일종의 원형극장 같은 구실을 하게 된다.

그리고 광장의 남쪽 끝에는 인터렉티브 플레이 분수가 설치된다. 잔디밭은 프로젝트 진행 지역의 양쪽 끝에 위치하는데, 가벼운 놀이나 피크닉 등의 용도로 활용된다. 수풀과 곳곳에 식재된 은행나무, 느릅나무, 커피나무 등은 더운 여름에 그늘을 제공해주는 동시에 냉방에 따른 인근 건물들의 부담을 덜어준다. 미식축구 시즌이 한창인 동안에는 나무들이 밝은 노란색을 띄게 되어, 시민들이 사랑하는, 그린 베이 패커스Green Bay Packers 미식축구팀의 반은 초록 반은 황금색인 상징색을 자연스럽게 보여준다.

초록색의 경우 특별 제작한 콘크리트 보도concrete paver를 통해 뚜렷이 나타나는데, 물고기 비늘 모양의 포장면에는 구멍이 뚫려 있어 빗물이 통과하기에 용이하다.

지속가능성

배수용 수로, 투과성 보도, 그리고 잔디밭 및 식재를 통해 프로젝트 진행 지역의 상당 부분이 다공성을 띄게 된다. 이러한 전략은 지하수의 보충, 노후한 배수 시스템으로의 물 유입 감소, 그리고 증대된 식물 자원에 대한 물 공급 확대 등의 성과를 낳는다. 이처럼 통합된 물 관리 전략 덕분에 프로젝트 진행 지역처럼 상당 부분이 보도로 덮인 환경에서 살아갈 수 있는 것보다 훨씬 많은 숫자의 나무들이 자랄 수 있게 되었으며, 장기적 관점에서는 워터프론트 지역 및 인근 건물들의 온도를 낮출 수 있게 되었다. 보드워크와 벤치 등은 지속가능한 방식으로 생산된 목재로 만들어졌는데, 이례적으로 긴 수명과 유지 관리의 용이함을 그 특징으로 한다. 또한 차단벽을 제거하기 보다는 그 위로 보드워크 등의 시설을 설치함으로써, 말 그대로 차단벽의 "재활용"이 이루어질 수 있고, 수백만 달러의 자금을 절약하는 효과를 거두는 셈이 되었다.

Large boats that occasionally glide up the Fox River seem almost close enough to touch ©Mike Roemer

PHILIP R. CLARKE
PHILIP R. CLARKE
DULUTH MN.

The CityDeck is the heart of a multi-phase redevelopment project along Green Bay's Fox River. The project aims to allow for significantly increased access to the river and to diversify social and ecological life along it.

EXISTING CONDITIONS + CHALLENGES

The site is a 2-acre strip of land, typically measuring 50 to 60 feet wide, that runs along the edge of the Fox River in downtown Green Bay. It is about one-quarter-mile in length and is situated between two bridges that cross the river. At the project's beginning, adjacent parcels were empty, abandoned (a large yellow warehouse), or in use as parking lots. Nearby buildings turned their back on the riverfront.

Unsurprisingly, there was little social or civic life here, and no reason to visit; the elevated walk along existing bulkhead walls prevented any direct access down to the river-as well as up to the city from boats. In terms of infrastructural constraints, the site was formerly home to rail lines and was marked by a number low-level contamination spots. The bulkhead wall was constructed in segments in at least six different stages; each of the walls has a distinct tieback and foundation system, which any new design would need to negotiate. The site also has a high groundwater table and is laced with major city utilities. The river typically freezes during the winter and is subject to surface ice flows. In addition to any new open space programs, the site was required to accommodate fire truck access along it, a challenge in such a narrow strip of land.

DESIGN STRATEGY

To address these challenges, the design team tasked itself with identifying broader urban design strategies for new open space and development along the river. These financial and programmatic ideas would positively transform about six square blocks of urban fabric and would reach back into downtown. The team sought to reconnect city streets and create new development parcels where symbiotic programmatic relationships between proposed buildings and open space would reinforce one another. Phase one of The CityDeck grew out of these urban design studies and strategies, which are now being developed in parallel with the open space. All was developed in close collaboration with City leaders and various local, regional, state, and federal regulatory agenciesas well as with the broader public.

DESIGN ELEMENTS

As conceived, Phase 1 of The CityDeck negotiates an infrastructural landscape of physical, environmental, and code complexities, and responds to the need for social and economic re-activation. The project establishes a new downtown waterfront; a new front porch for the city on the region's most precious environmental and economic resource, the Fox River.

The project starts as a simple boardwalk

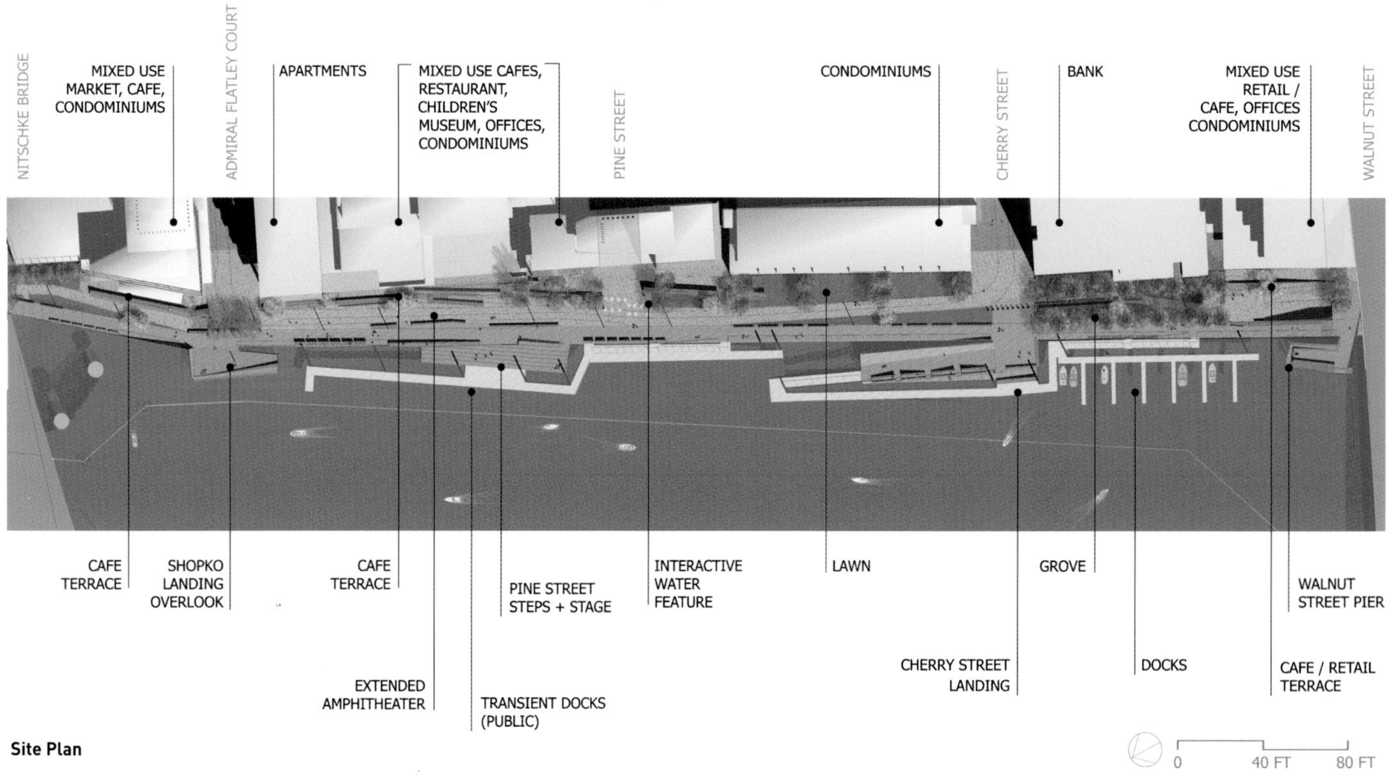

Site Plan

deployed at the edge of city and river. The highly articulated wooden boardwalk undulates, folding in response to technical, code, and programmatic issues. At the scale of the human body, these folds create diverse seats, benches, and chaise lounges that allow for choice and flexibility: some are close to the water, others further back but overlooking it; some are clustered and assembled in long rows, while others are a bit more solitary. The idea was to give people many choices about where to sit, depending on their own desires, their body type, their mood, and their attraction to various ambient light, heat, or weather conditions.

The wood surface folds up and over the existing bulkhead wall at the north end of the site, rising to form a dramatic overlook perched above the river on piles-a great place to watch passing lake barges and small recreational boats. At the city edge, the surface folds up again, affording adjacent buildings required protection from flooding and creating retail and dining terraces, seating, and communal chaise lounges looking out to the water. A flexible upland plaza floats atop fill between the perched terraces and the undulating boardwalk, creating a free-zone to be inhabited by festivals, vendors, and spontaneous activity; it doubles as an informal amphitheater for performances and is marked at its southern end by an interactive play fountain.
Lawns are located at both north and south ends of the project, allowing for casual play and picnicking. Groves and scatterings of gingkos, elms, and coffeetrees offer shade in the hot summer sun and reduce adjacent buildings' cooling loads. During football season, the trees turn bright yellow, half of the green and gold color scheme of the city's beloved Green Bay Packers football team; the green is manifest in custom-designed concrete pavers (with a green aggregate), shaped to resemble fish scales and perforated to allow for stormwater infiltration.

Even amidst the crowds it's still possible to break away for a quick ride through the interactive water feature ©Stoss Landscape Urbanism

SUSTAINABILITY

Much of the site is rendered porous, with infiltration channels integrated along terrace seams; permeable pavers throughout; and areas of lawn and planting. These strategies allow for re-charge of groundwater, reduce inputs to the city's aging infrastructure, and feed extended underground structural planting areas for trees. This integrated irrigation strategy allows for a greater number of trees than would typically be possible in a largely paved setting and, over time, cooling the waterfront and the adjacent buildings. The boardwalk and benches are constructed from sustainably harvested ipe wood, which has an extraordinarily long lifespan and reduced maintenance requirements. And, by developing design strategies that allow surfaces to move up and over the bulkhead walls-rather than cutting them down- we were able to save millions of dollars and essentially "recycle" these walls in place.

Design _ Stoss Landscape Urbanism
Chris Reed, principal(lead designer), Scott Bishop(project manager)
Design Team _ Tim Barner, Cathy Braasch, Steve Carlucci, Jill Desimini, Adrian Fehrmann, Carl, Frushour, Kristin Malone, Chris Muskopf, Susan Fitzgerald, Jana Kienitz, Lisl Kotheimer, Bryan Miyahara, Graham Palmer, Megan Studer, Sarah Wright
Client _ City of Green Bay
Location _ Green Bay, Wisconsin, USA
Area _ 2.5 acres(Phase 1_ 1.75 acres / phases 2, 3(in 2011~2012) _ 0.75 acres)
Photograph _ ©Mike Roemer
Completion _ Phase 1_ 2009 and 2010 / Phases 2, 3 _ 2011~2012
Text & Material _ Stoss Landscape Urbanism

orientation

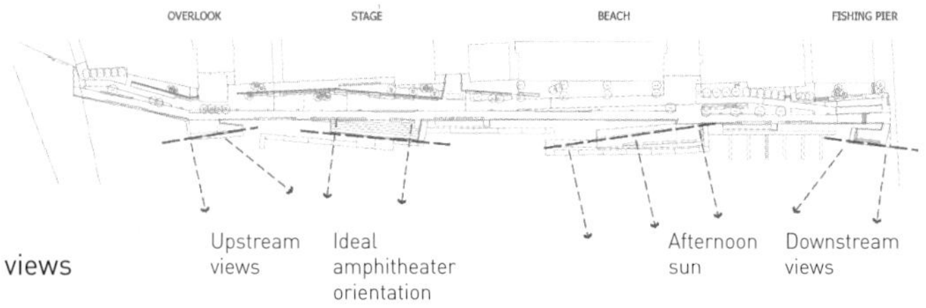

views

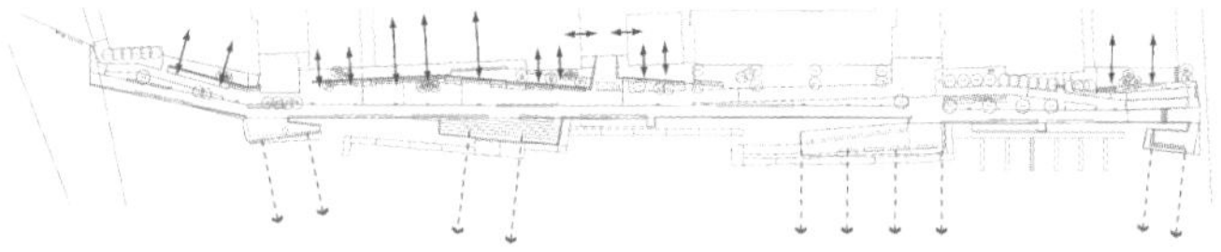

upland programs

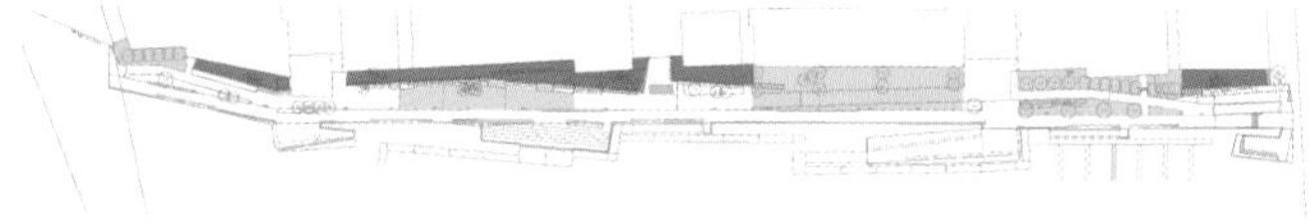

pedestrian circulation

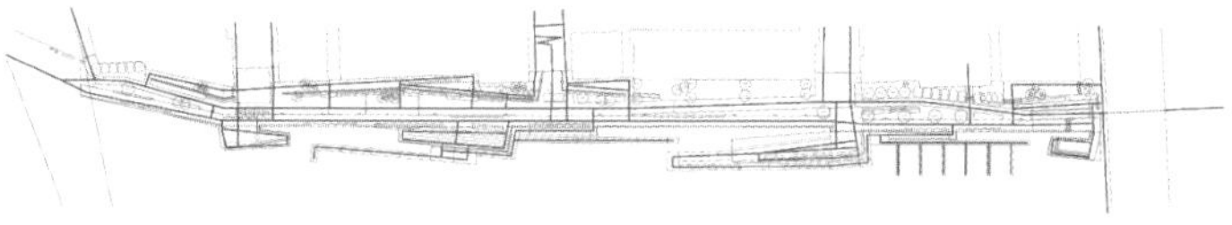

connections

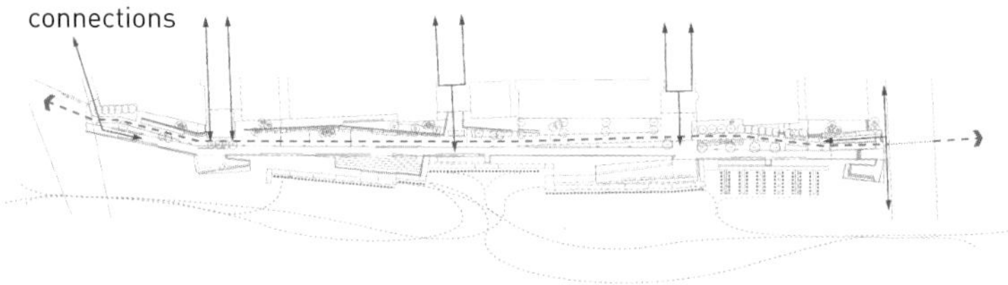

event space

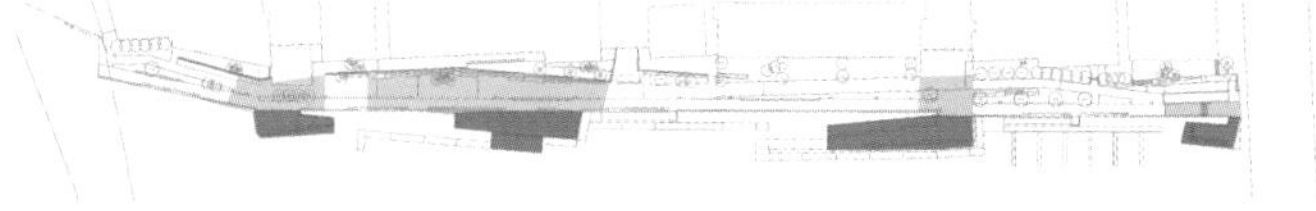

The project re-imagines the riverfront as the new center of civic life - Green Bay's new front porch on the river. The linear corridor is rendered as a series of discrete activity spaces oriented to the river and designed to encourage connections from the city to the river and vice-versa. Mixed use development projects are conceived in concert with the new open spaces, so that groundfloor retail and cafe spaces open directly to The CityDeck and the Fox River

CityDeck is designed for year-rounduse

A play fountain in the center of the project has become the heart of The CityDeck, an attraction for all ages, and an enduring symbol of the city's ongoing civic renewal ©Jeff Mirkes

The riverfront boardwalk is a pleasant place for an afternoon stroll ©Mike Roemer

The most rambunctious of the bench forms is rendered as a large chaise lounge. Children utilize it as a play surface, while adults take advantage of its recline to watch river activity, directly to the left ©Stoss Landscape Urbanism

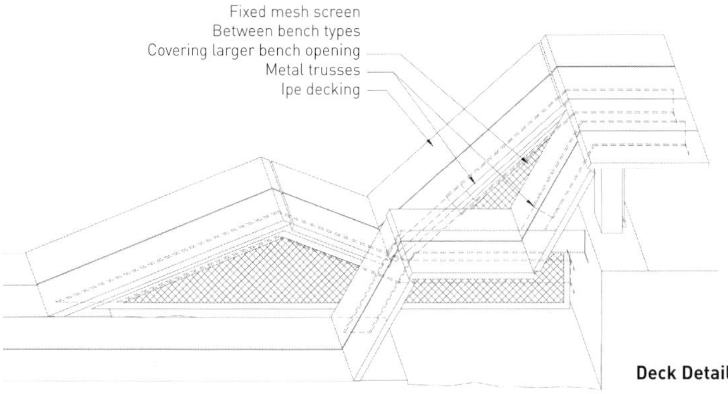

Deck Detail

The wooden surface expands at the Shopko Landing, rising up as a dramatic overlook and fishing pier. Here people are projected directly over the river and can utilize riverfront seating for quiet contemplation
©Stoss Landscape Urbanism

The benches are a great vantage point to watch the sun drop below the horizon ©Mike Roemer

Park am Gleisdreieck

Atelier LOIDL

Landscape Architecture _ Atelier LOIDL
Location _ Berlin, Germany
Completion _ 2011
Photograph _ Julien Lanoo
Text & Material _ Atelier LOIDL

모범적인 현대식 베를린 공원

우리는 베를린에 특화된 공원을 짓는 비전을 가지고 있었다. 강인하고 단단하되, 다양한 용도와 라이프 스타일에 부응할 수 있는 감성과 유연성을 지닌 공원. 파크 암 글라이스드라이에크는 그 활용에 있어 몇 가지 선택의 여지를 열어 놓는 데 그치지 않고, 이용자 스스로 공간을 창의적이고 유연하게 이용할 수 있는 폭넓은 가능성을 제공하고 있다. 공원의 모든 요소들은 이러한 미학적 전제를 염두에 두고 디자인되었다. 감각적 표면으로 이루어진 널찍한 공간들은 내구성이 뛰어난 대규모 야외용 가구들과 어우러지고, 그윽한 자태의 수풀 및 목초와 더불어 독특한 도시 경관을 자아낸다.

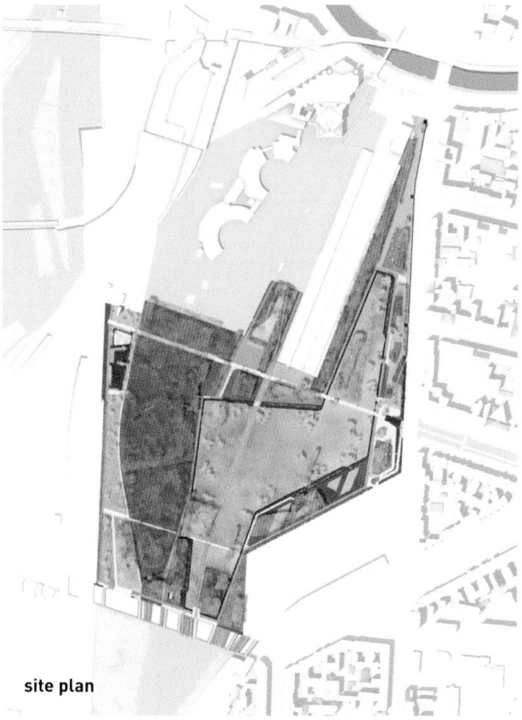

베를린 동부 지역의 대규모 신규 도심 공원인 파크 암 글라이스드라이에크가 크로이츠베르크Kreuzberg 한복판에 금년 여름 개장했는데, 이곳은 과거 삼각형 모양의 교차로로 활용되었던 공간이다. 20세기 건설된 삼각형 형태의 고가 철로의 이름을 따서 지어진 글라이스드라이에크는 1945년 이래로 버려진 땅으로 남아 있었다. 과거 안할터Anhalter 및 포츠다머Potsdamer 조차장 등이 자리한 지역은 독일 국영 철도인 '라이히스반Reichsbahn'이 수십 년 동안 독점적으로 이용해왔다. 이제 처음으로 이 지역이 도시 구조의 한 부분으로 재통합되게 된 것이다. 공원 건립과는 별도로 16헥타르에 달하는 공원 주변 도심 지역의 개발을 위한 기본 협약이 마련되었다. 파크 암 글라이스드라이에크에 곧바로 연결될 수 있는 조건을 충족시키는 것을 비롯한, 지속가능한 도시 계획을 수립한다는 목표를 달성하기 위해, 양적으로 충분한 주거 공간, 세대를 아우르는 동시에 탄소 배출이 없는 생태친화적 생활 환경, 그리고 통합된 워크숍 등이 개발의 중심이 될 것이다.

이 공원을 통해서 조경의 필수 요건에 초점을 맞춘 현대적 도심 공간이 창조되었다. 일체의 꾸밈을 배제한 하나의 공간이 탄생한 것이다. 이 공간은 그 자체의 단순성을 최대한 유지하면서도 섬세한 디테일, 감각적 소재와 식생을 활용해 강하고 시적인 효과를 창출해 낸다. '스스로 자라나는' 자연과 인공적으로 조성된 요소들 사이의 대조를 보여주기 위해 식생과 관련된 요소들을 의도적으로 배치하였다. 시적인 경관들은 하나의 아름답고 거대한 경치로 통합된다. 도시 안의 '녹색 휴식 공간'인 이곳은 빈 공간에 대한 사색적이고 고무적인 경험을 함께 제공함으로써 도시에 대한 정선되고 감각적인 인식을 갖게 해준다. 베를린의 표고보다 4미터 높은 곳, 과거 철도 교차로의 잔존물 위로 마치 고원 지대 같이 자리 잡은 공원의 형태는 그 인상적인 면적과 이국적 풍모를 통해 독특한 매력을 물씬 뿜어내고 있다. 굉장히 큰 규모와 분명한 구성을 통해 시적 성격을 지닌 많은 경치가 탄생하는 동시에 하나의 거대한 경관이 창조되었다. 초지의 사유, 나무의 장막, 숲, 묘목장, 대규모 테라스, 작은 숲, 육상 트랙, 그리고 중앙 광장 등이 조성된다. 단단하고 수명이 긴 재료는 성공적인 조경 컨셉 및 공원의 향후 활용에 있어서 수적 요소이다. 테라스에 설치된 네 개의 80미터짜리 벤치 구조물과 공원을 가로지르는 다양한 형태의 조명 시설을 통해 하나의 거대한 조각품이 만들어져, 공원 전체의 성격을 특징짓게 된다. 컨셉을 요약하자면, 우리는 철도의 역사나 이 지역에서 창조된 자연에 향한 신화 보다는 향후의 개발 및 해당 지역의 새로운 이미지에 더 큰 관심을 기울였다. 이 지역의 역사는 새로운 항해를 떠나는 출발점이 되어 줄 것이다.

새로운 공원은 이 지역에 생동감을 불어넣고, 공간 자체를 재창조할 뿐만 아니라, 낡은 것을 새롭게 보이게 하는 한편, 지역민들 및 방문객들이 시간을 보내고 싶은 장소가 될 것이다. 주변을 둘러싸고 있는 도시와 확연히 다른 모습을 보여줌으로써, 공원은 사람들에게 휴식과 여가의 시간을 마련해줄 것이다. 파크 암 글라이스드라이에크가 베를린의 진정한 성격을 보여줄 수 있다면 이상적일 것이다. 다문화적이고, 뽐내지 않으면서도 세련되고, 현대적이면서 유연하며, 즐거움을 추구하는, 그리고 그 무엇보다도 감각적인 베를린의 모습 말이다. 마지막으로 우리는 이 공원이 구시가지 지역과 포츠다머 플라츠 Potsdamer Platz의 새로운 주거지를 연결하는 가교가 되기를 기대한다. 파크 암 글라이스드라이에크가 2011년 9월 2일 개장한 이래로 베를린 거주자들이 쓸모 있는 현대적 도시 공원에 대한 우리의 비전을 긍정적으로 받아들여주기를 간절히 기대하고 있다.

"We had the vision to build a park that is very peculiar for Berlin - rough and robust, but still very sensual and adjustable to different uses and lifestyles. The 'Park am Gleisdreieck' predetermines not only a few options for use, but rather provides vast areas for a creative and informal adoption of the location by the visitor. All elements of the park were designed with these aesthetical premises in mind. Large spaces with haptic surfaces assemble to an arrangement of large-scale, indestructible outdoor furniture fusing with mellow tree groves and meadows into a very unique cityscape."

In the heart of Kreuzberg, the Eastern part of Berlin's new, big inner-city park was opened this summer: "Park am Gleisdreieck", a former triangular junction. It will be the first half of an altogether 36 hectares area spanning in the Western part of Berlin. Named after the turn-of-the-20th-century viaducts of the overhead railway, which form a triangle here, since 1945 the Gleisdreieck has been waste land. Before, the area of the Anhalter and Potsdamer railway yards had been an enclave of the German state railway "Reichsbahn" for decades. Now, for the first time, this tract of land has been reintegrated into urban structure.

The town building basic agreement provides, besides the realization of the park, for the development of about 16 hectares of urban quarters to round off the park on diverse areas. For the purpose of a sustainable town planning with direct access to the Park am Gleisdreieck new urban quarters with qualitatively valuable housing spaces, cross generational and eco-friendly living areas with a zero carbon environmental impact together with integrated workshops will be developed.
With the Park am Gleisdreieck a modern urban location has been created focusing on the basic essentials of landscape architecture. Without any decoration, a location is formed, which keeps it as simple as possible but uses fine details, sensual materials and vegetation, which together unfold a strong, poetical effect.

The contrast between "grown" nature and artificially built elements, vegetative elements has been purposely put in scene. Poetical landscapes unify to one big beautiful scenery. As a "green break" in the city, the Park am Gleisdreieck stands at the same time for contemplative and stimulative experience of free space, targeting at a refined, sensual perception of the city.

The impressive expanse and the other-worldliness of the plateau-like grounds, which lie four meters above city level as well as the relicts of the former railway junction, make the park unique in Berlin. By means of an exceptionally large scale and clear configuration many poetical types of scenery are created, together forming one big landscape: the freedom of the meadows, the backdrops of trees, the forest, the nursery, the large terraces, the small woods, the sport tracks, and the central plaza.

Robust and long-living materials are essential criteria for a successful landscape architectonic concept and the later use of a park. With four 80 meters long bench sculptures on the terraces and the luminaires, crossing the park as differently folded masts, an own large sculpture is formed, which characterizes the entire site. Summing up our concept, we have put more focus on the future development and the new image of the site than on railway history or the nature myth created by the very special absence of man which will change in any case due to his future presence. The history of the area is the starting point for a new voyage and not to be considered conservational.
The new park will put something into motion in this location, change the site itself, let something old appear new and will above all be a place where neighbours and visitors will like to spend their time. As a change from the surrounding city, people will experience here relaxation and leisure.
Ideally, the Park am Gleisdreieck can show how Berlin really is: multi-cultural, sophisticated without showing off, modern, flexible, fun-loving, and above all sensual. Finally, we hope that the park will build a bridge between the old quarters and the new life at the Potsdamer Platz.
Since the Park am Gleisdreieck was opened only recently (the 2nd September of 2011), as landscape architects and citizens of Berlin, we strongly believe that our vision of a decent, contemporary urban park will be adopted positively by Berlin's inhabitants.

Toronto Central Waterfront

West 8 urban design & landscape architecture

Landscape Architecture _ West 8 urban design & landscape architecture
Client _ Waterfront Toronto
Location _ Toronto, Canada
Area _ 3.5km length
Joint Venture _ du Toit Allsopp Hillier (DTAH)
Association _ Schollen & Company, Diamond + Schmitt Architects, Arup, Halsall Associates, David Dennis Design, Mulvey + Banani
Design & Realization _ 2006~present
Construction Value _ 192 million CDN
Text & Material _ West 8 urban design & landscape architecture

New public promenade and boardwalks

토론토에서 가장 소중한 자산 중 하나인 센트럴 워터프론트Central Waterfront는 온타리오호Lake Ontario로부터 3.5킬로미터 떨어져 위치하면서 도심의 상업 지구와 인접해 있다. 하지만 수십 년간의 계획과 부분적인 개발 프로젝트들이 있어왔음에도 불구하고, 시각적으로나 물리적으로 전체를 하나로 아우를 만한 일관된 비전이 부재한 것이 사실이다. 이러한 맥락에서 본 프로젝트의 본질적 목표는 건축과 기능성이라는 두 가지 측면에서 센트럴 워터프론트의 일관성 있고 또렷한 이미지를 창출해냄으로써 지금까지의 문제를 해결하는 것이다.

Masterplan Competition Image

West 8은 워터프론트 토론토Waterfront Toronto가 실시한 이노베이션 디자인 공모를 통해 센트럴 워터프론트의 종합적인 비전을 제시하였다. 이는 강렬함과 단순함을 토대로 현존하는 시각 공해를 극복하는 한편, 연관성과 통일감을 자아낼 수 있는 강력한 디자인 언어를 구축하는 것이었다. 도시와 온타리오호가 발산하는 활력을 연계하는 것과 지속적으로 대중의 접근이 용이하도록 워터프론트를 만드는 것이 본 계획의 최우선 과제이다. 그리고 토론토의 풍요로운 문화 자원과 지속 가능하고 생태적으로 효율적인 환경Green foot을 접목하고자 하는 비전을 담았다. 프로젝트에서 워터프론트 전역을 관통하는 일관성과 연속성을 엿볼 수 있는데, 표면적으로는 비교적 단순한 실천 방안들을 통해 신개념의 "복합 워터프론트Multiple Waterfront"를 구현하고 있다. 구체적으로 살펴보면 일련의 보행자용 교량을 비롯한 수변 산책로로 구성된 제1 워터프론트Primary Waterfront, 재정비된 퀸스퀘이 대로Queens Quay Boulevard와 새로운 도심 산책로 및 공공 공간으로 이루어진 제2 워터프론트Secondary Waterfront,로 나눌 수 있다. 그리고 호수와 연계된 공공 공간과 새로운 선박 계류장으로 활용될 일련의 부양식floating 설비로 구성된 플로팅 워터프론트Floating Waterfront 토론토의 다채로운 주변 지역과 수변 지대를 연결시켜줄 시티 컬쳐스Cultures of the City 등을 꼽을 수 있다.

Promenade

Queens Quay with four WaveDecks

공공 영역에서 이루어질 수 있고, 또 반드시 이루어져야 하는 여러 가지 활동들뿐만 아니라 위와 같은 시설들을 보다 발전시키려는 노력이 앞으로 전개될 것이다. 도심과 수변 지역을 확실히 연계시키고, 대중들에게 지속적 접근성을 제공하는 것이 최우선 과제가 될 것이다. 본 계획을 통해 대중적이고 다채로우며, 다양한 경험을 통해 느낄 수 있는 워터프론트를 조성할 수 있을 것이다. West 8은 이미 센트럴 워터프론트를 위한 전략적 마스터플랜을 수립했으며, 현재 다양한 부문의 디자인 및 시행에 참여하고 있다. 그 예로는 승용차, 대중교통, 보행자, 그리고 자전거 사이의 균형을 목표로 하는 퀸스퀘이 대로 재정비, 이스트 베이프론트East Bayfront 개발을 위한 초기 가로 정비 사업, 그리고 수변 공공 부분의 웨이브데크WaveDeck 건설 등을 들 수 있다.

Rees WaveDeck

Rees WaveDeck

Rees WaveDeck

Simcoe WaveDeck

Simcoe WaveDeck

SIRIUS

Simcoe WaveDeck

The Central Waterfront, 3.5 km of Lake Ontario shoreline immediately adjacent to the downtown business district, is one of Toronto's most valuable assets. Yet, despite decades of planning and patchwork development projects, there is no coherent vision for linking the pieces into a greater whole -visually or physically. In this context, the fundamental objective of the project is to address this deficiency by creating a consistent and legible image for the Central Waterfront, in both architectural and functional terms.

In response to an innovative design competition launched by Waterfront Toronto, West 8 submitted a comprehensive vision for the Central Waterfront that produced a powerful design language with the strength and simplicity to overcome the existing visual noise and create a sense of interconnectedness and identity. Connectivity between the vitality of the city and the lake and a continuous, publicly accessible waterfront are the plan's priorities. The plan expresses a vision for the Central Waterfront that brings a sustainable, ecologically productive "green foot" to the rich culture of the metropolis. It suggests a new coherence and continuity along the waterfront produced by four seemingly simple gestures that create a new "Multiple Waterfront": the Primary Waterfront - a continuous water's edge promenade with a series of pedestrian bridges, the Secondary Waterfront - a recalibrated Queens Quay Boulevard with a new urban promenade and public spaces at the heads-of-slips, the Floating Waterfront - a series of floating elements that offer new boat moorings and public spaces in relation to the lake, and the Cultures of the City - connections from Toronto's diverse neighborhoods towards the waterfront.

Spadina WaveDeck

Spadina WaveDeck

Having been awarded the commission, further elaboration of this vision seeks to develop these elements, as well as the activities that can and should be sustained in the public realm. Articulating the point of contact between the city and the water and providing continuous public access are key priorities. The proposal creates a waterfront that is public, diverse and expressed through a multiplicity of experiences. West 8 has completed the strategic master plan for the Central Waterfront and is currently engaged in design and implementation of various components of the plan, including the reconstruction of Queens Quay Boulevard to create a new balance between automobiles, public transportation, pedestrians and cyclists, the implementation of the first parts of streetscape for the new East Bayfront development and the construction of wavedeck public spaces at the heads of slips.

Lincoln Park

Miami Beach Sound Scape

West 8 urban design & landscape architecture

Landscape Architecture _ West 8 urban design & landscape architecture

Location _ Miami Beach, USA

Area _ 10,000m^2

Client _ City of Miami Beach

Design _ 2009~2010

Completion _ 2010~2011

Photograph _ West 8, Claudia Uribe, Tomas Loewy

Text & Material _ West 8 urban design & landscape architecture

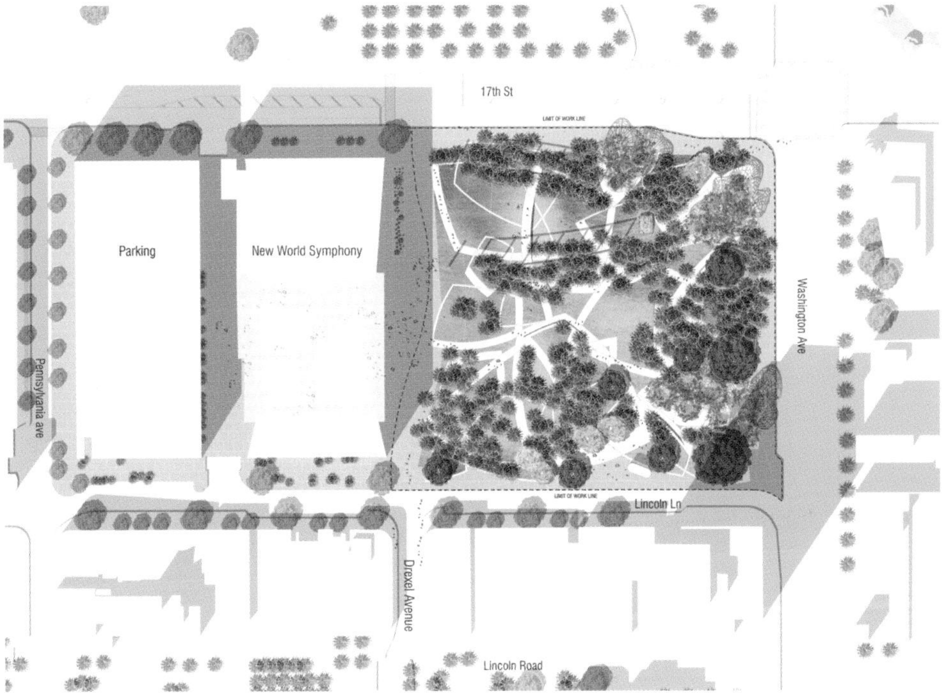
17th St
LIMIT OF WORK LINE
Parking
New World Symphony
Washington Ave
Pennsylvania ave
LIMIT OF WORK LINE
Lincoln Ln
Drexel Avenue
Lincoln Road

Master plan

©Claudia Uribe

©Tomas Loewy

©Claudia Uribe

도심에 위치한 링컨 공원은 1만㎡가 약간 넘는 작은 규모로, 새로운 선례가 될 만한 공원을 조성하기 위해 고군분투하고 있는 플로리다Florida주 남쪽 마이애미시 비치의 워싱턴가와 17번가에 걸쳐 위치해 있다. 이러한 작은 도시공원들은 종종 부드러운 외관을 강조하기 보다는 포장면을 강조하는 디자인을 선호하는 경향이 있는데, 링컨 공원은 부지가 가지는 특성과 프로그램들을 통해 독특한 해결책을 이끌어 내었다. 이 공공 공간은 초기 계획 단계부터 '녹음'을 느끼도록 하고 공원을 더욱 좋아할 수 있도록 설계하였다.

West 8 은 광장이 아닌 녹음이 있는 공원, 친밀함을 느낄 수 있고 나무 그늘이 어우러지는 편안한 공원, 세계적인 명소인 New World Symphony 빌딩과 어울릴 수 있는 공원 조성이라는 과제를 수행하면서 확실한 입지를 다지게 되었다. 링컨 공원은 마이애미 해변의 정신과 활기를 반영하고 있으며, 낮에는 나무 그늘 아래서, 밤에는 별이 빛나는 하늘 아래서 다양한 이용 행태가 일어날 수 있도록 조성되었다.

링컨 공원에서 매우 특이한 점은 독특한 시설물이 있다는 것이다. 첫째로, 공원 경계에 여러 개의 퍼골라가 있다. 퍼골라의 모양은 남 플로리다의 열대성 기후에서 볼 수 있는 뭉게구름에서 영감을 받았다. 손으로 직접 제작하여 색을 입힌 알루미늄 구조물은 그늘을 제공할 뿐만 아니라 부겐베리아bougainvillea 넝쿨이 장관을 이루고 꽃을 피울 수 있도록 지지대의 역할을 한다. 이 고급 예술작품 역시 이 공원에서 중요한 요소이다. New World Symphony Hall 건물 근처에 있는 영상 투영벽은 예술계에서 나타난 최신 예술 사조와 흥미진진한 예술적 표현을 시도하는 비디오 아티스트들을 위한 이상적인 '도화지' 역할을 한다. West 8은 공원 내에 대규모의 멀티미디어 시설을 수용할 수 있는 영상 타워와 'Ballet Bar' 를 설계한 적이 있다. 공원에 있는 건축적인 요소들 사이 사이에 일관성 있게 이 요소들을 표현한 것이다. 이들은 국내외 예술가들이 전통적인 형태의 전시관의 한계를 외부로 이끌어내며 변화무쌍한 전시품들을 보여줄 수 있도록 다양한 가능성을 제시하였다.

부드럽게 굴곡진 공원 지형은 구불구불하게 흰색 콘크리트 모자이크로 길을 조성해 시각적으로 강조되어 보인다. 그리고 흰색 콘크리트 앉음벽은 편안하게 앉을 수 있게 만들었다. 공원 디자인에서 중요한 이 두 가지 요소들은 링컨 공원이 작은 부지 규모에도 불구하고 더욱 크게 보이는 착시 효과를 갖게 한다. 야자수의 장막과 표본 식재된 나무들은 오아시스 안에 있는 듯한 느낌을 들게 하며 시야를 가리기도 하고 더 멀리 조망할 수 있게 하기도 한다.

2011년 1월 시민들에게 공개된 링컨 공원은 시민들의 여가 활동 및 휴식, 문화 활동을 위한 통합 공간이라고 할 수 있다. Symphony halls의 활용 및 유명한 건축물과 함께 the New World Symphony 단지는 음악과, 디자인, 경험이 결합된 세계 수준으로 거듭날 것이다.

The Lincoln Park site is a small — slightly larger than 1 hectare in size — urban site located at Washington Avenue and 17th Street in South Florida that strives to establish a new precedent for parks in the City of Miami Beach. While an urban park this size might often receive a design that has more hard surface than soft, Lincoln Park's site-specific conditions, context and program elicited a unique response. A decision was made early in the design process for this public space to feel "green" and more like a park.

With West 8 firmly positioned to deliver its mission of a green park, not a plaza, a park that feels intimate, shady, and soft was created; a park that will support the world-class attraction of the New World Symphony Building. Lincoln Park reflects the spirit and vitality of Miami Beach and will support a multitude of day and night uses, either under the shade of the trees or a starlit sky.
Lincoln Park will also have the wonder of some totally unique features that are one of a kind. First, several pergolas embrace the park edges; their shape inspired by the puffy cumulous clouds inherent in South Florida's tropical climate. The hand-fabricated painted aluminium structures not only provide shade but will support the spectacular blooms of bougainvillea vines; highlighting a threshold of colour at the parks points of entry. High quality artwork is equally important here, and the projection wall of the adjacent Symphony Hall building is an ideal "canvas" for video projection artists - an emerging and exciting discipline within the art world. West 8 has designed a projection tower and "Ballet Bar" to house the extensive multimedia equipment provided within the park. These elements provide a consistent language among the park's unique architectural elements, providing a wide range number of possibilities for both local and international artists to present an ever-changing exhibit that would occur outside the confines of a traditional museum experience.

Soft, undulating topography is reinforced visually by a white concrete mosaic of meandering pathways, and white concrete seating walls that providing options for informal seating. These two critical elements of the park design allow Lincoln Park to convey the illusion of a park larger than its humble inherent size. "Veils" of palm and specimen tree planting conceal and reveal views further reinforcing the experience of being within an oasis that is much larger.

Open to the public in January 2011, Lincoln Park is a unified expression of recreation, pleasure and culture. Combined with the momentum of the symphony halls uses and outstanding architecture, the New World Symphony campus will be a world class destination that marries music, design, and experience.

Uptown Normal Circle

Hoerr Schaudt Landscape Architects

Landscape Architect and Prime Consultant _ Hoerr Schaudt Landscape Architects

Civil Engineer and Traffic Engineer _ Clark Deitz

Subsurface Infrastructure Engineer _ Farnsworth Group

Irrigation Consultant _ Landtech

Client _ Town of Normal, IL

Location _ Normal, Illinois, USA

Photograph _ Scott Shigley

Text & Material _ Hoerr Schaudt Landscape Architects

배경 및 목적

미국 전역에 있는 지역사회들이 거대 도시공간을 조성하면서도 지속가능성에 대한 그들의 노력을 표현할 수 있는 방법을 모색해왔는데, 이 가운데 일리노이주 Normal Town의 중심가는 중심업무지구CBD, Central Business District 조성의 사례로 자리매김하게 되었다. 환경원리를 기본으로 한 진보적인 재개발 계획에 중점을 두고 있는 Uptown Normal Circle은 급성장하고 있는 이 지역에서 새로운 변화를 모색하면서 도시의 정체성과 가치를 창조할 수 있는 촉매제 역할을 할 수 있도록 조성되었다. Hoerr Schaudt에서 설계한 이 서클은 우수의 자연정화, 공공공간 및 교통체계 조절의 역할을 동시에 수행하는 살아 있는 광장이 되었다.

이 서클은 Normal Town이 주도한 다면적인 재개발계획인 Uptown 재개발 계획의 일환으로 설계되었다. 이 재개발 계획은 몇 년동안 쇠락해가던 이 지역에 새로운 활력소를 부여하고 정체성을 확립하는 것을 목적으로 하고 있다. Uptown Normal 지역을 활성화하기 위해 Dong Farr Associates에서 설계한 마스터플랜은 경제적 재활을 위한 전략으로서의 지속가능성을 위해 매우 진보적인 제안을 담고 있다. 이 전략은 7,500제곱피트 이상의 신축건물에 대한 최소한의 LEED 요건을 시행할 수 있는 법령제정, 중심부에 위치한 다양한 형태의 교통수단과 지역 및 지구단위의 교통체계와의 연계, 재구성되어 밀도가 높아진 주차장 계획 등을 포함한다. 이 서클은 전체 계획안에서 중요한 부분을 차지하고 있으며 2010년 완성되었다.

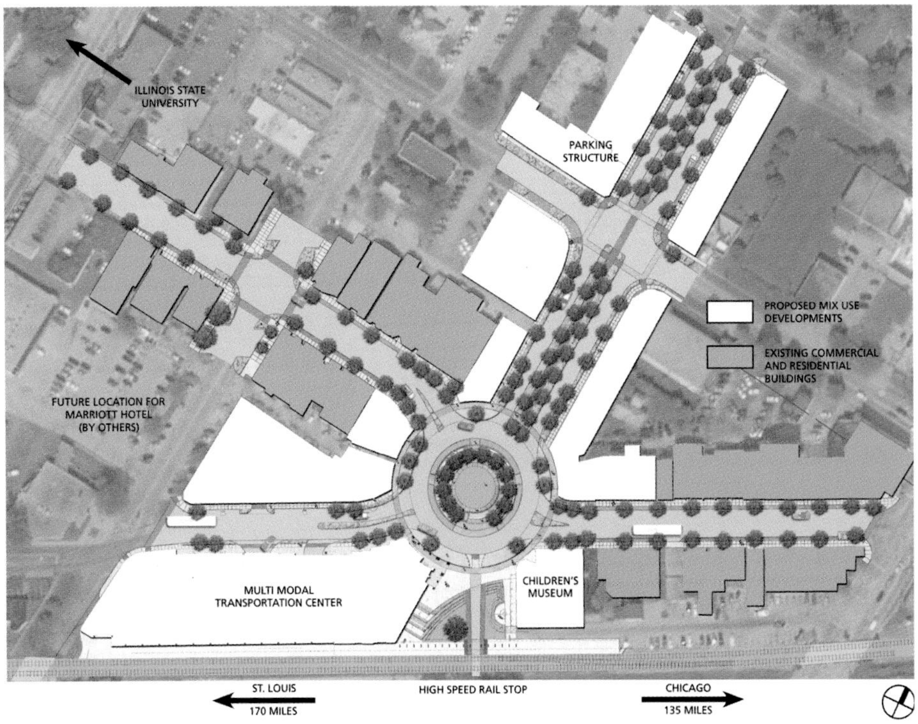

디자인

과거 두 개의 철로와 하천의 합류지점으로 시내 중심부를 두 개의 구역으로 분절시키고 '사람이 살지 않는 땅'이었던 이 서클 지역은 도로교통의 안정성을 확보하는 동시에 다섯 개의 거리가 만나는 위험한 교차로를 해결한 새로운 형태의 서클로 거듭났다. 이 서클은 Uptown Normal의 중심부로서의 역할을 하는 동시에 2012년 완공될 다양한 교통 형태의 수단을 이용할 수 있는 인근의 역으로부터 남부 지역에 이르는 범위를 아우르는 지역사회의 관문 역할을 하고 있다. 이 서클의 중심부는 공원으로 이용되며 벤치, 수공간, 그늘 및 광장이 있는 중앙녹지가 조성되어 있다.

이 프로젝트의 중요한 요소 중의 하나는 Uptown Normal에서 발생하는 대부분의 우수를 집수 및 저장, 정화와 재활용하는 지속가능한 우수관리에 있다. 서클 근처 여러 개의 거리에서 모아진 표면유거수는 7만5천 갤런에 이르는 지하 물탱크에 저장된다. 이 물탱크는 기반시설개선사업으로 인해 버려진 지름 6인치의 하수관을 재활용하여 만들었는데 지역사회의 집수구에 안정적인 물공급을 위한 저장장치로서의 역할을 한다. 물탱크에 모아진 물은 이 구역 내 잔디 및 기타 식물을 위한 관개용수로 이용되거나 서클 내로 끌어들여 광장을 통해 흐르게 된다. 이 물의 흐름은 도시환경에서 적용된 지속가능성을 확실하게 입증하며 '살아 있는 광장'을 만들고 있다.

서클 내에서 물탱크에 저장된 물은 서클을 두르고 있는 낮은 둑 주변 식재지나 우수관을 통해 테라스 형태의 여과습지에 모아진다. 이 지점에서 물은 다시 지하 저류조로 흘러들어가고 UV 여과장치에 의한 처리과정을 거쳐 얕은 개울의 형태나 수공간의 형태로 순환된다. 공원 이용자들은 원주를 따라 흐르며, 마치 서클 너머에 있는 교통의 흐름을 투영한 듯 흐르는 상당히 매력적인 수로에 접근이 가능하다. 다양한 형태를 가진 이 수로는 주변 교통 소음을 막아주는 자연스런 완충제 역할을 하며 지역사회로 들어오는 관문의 역할을 수행한다. 또한, 도시열섬효과를 완화하며 우수로 인해 발생한 표면유거수의 증발을 유도한다.

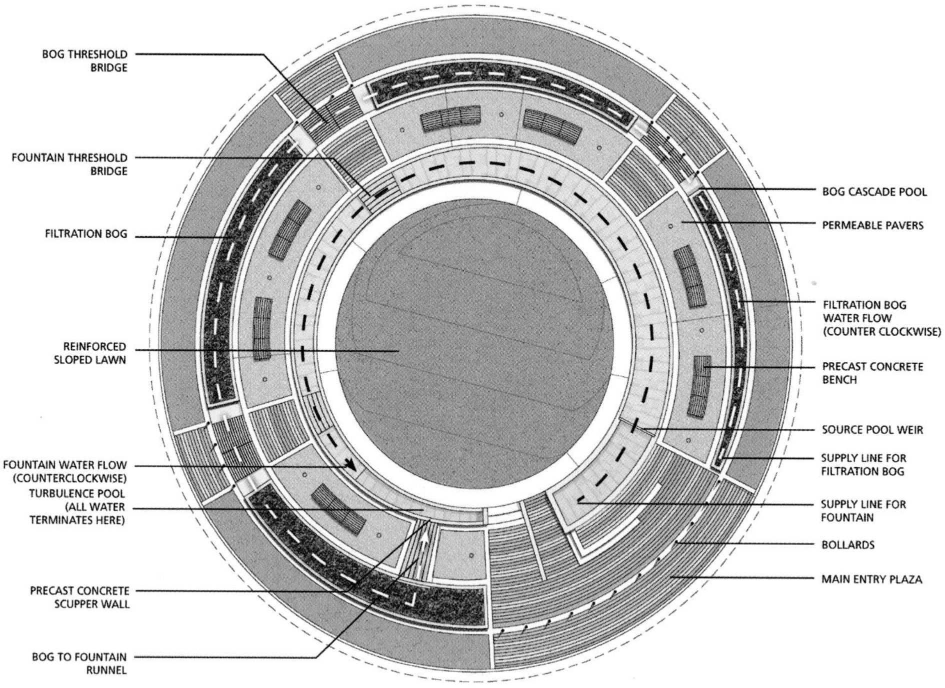
BOG THRESHOLD BRIDGE
FOUNTAIN THRESHOLD BRIDGE
FILTRATION BOG
REINFORCED SLOPED LAWN
FOUNTAIN WATER FLOW (COUNTERCLOCKWISE)
TURBULENCE POOL (ALL WATER TERMINATES HERE)
PRECAST CONCRETE SCUPPER WALL
BOG TO FOUNTAIN RUNNEL
BOG CASCADE POOL
PERMEABLE PAVERS
FILTRATION BOG WATER FLOW (COUNTER CLOCKWISE)
PRECAST CONCRETE BENCH
SOURCE POOL WEIR
SUPPLY LINE FOR FILTRATION BOG
SUPPLY LINE FOR FOUNTAIN
BOLLARDS
MAIN ENTRY PLAZA

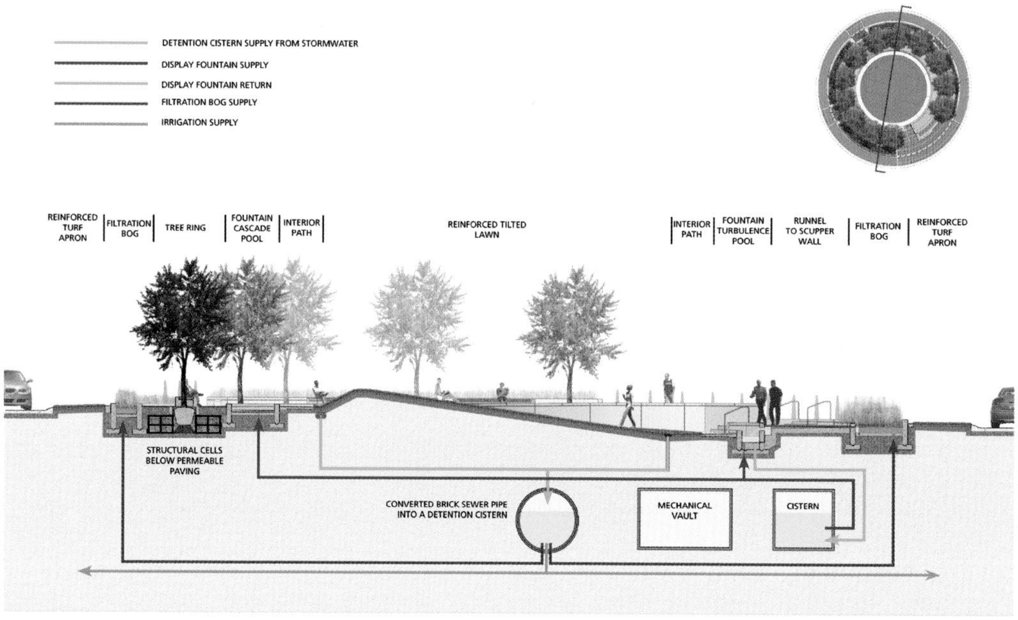
DETENTION CISTERN SUPPLY FROM STORMWATER
DISPLAY FOUNTAIN SUPPLY
DISPLAY FOUNTAIN RETURN
FILTRATION BOG SUPPLY
IRRIGATION SUPPLY
REINFORCED TURF APRON
FILTRATION BOG
TREE RING
FOUNTAIN CASCADE POOL
INTERIOR PATH
REINFORCED TILTED LAWN
INTERIOR PATH
FOUNTAIN TURBULENCE POOL
RUNNEL TO SCUPPER WALL
FILTRATION BOG
REINFORCED TURF APRON
STRUCTURAL CELLS BELOW PERMEABLE PAVING
CONVERTED BRICK SEWER PIPE INTO A DETENTION CISTERN
MECHANICAL VAULT
CISTERN

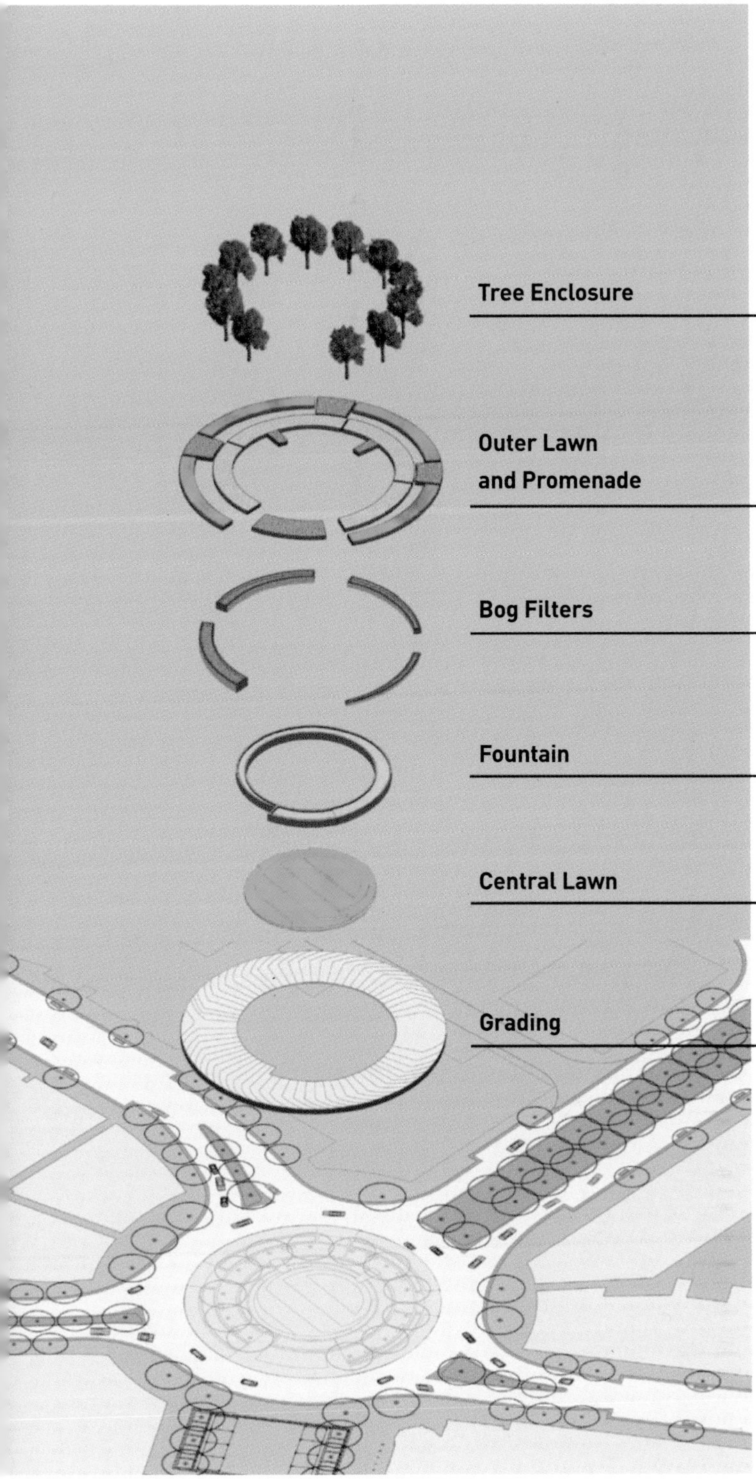

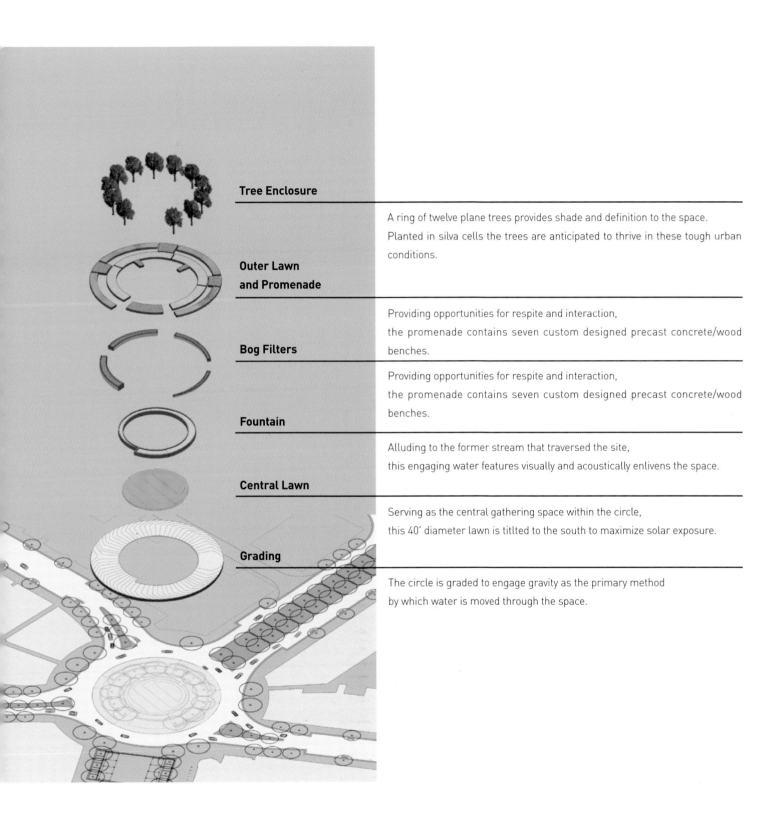

Tree Enclosure

A ring of twelve plane trees provides shade and definition to the space. Planted in silva cells the trees are anticipated to thrive in these tough urban conditions.

Outer Lawn and Promenade

Providing opportunities for respite and interaction, the promenade contains seven custom designed precast concrete/wood benches.

Bog Filters

Providing opportunities for respite and interaction, the promenade contains seven custom designed precast concrete/wood benches.

Fountain

Alluding to the former stream that traversed the site, this engaging water features visually and acoustically enlivens the space.

Central Lawn

Serving as the central gathering space within the circle, this 40' diameter lawn is titlted to the south to maximize solar exposure.

Grading

The circle is graded to engage gravity as the primary method by which water is moved through the space.

이 프로젝트는 전형적인 도시 거리 경관 프로젝트와는 차별되는 다양한 혁신적인 기술을 도입하였다. 다른 무엇보다도, 이 서클은 훌륭한 고성능 기반시설의 사례라고 할 수 있는데 하나의 단일 프로젝트에 도로, 보행자 전용도로, 우수의 양과 질을 고려한 관리방안, 공공공간의 조성 등의 다양한 도시 요소가 통합된 특별한 사례라고 할 수 있다. 도시설계에 대한 이러한 접근 방식은 종종 불필요하다고 여겨지는 프로젝트들에 투자되는 제한된 공공기금으로 새로운 공원과 도시공간을 만들어 내는 일을 주장하기가 어려웠던 때에 전개되었다. 이 통합계획이 실행됨에 따라 Uptown Normal은 다양한 공공의 요구를 일제히 다룰 수 있게 되었다. 이 프로젝트는 우수 집수 시스템뿐만 아니라 거리 환경 내에서 다양한 지속가능한 개발을 위한 요소들을 이끌어 내고 있다. 이러한 요소들은 근처의 보도 및 건물에서 우수의 유입을 유도하는 보도변 여과 플랜터 설치, 구조적인 단위식재 및 우수저장의 가능성을 높이고 건강한 식물 생육을 증진하는 우수 관리 시스템 등을 포함한다.

Project Purpose and Background

As communities across the U.S. search for ways to articulate their commitment to sustainability while creating great civic spaces, the central Illinois town of Normal has set an example in its central business district. The focal point in a progressive redevelopment plan rooted in environmental principles, the Uptown Normal Circle is intended to serve as an urban catalyst, creating identity and value while encouraging new growth in this burgeoning district.

The Circle, designed by Hoerr Schaudt Landscape Architects in Chicago, IL, is a living plaza where naturally-cleansed stormwater, public space, and transportation work in unison.

The Circle is one portion of The Uptown Renewal Project, a multiphase redevelopment plan led by the Town of Normal. The plan aims to revitalize and intensify Normal's downtown, which has been in decline for decades. The town's master plan for a thriving "Uptown Normal" district, designed by Doug Farr Associates, offered an unusually progressive sensitivity to sustainability as a strategy for enhancing economic revitalization, including the first ordinance in the country to enforce minimum LEED requirements for new buildings over 7500 square feet, centrally-located multimodal links to regional and local transit, and restructured and densified parking. The Circle is an important piece of the overall plan and was completed in 2010.

Project Design

Historically a "no man's land" at the confluence of two railways and a former stream that created two disconnected segments of downtown, the Circle is a new traffic circle resolving the once awkward intersection of five streets while simultaneously calming traffic. It acts as the heart of Uptown Normal and as a gateway to those entering the community from the adjacent multi-modal transportation station to the south, scheduled for completion in 2012. At the center of the Circle is a park that provides a central green gathering space with seating, a water feature, shade, and an open plaza.

One of the key elements of the project is sustainable stormwater management; capturing, storing, cleansing and recycling much of the stormwater in Uptown Normal. Runoff is collected from several streets adjoining the Circle and is stored in a 75,000 gallon underground cistern. This cistern, which was recycled from a 60" diameter storm sewer line being abandoned as part of the associated infrastructure improvements, serves as a detention device for water providing relief to the community's watershed. Water captured and retained in the cistern is then either used for irrigation of turf and plant material in the district or is introduced into the Circle where it begins a journey through a "living plaza" creating a legible demonstration of sustainability in an urban environment.

In the Circle, water collected in the cistern is pumped from into a series of terraced filtration bogs where it is cleansed as it flows slowly through the plant material around the circle passing over several weirs and through a scupper wall into a collection pool. At this point, water is pumped into an underground reservoir, and treated by a UV filter and then circulated through a shallow stream-like water feature. Park visitors have access to this highly engaging watercourse as it flows around the circumference of the circle, mirroring the flow of traffic beyond and those entering the community from the adjacent multi-modal providing an acoustic buffer to the sound of traffic. This feature also creates the added benefit of encouraging evapotranspiration of water that would have runoff as part of a storm event while ameliorating the heat-island effect in this urban district.

The project incorporated numerous innovative techniques that distinguish it from typical urban streetscape projects. First and foremost, the Circle is an excellent example of high-performance infrastructure, integrating multiple civic elements such as roadways, pedestrian corridors, stormwater quantity and quality control and public space into a single project. This approach to urban design comes at a time when it is difficult to advocate for the creation of new parks and civic spaces with limited public funds for projects that are often perceived as unnecessary. By following this practice of integrated design, the Uptown Normal Circle has addressed several public needs simultaneously.

In addition to the stormwater harvesting system the project includes several sustainable elements in the streetscape.
These include infiltration planters along the sidewalks that facilitate inflow from adjacent sidewalks and buildings as well as a structural cell tree and stormwater management system to enhance water storage capacity and promote healthy tree growth.

Garden

Gardens by the Bay

Side Effect

Sensational Garden

Gardens by the Bay will provide a unique leisure destination for local and international visitors
가든스 바이 더 베이는 지역민과 해외관광객 모두에게 독특한 여가 체험의 기회를 제공하게 될 것이다

Gardens by the Bay

Grant Associates

Landscape Architects _ Grant Associates

Architects _ Wilkinson Eyre Architects

Client _ National Parks Board of Singapore

Engineers _ Atelier One, Atelier Ten

Quantity Surveyors _ Davis Langdon and Seah

Collaborators _ Thomas Matthews

Location _ Singapore

Site Area _ 54 Hectares

Photograph _ Courtesy of Grant Associates

Text & Material _ Grant Associates

싱가포르가 야심차게 추진하고 있는 가든스 바이 더 베이Gardens by the Bay 프로젝트의 1단계 구역인 베이 사우스 가든Bay South Garden이 지난 6월 29일 일반에 공개되었다. 싱가포르 국립공원운영이사회National Parks Board of Singapore가 발주한 이 프로젝트는 지난 2006년 국제공모를 통해 영국의 그랜트 어소시에이츠가 이끄는 설계팀을 베이 사우스 가든에 대한 설계사로 선정하였다.

가든스 바이 더 베이는 비슷한 성격의 프로젝트로는 세계에서 가장 큰 규모의 정원 프로젝트 중 하나이다. 공원의 전체 부지는 101헥타르에 이르며, 베이 사우스Bay South, 베이 이스트Bay East, 베이 센트럴Bay Central 등 총 세 곳의 개성 넘치는 공원들로 채워질 예정이다. 싱가포르의 새로운 도심으로 급부상하고 있는 마리나 베이Marina Bay의 간척지에 위치한 가든스 바이 더 베이는 지역민과 해외관광객 모두에게 독특한 여가 체험의 기회를 제공하게 될 것이다. 이 중 베이 사우스는 가든스 바이 더 베이에서 가장 큰 규모의 공원이며, 마리나 베이 샌즈Marina Bay Sands와 인접한 54헥타르 넓이의 부지에 자리 잡고 있다.

이 프로젝트는 싱가포르의 미래 비전인 "공원 속의 도시City in a Garden"의 핵심 사업 가운데 하나이며, 싱가포르의 국가적 위상을 제고하는 한편, 세계 최고 수준의 원예 및 정원 조성 기법을 보여주는 것을 목표로 설계되었다.

난초의 형태에서 영감을 얻은 그랜트 어소시에이츠의 마스터플랜에서는 자연, 기술, 그리고 환경 관리의 조화로운 결합을 엿볼 수 있다. 눈이 휘둥그레질 만큼 멋진 건축물들이 다채로운 원예 시설물, 햇빛과 음향 효과, 호수, 숲, 이벤트 공간, 그리고 다수의 음식점 및 상업시설 등과 절묘하게 어우러져 있다. 전체 계획에 지능형 환경 기반시설을 포함시킴으로써 일반적인 환경에서라면 결코 싱가포르에서 생장할 수 없는 멸종위기 식물들이 잘 자라날 수 있도록 했으며, 여가와 교육적 측면에서 이점을 취할 수 있도록 하였다.

The first phase of Singapore's dramatic Gardens by the Bay project opens to the public on 29th June following completion of the 54-hectare £500m Bay South Garden by a world-class British design team led by Bath-based landscape architects, Grant Associates.

Gardens by the Bay is one of the largest garden projects of its kind in the world. Ultimately, the site will total 101 hectares comprising three distinct gardens — Bay South, Bay East and Bay Central. Located on reclaimed land in Singapore's new downtown at Marina Bay, the site will provide a unique leisure destination for local and international visitors.
Bay South is the largest garden at Gardens by the Bay and it stands at 54 hectares located next to the Marina Bay Sands.

The project is an integral part of Singapore's "City in a Garden" vision, designed to raise the profile of the city globally whilst showcasing the best of horticulture and garden artistry.

A Great British Collaboration

Following an international design competition, a team led by landscape architecture firm Grant Associates was appointed in 2006 by the National Parks Board of Singapore to masterplan Bay South Garden, the first and largest of the three planned gardens at Gardens by the Bay.

A Fusion of Nature and Technology

Taking inspiration from the form of the orchid, Grant Associates' masterplan is a rich fusion of nature, technology and environmental management. Stunning architectural structures are combined with a wide variety of horticultural displays, daily light and sound shows, lakes, forests, event spaces and a host of dining and retail offerings. The whole plan has an intelligent environmental infrastructure, allowing endangered plants, which could not normally grow in Singapore to flourish, providing both leisure and education to the nation.

Supertree Grove is lined by a 300m long colonnaded walkway providing shaded and dry connection across the site
수퍼트리 그로브에는 300미터 길이의 산책로가 자리 잡고 있는데, 이 길을 통해 방문객들은 선선한 그늘을 즐기며 공원을 둘러볼 수 있다

An aerial walkway suspended from the Supertrees offers visitors a unique perspective on the gardens
수퍼트리로부터 공중에 매달린 산책로에서 방문객들은 정원 전역에 대한 독특한 전망을 즐길 수 있다

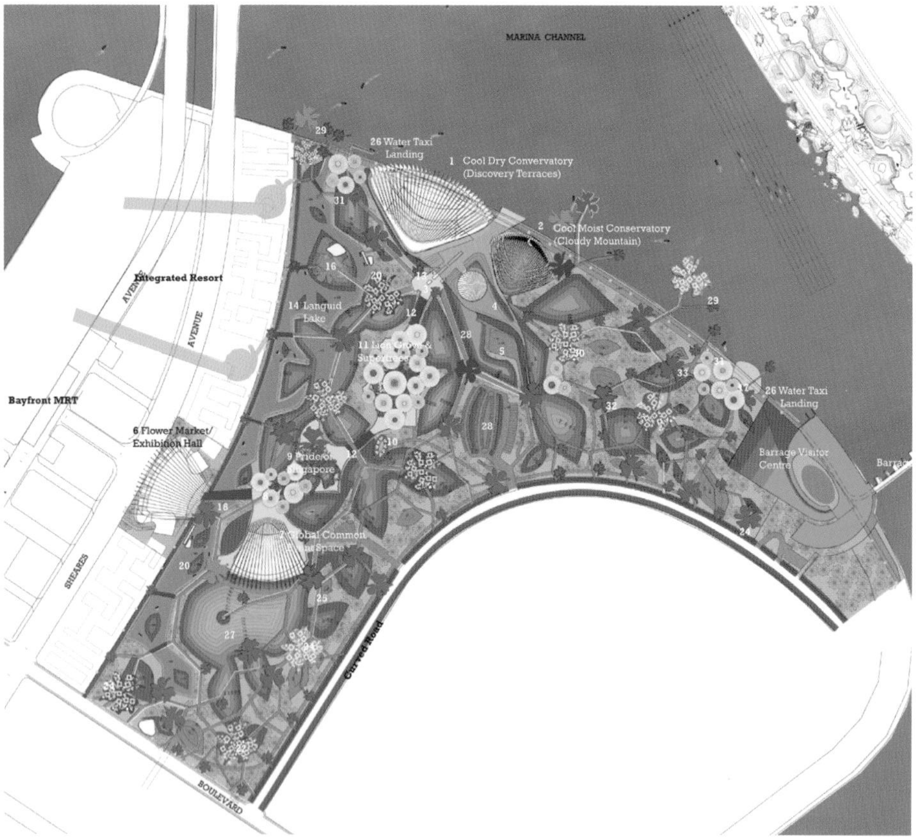

Master Plan

수퍼트리

25미터에서 50미터의 높이9~16층로 제작된 18개의 수퍼트리는 상징적 의미가 강조된 수직 형태의 정원이다. 방문객들에게서 "와!"하는 탄성을 자아내는 데 주안점을 두고 제작된 수퍼트리에는 열대의 덩굴 및 착생식물, 그리고 양치식물 등을 수직적으로 배치하였다. 밤이 되면 수퍼트리의 캐노피들은 조명과 다양한 매체를 통해 새로운 활기를 얻게 된다. 수퍼트리로부터 공중에 매달린 산책로에서 방문객들은 정원 전역에 대한 독특한 전망을 즐길 수 있다. 수퍼트리에는 저온 온실Cooled Conservatories의 냉방에 반드시 필요한 지속가능한 에너지 및 수자원 관리 기술이 적용되었다. 싱가포르의 적도성 기후를 고려했을 때, 수퍼트리의 캐노피가 자아내는 그늘 및 휴식공간은 방문객들에게 적잖은 편의를 제공하게 된다.

수퍼트리 가운데 가장 높은 나무의 꼭대기에는 윌킨슨 에어 아키텍츠Wilkinson Eyre Architects가 설계한 바가 자리하고 있으며, 지상 20미터 높이에는 그랜트 어소시에이츠가 설계한 공중 산책로가 위치해 있다.

Supertrees

Between 25 and 50 metres in height (9 to 16 storeys), the 18 Supertrees designed by Grant Associates are iconic vertical gardens, with emphasis placed on creating a "wow" factor through the vertical display of tropical flowering climbers, epiphytes and ferns. At night, these canopies come alive with lighting and projected media. An aerial walkway suspended from the Supertrees offers visitors a unique perspective on the gardens. The Supertrees are embedded with sustainable energy and water technologies integral to the cooling of the Cooled Conservatories.

Given the equatorial climate, the grove of Supertrees will help to ameliorate discomfort by providing shade and shelter with the canopy. The Supertrees support a bar at the top of the tallest tree (designed by Wilkinson Eyre Architects) and an aerial walkway experience 20m above the ground (designed by Grant Associates).

수퍼트리는 열대의 덩굴 및 착생식물, 양치식물 등이 수직적으로 배치된 상징적 의미가 강조된 수직 정원이다

Supertrees are iconic vertical gardens, with the vertical display of tropical flowering climbers, epiphytes and ferns

저온 온실

온실 컴플렉스Conservatory Complex는 건축적 상징성을 지니는 한편 원예와 관련된 볼거리를 제공하는 동시에 지속가능한 에너지 관리 기술을 선보인다. 윌킨슨 에어 아키텍츠가 설계한 플라워 돔Flower Dome, 1.2ha과 클라우드 포레스트 돔Cloud Forest Dome, 0.8ha 등 두 개의 거대한 생물계에는 지중해성 기후부터 열대 산간 지방에 이르는 다양한 지역의 식물 및 꽃들이 전시되어 있으며, 관람객들은 전천후 "에듀테인먼트" 공간을 만끽하게 된다.

온실의 환경친화적 에너지 관리를 확보하기 위해 국립공원이사회는 에너지 모델링 연구를 의뢰한 바 있다. 이 연구에 따르면 최신 냉방 기술을 적용시킴으로써 온실의 에너지 사용량은 비슷한 크기를 가진 싱가포르의 평균적 상업용 건물의 그것과 견줄 수 있는 수준으로 유지할 수 있다고 한다.

The Conservatory Complex is an architectural icon, a horticultural attraction and a showcase of sustainable energy technology
온실 컴플렉스는 건축적 상징성을 지니는 한편 원예와 관련된 볼거리를 제공하는 동시에 지속가능한 에너지 관리 기술을 선보인다

Cooled Conservatories

The Conservatory Complex is an architectural icon, a horticultural attraction and a showcase of sustainable energy technology.

Two giant biomes designed by Wilkinson Eyre Architects — the Flower Dome (1.2 hectare) and the Cloud Forest Dome (0.8 hectare) — display plants and flowers from the Mediterranean-type climatic regions and Tropical Montane (Cloud Forest) environments and provide an all-weather "edutainment" space within the Gardens.

To ascertain the environmentally sensitive energy requirements of the Conservatory, NParks commissioned an energy modeling study. The study shows that, by applying the latest cooling technologies, the energy consumption for the Conservatory is comparable to that of an average commercial building in Singapore of the same footprint and height, normalised to a 24-hour cooling period.

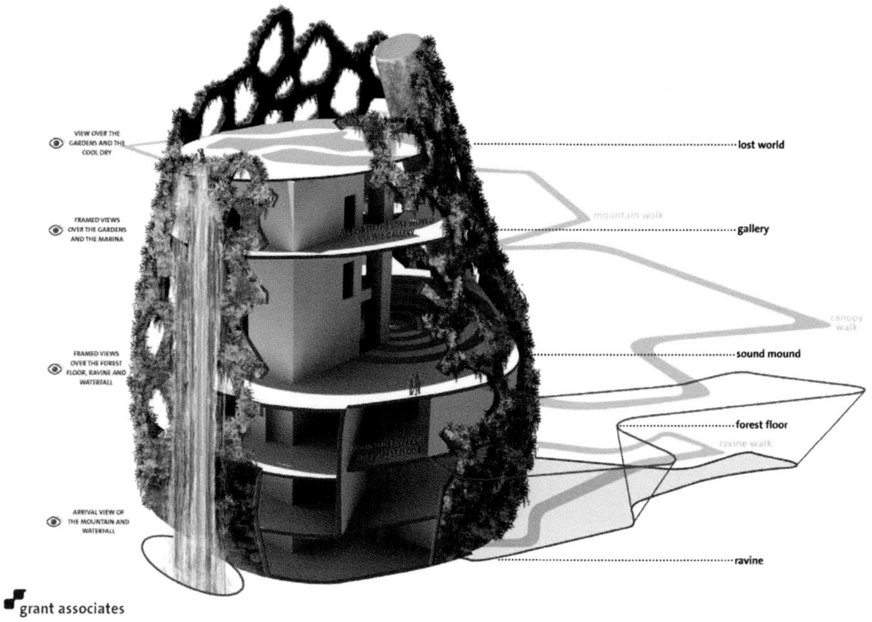

The project is an integral part of Singapore's "City in a Garden" vision, designed to raise the profile of the city globally whilst showcasing the best of horticulture and garden artistry

이 프로젝트는 싱가포르의 미래 비전인 "공원 속의 도시"의 핵심 사업 가운데 하나이며, 싱가포르의 국가적 위상을 제고하는 한편, 세계 최고 수준의 원예 및 정원 조성 기법을 보여주는 것을 목표로 설계되었다

Eco System

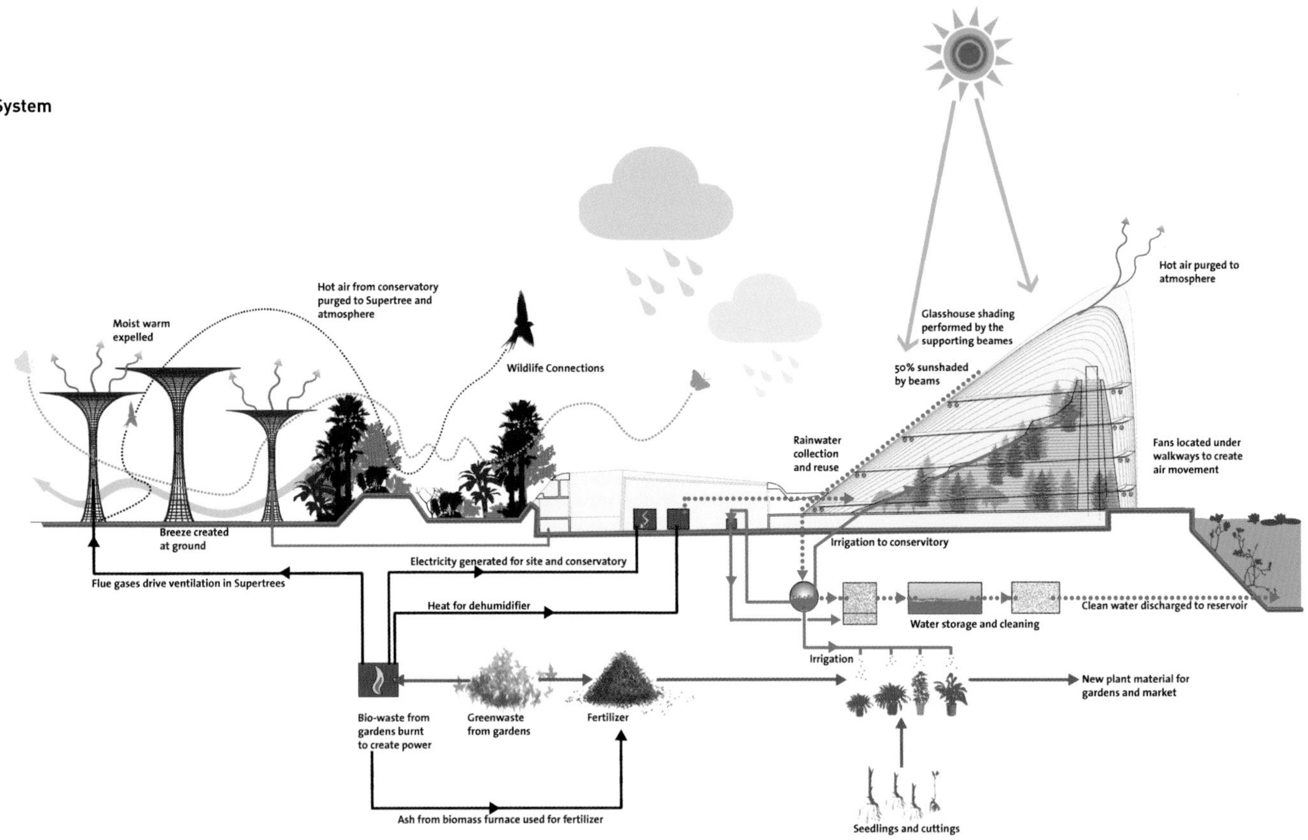

원예 정원

헤리티지 가든Heritage Garden과 식물의 세계The World of Plants는 각각 '식물과 인간' 그리고 '식물과 지구'를 그 주제로 삼고 있다. 이들 시설은 수많은 꽃과 다채로운 빛깔의 잎사귀로 이뤄진 주변 경관과 절묘한 조화를 이뤄, 색, 질감, 그리고 향기가 가득한 장관을 연출함으로써 방문객들에게 매혹적 경험을 선사한다.

기타 볼거리들

대상지의 중앙에 위치한 수퍼트리 그로브Supertree Grove는 12개의 수퍼트리가 모여 있는 최대 규모의 정원이다. 이 정원에는 300미터 길이의 산책로가 자리 잡고 있는데, 이 길을 통해 방문객들은 선선한 그늘을 즐기며 공원을 둘러볼 수 있다. 또한 기근을 위한 퍼골라가 설치되어 있어 열대 덩굴식물이 자라나는 모습을 관람할 수 있다.

잠자리 호수Dragonfly Lake는 1킬로미터 길이의 호수로서 수퍼트리 및 온실과 함께 드라마틱한 경관을 자아낸다. 독특한 형태의 잠자리 다리Dragonfly Bridge는 도심과 정원 중심부를 연결해준다. 호수 주변으로는 보드워크와 수변 공원이 마련되어 있고, 더불어 정수 시스템이 설치돼 가든스 바이 더 베이 전역에 걸친 수질 관리에 보탬이 되도록 했다.

Horticultural Gardens

Two collections The Heritage Gardens and The World of Plants centre on 'Plants and People' and 'Plants and Planet'. Together with mass flowering and coloured foliage landscape, they form a spectacle of colour and texture and fragrance within the Gardens, providing a mesmerising experience for visitors.

Other Bay South Garden Attractions

Supertree Grove is the largest garden at the heart of the site featuring a cluster of 12 Supertrees. The garden is lined by a 300m long colonnaded walkway providing shaded and dry connection across the site and by a display of Aerial Root pergolas displaying tropical climbing plants.

Dragonfly Lake is a 1km long lake creating a dramatic setting to the Supertrees and Conservatories. The distinctive Dragonfly Bridge connects the city to the central gardens. The lake is lined by boardwalk and special aquatic gardens and a system of filter beds that are part of the water quality management for the site.

Given the equatorial climate, the grove of Supertrees will help to ameliorate discomfort by providing shade and shelter with the canopy

싱가포르의 적도성 기후를 고려했을 때, 수퍼트리의 캐노피가 자아내는 그늘 및 휴식공간은 방문객들에게 적잖은 편의를 제공하게 된다

Side Effect

Amir Lotan

Design _ Amir Lotan, Landscape Architect

Location _ Intersection of Ort Israel and Melacha Streets, Bat Yam, Israel

Area _ 2,000㎡

Completion _ 2010

Photograph _ Ben Herzog

Text & Material _ Amir Lotan

The site on which 'Side Effect' is located is at the fault line between the city's residential and industrial areas, in what can be called an 'intermediate' zone

'사이트 이펙트'가 위치한 대상지는 도시의 거주지역과 공업지역의 경계선상, 즉 '중간'지대라고 부를만한 곳에 있다. 이 지역은 도시계획의 목적에 부합하지 못하여 버려졌다

건설과 도심 개발엔 종종 예상치 못한 파편화된 부작용이 있고, 이것의 결과물은 독특한 경관을 형성한다. 사회에서 우리는 책임을 부인하며 한 공간에서의 건축 행위의 결과를 무시하고, 억압하고, 은폐하고자 한다. 이러한 결과는 대부분 전통적인 도시생활 밖에 존재하고, 그곳의 정체성과 미학, 법적 정의는 독특하며, 건축 대상지 가장자리에서 자라는 식물계가 일반적인 '결과물'로, 가장자리는 특정한 환경에서 자라나 번성하는 다양한 종과 식물들의 서식지가 된다. 이 서식지에는 주변 생태계를 위협할 수 있는 침입종과 잠재적으로 해로울 수 있는 식물종이 우세하다. 대부분의 경우 거친 땅에서 자라는 식물들이 나타나면 우리는 이것들을 제거하곤 한다. 하지만 이런 정의는 건축되고 조경된 도시환경의 맥락과 과연 관련이 있는 것일까?

이러한 서식지의 표면은 대개 건축 폐기물이나 기반시설의 잔해, 쓰레기 산과 버려진 아스팔트 더미 같은 원자재로 이루어져 있다. 바트 얌의 산업지대현재 다목적 상업구역으로 바뀌고 있다는 여러 면에서 '변두리'이다. 이곳은 도시의 주요 도로에서 떨어진 주거 밀집 지대이고 버려진 건물들이 많으며, 일부는 도시의 경계 근처에 위치하여 황폐해진 도시 조직을 드러낸다. 여기에서 작업하는 동안 나는 앞서 말한 특징과 재료에 맞닥뜨렸다. 따라서 이들을 통해 규정되고 간과되어 온 지역들을 부각시키고자 했다. 예를 들어 대상지의 경계를 정의하는 '침략적인' 식생을 수용하고 의도적으로 더 도입하여 이 지역의 자연적 미학과 텍스처를 강조하고 강화할 수 있었다. '사이드 이펙트'는 도시경관을 현존하는 대상지의 새로운 정체성을 형성하는데 있어 다시 상상하거나 다시 사용하기 위해 그것을 세운 바로 그 요소들로 바꾸고 해체하고자 하였다.

An area's natural aesthetic and texture can be highlighted and strengthened by accepting and purposefully introducing more of the 'invasive' vegetation that defines the site's edges

대상지의 경계를 정의하는 '침략적인' 식생을 수용하고, 의도적으로 더 도입하여 이 지역의 자연적 미학과 텍스처를 강조하고 강화하였다

Construction and urban development often have unpredictable and fragmented side effects, the sum of which form specific landscapes. As a society, we tend to ignore, repress and suppress the consequences of our own building actions on a space, denying our responsibility. These consequences mainly exist outside traditional urban life and have unique identities, aesthetics and statutory definitions. A common 'consequence' is the plant-life that grows on the edge of built sites. These margins become habitats for various species and plants that thrive and grow in that particular environment. Predominant to said habitats are invasive and potentially harmful plant species, which may threaten surrounding ecosystems. In most cases, when these ruderal plants appear, we try to get eliminate them. However, are these definitions relevant in the context of built and landscaped urban environments?

The surface of these habitats is mostly comprised of raw materials such as construction debris, infrastructure leftovers, hills of dirt and piles of abandoned asphalt. Bat-Yam's industrial zone (now undergoing a transformation into a multi-purpose business district) is a 'margin' in many ways; it is a dense residential area apart from the city's main arteries, it is home to many abandoned buildings, parts of it are located adjacent to the city limits, and it reveals a dilapidated urban tissue. During my work there, I encountered said characteristics and materials, and therefore sought to spotlight the ignored areas that were defined by them. For example, an area's natural aesthetic and texture can be highlighted and strengthened by accepting and purposefully introducing more of the 'invasive' vegetation that defines the site's edges. 'Side Effect' attempts to alter and deconstruct the urban landscape into the very elements that constructed it, in order to re-imagine and re-use them to create a new identity for an existing site.

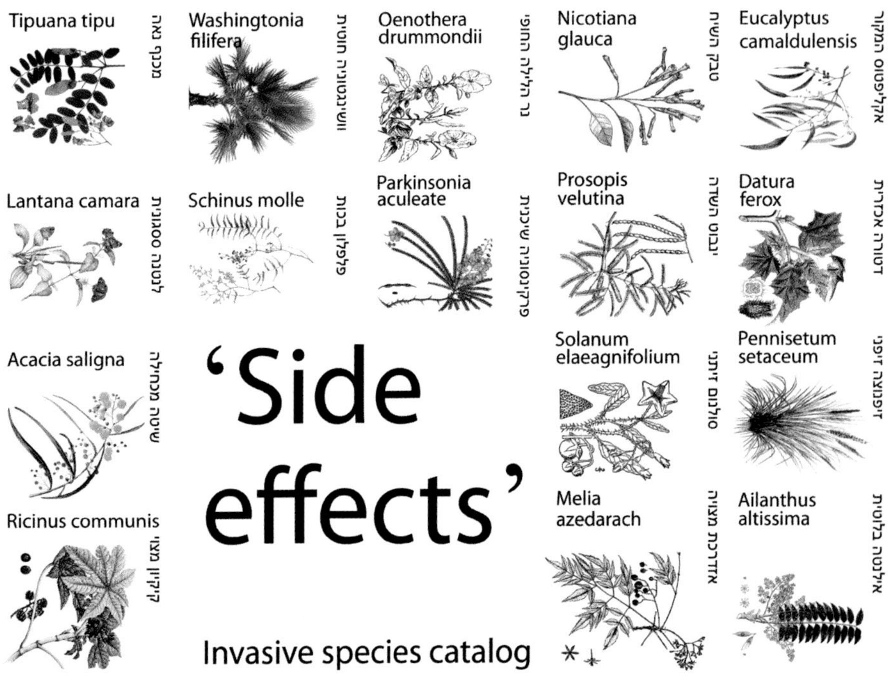

대상지

'사이트 이펙트'가 위치한 대상지는 도시의 거주지역과 공업지역의 경계선상, 즉 '중간'지대라고 부를만한 곳에 있다. 이 지역은 도시계획의 목적에 부합하지 못하여 버려졌다.

대상지 자체는 콘크리트 담장과 철조망으로 둘러싸인 건물들로 이루어져 있다. 프로젝트 이전에 버려진 건물 골조는 주변의 주민과 사업주들의 쓰레기장으로 쓰여 인근 자동차 정비소에서 나오는 폐기물을 포함한 쓰레기로 가득했다. 대상지 주변에는 공업시설과 주거시설, 고등학교와 신학교, 제지공장, 몇 개의 작은 상점이 있다. 계획에는 공업지역과 주거지역 사이에 다리를 놓고자 했다. 대상지의 건물 골조가 작업의 기초가 되었으며, 구조를 축소하고 주변의 부가적 공간을 규정하여 새로운 대상지가 만들어졌다. 석면 지붕을 제거하자 인상적인 철골 구조물이 드러났다. 내벽은 안전상의 이유로 제거되었고, 외벽에 새로운 문을 몇 개 만들어 건물을 주변과 연결했다. 뿐만 아니라 대상지를 거리와 건물로부터 차단하던 철조망을 높이 올린 콘크리트 담장도 제거되었다. 이 콘크리트는 얇게 잘려 대상지의 새로운 입구를 경계 짓는 수평면을 만드는데 재사용되었다.

이렇게 하여 건물의 어떤 부분은 깎이고 분해되어 대상지를 새롭게 만드는 원자재로 사용되면서 빌딩은 어느 정도 '소화'되었다. 이 조각들은 새롭게 구축된 대상지의 재탄생을 상징한다. 구조의 외벽에 있던 시멘트–조개 혼합물 블록 코팅은 남았지만 내벽은 보통 '위험' 사인에 쓰이는 노란색으로 칠해져 침입종에 의한 생태계적 위협을 시각적으로 표현했다. 대상지의 바닥은 일종의 구멍 난 아스팔트 '카펫'으로 구상되었다. 이 새로 만들어진 구멍에는 인도먹구슬나무를 포함하여 거친 땅에서 자라는 식물들을 심었다.

주변 자동차 정비소에서 가져온 낡은 타이어로 식재 구멍의 가장자리를 두르고, 새로 노출된 철제 지붕에 스프링클러를 달아 주변 고등학교의 쉬는 시간에 맞춰 하루에 세 번 공기 중에 물을 뿌린다.

따라서 대상지는 지역 주민들, 특히 이곳을 교정의 비공식적 연장이라고 보는 학생들의 휴게공간이 되었다. 대상지는 또한 주변 상점주와 판매자들이 점심시간 동안 쉴 수 있는 공간으로도 쓰인다. 앞서 언급한 자동차 정비소의 주인은 대상지의 비공식 관리자가 되어 반달리즘이나 다른 위협으로부터 이곳을 지킨다. 이제 활기가 넘치는 대상지에서 도시는 대안적인 사교활동과 장소를 탐색할 수 있다.

The floor of the site was planned as a kind of perforated asphalt 'carpet'. In the holes of this newly created floor ruderal plants were planted, including Margosa trees. The planting holes were bordered by old tires from the nearby garage

대상지의 바닥은 일종의 구멍난 아스팔트 '카펫'으로 구상되었다. 이 새로 만들어진 바닥 구멍에는 인도먹구슬나무를 포함하여 거친 땅에서 자라는 식물들을 심었다. 주변 자동차 정비소에서 가져온 낡은 타이어로 식재 구멍의 가장자리를 댄다

'Side Effect' attempts to alter and deconstruct the urban landscape into the very elements that constructed it, in order to re-imagine and re-use them to create a new identity for an existing site

'사이드 이펙트'는 도시 경관을 현존하는 대상지의 새로운 정체성을 형성하는데 있어 다시 상상하거나 다시 사용하기 위해 그것을 세운 바로 그 요소들로 바꾸고 해체하고자 하였다

THE SITE

The site on which 'Side Effect' is located is at the fault line between the city's residential and industrial areas, in what can be called an 'intermediate' zone. The area does not fulfill its purpose, according to the city's plan, and is therefore abandoned. The site itself comprises of a building, surrounded by a concrete wall and barbed wire. Prior to the project, the abandoned building skeleton was used as a dumping ground by the surrounding residents and business owners, filled with refuse material including that from a nearby garage. The site is bordered by industry and residences and public facilities including a high school, a religious school, a paper mill and a few small stores. In my plan, I tried to create a bridge between the industrial zone and the residential one. The building skeleton at the site was the basis of the work. By paring down the structure and defining additional space around it, a new site was created. After the removal of the Asbestos roof, an impressive steel construction was exposed. The interior walls were dismantled for safety reasons and some new openings were created through the external walls, so as to connect the building with its surroundings. Furthermore, another concrete wall with an elevated wire fence that originally blocked the site from the street and buildings was removed. The concrete was then sliced up and recycled to form a horizontal plane that defines a new entrance to the site. By doing so, of the building was semi 'digested'; as certain parts of the building were carved and dismantled, they were used as the raw materials for reshaping the site. These pieces symbolize the rebirth of the newly constructed site. The structure's external walls' original coating of cement-seashell compound blocks was left, while the internal walls were painted in the shade of yellow that is typically used for 'Hazard' signs; a visual expression of the ecological threat of the invasive species. The floor of the site was planned as a kind of perforated asphalt 'carpet'. In the holes of this newly created floor ruderal plants were planted, including Margosa trees. The planting holes were bordered by old tires from the nearby garage. In addition, sprinklers were hung from the newly exposed steel roof, to mist the air three times a day, in coordination with the adjacent high school's recesses. Thus, the site was transformed into a refreshing space for the people of the area, especially for the students who now see it as an informal extension of their schoolyard. The site also serves the local business owners and vendors as a place of rest during their lunch hour. The owner of the previously mentioned garage has become the site's informal caretaker, protecting it from vandalism and other threats. The now active site allows the city to explore alternative social activities and locations.

Sprinklers were hung from the newly exposed steel roof, to mist the air three times a day, in coordination with the adjacent high school's recesses
새로 노출된 철제 지붕에 스프링클러를 달아, 주변 고등학교의 쉬는 시간에 맞춰 하루에 세 번 공기 중에 물을 뿌린다

During the 2010 Bat-Yam Biennale of Landscape Urbanism the site was home to various activities

2010년 바트 얌 랜드스케이프 어바니즘 비엔날레 기간 동안, 대상지에서는 다양한 활동이 이루어졌다

The performance Shirana, which is led by a choir of Jewish, Muslim and Christian women from Jaffa, who sing in response to one another.

The now active site allows the city to explore alternative social activities and locations

야파의 유대교, 이슬람교, 기독교 여성들이 서로에게 응답하며 노래하는 합창단이 이끄는 Shirana 공연이 있었다. 이제 활기가 넘치는 대상지에서 도시는 대안적인 사교활동과 장소를 탐색할 수 있다

Sensational Garden

Nabito Architects and Partners

이탈리아 프로시오네Frosione시 꼬르소 라치오Corso Lazio지역에 사람들이 25년 동안 기다려온 최초의 공공 공간이 마침내 마련되었다. 센세이셔널 가든은 주로 주거 용도인 해당 지역의 공공 공간 및 서비스를 혁신, 통합하고자 수립된 거대 마스터플랜의 출발점이 될 것이다. 공공 공간의 부재로 인하여 이 지역 전체의 가치가 심대하게 하락하였을 뿐만 아니라, 지속가능성 역시 훼손되었다. 이러한 문제 의식을 바탕으로 센세이셔널 가든은 관계지향적 공간 아이디어를 한층 확장시켜, 폭발력 있고, 즐거우며, 감각적인 동시에 상호적인, 마치 개인의 거실과도 같은 친밀한 공간을 사회적 맥락 속에 구축하고자 한다. 센세이셔널 가든에서는 인공적 요소들과 자연적 요소들이 지속적 긴장 관계를 유지하게 된다. 센세이셔널 가든에서 방문객들과 시민들은 삶의 즐거움을 발견하고, 다시금 서로를 알아가게 될 것이며, 지역 전체에 대해 더 큰 친근감을 느낄 것이다. 이를 바탕으로 이 지역의 사회적 지속가능성에도 혁신이 이뤄지게 된다.

공공 공간을 누릴 수 있는 시민의 권리를 보장, 획득하기 위한 지속적 투쟁을 통해 이번 건설 사업의 성격을 분명히 확인할 수 있다. 이 경우 대단히 커다란 역설을 목도하게 된다. 공공 부문을 통해 사업 의뢰가 이뤄졌지만, 그 실현에 있어서는 우리들 민간 부문의 역할, 즉 시정부 및 공공사업과를 도와 목표를 완수하고자 하는 설계팀의 의지가 결정적 요소로 작용하였다. 설계를 맡은 Nabito Architects and Partners는 올해 본 프로젝트를 완성시키면서 시민의 권리를 찾기 위해 3년 전 시작된 싸움에서 승리를 거두었다. 본 프로젝트의 목적은 경관이 지속적으로 변화하는 경로로 사용자들을 인도하는 것이다. 사용자는 계속 달라지면서도, 일정한 성격을 유지하는 공간을 발견하는 느낌을 받게 될 것이다. 인간의 오감이 공간의 주된 테마가 되며, 재료의 사용과 식생의 배치 역시 이와 관련되어 있다. 사용자는 한 눈에 공원 전체를 조망할 수는 없을 테지만, 각기 다른 일련의 감각 기관을 통해서라면 가능할 것이다. 다양한 높낮이와 경사도 등은 이 공원에 유쾌한 독특함을 가져다주며 감각들은 거대한 메타포로 활용된다. 이 감각을 통해 우리들 자신을 주변 환경 및 다른 사람들과 연관 짓게 된다.

각각의 구역은 인간 오감 중 하나에 대한 메타포로 활용되며, 방문자는 방문자 자신과 공간 사이에 일정한 관계를 형성하라는 끊임없는 요청을 받게 된다. 경로는 발견이며, 공간은 방문자에게 그 모습을 조금씩 드러내도록 설계되었다. 이를 통해 방문자는 이러한 발견의 경험을 지속해나가게 된다. 파이브 빅 디바이시스Five Big Devices는 이러한 메타포의 본질 및 시적 아름다움을 품고 있다. 경로는 이들 사이의 연결고리가 된다. 아름다운 장미 정원은 시각을 즐겁게 하고, 과일 나무들은 미각을 자극하는 등 모든 감각이 정원을 직접 체험한다. 자연의 본질적 요소들나무, 관목, 그리고 꽃과 인공적 요소들시멘트와 합성수지의 균형적 조화를 통해 공원의 관리를 용이하게 할 수 있을 뿐만 아니라, 그 내구성 및 가변성을 높일 수 있다.

Design _ Nabito Architects and Partners
Design Team _ Alessandra Faticanti, Roberto Ferlito, Luca Faticanti(Architecture), Damiano Bauco (Engineering), Gianluca Sanità(Agriculture)
Client _ Frosinone's Municipality
Collaborators _ Davide Fois, Lucio Altana, Joanna Rodriguez Noyola, Agita Putnina, Furio Sordini
Location _ Frosinone, Italy
Completion _ 2011
Text & Material _ Nabito Architects and Partners

The project for the sensational garden amplifies the idea of a relational space filling the social void with an explosive, playful, sensorial and interactive intimate room, like a personal living room in a public realm

The neighbourhood of Corso Lazio, in the city of Frosinone, Italy, can finally enjoy its first public space, that it has been expecting for 25 years now. The sensational garden represents the starting point of a big masterplan to renew and integrate the public spaces and the services to the housing neighbourhood. This lack of public spaces generate an absolute degrade of the entire area, and the neighbourhood has become an unsustainable dormitory. For this reason the project for the sensational garden amplifies the idea of a relational space filling the social void with an explosive, playful, sensorial and interactive intimate room, like a personal living room in a public realm. The garden is constantly in tension between artificial and natural elements. It is a garden in which users and citizens can find the joy of life, love and get to know each other again and make themselves comfortable with the entire neighbourhood, thus renewing the social sustainability of this site in Frosinone. The continuous fight to obtain and respect a citizen's right to a public space has characterized the development of the building site. In this case we verify a very big paradox. The commission was public, but the realization was forced by our private will "helping" the city hall and department of public works to accomplish his duty: the good of the community. Nabito Architects and Partners won in 2011 an unsustainable battle for the citizens' rights that started three years ago.

The goal of the project is to invite users to a path in which the scene is always changing. The user will have the sensation of discovering an always-different space but with the same kind of characteristic. The five human senses are the main theme of the space; the materials and vegetation will relate to them. The user will not have an entire look over the park, but he will do through a series of the different

The goal of the project is to invite users to a path in which the scene is always changing

senses. The variation of height, inclination, and dimensional games is part of the ludic peculiarity of the park. We use the senses as a big metaphor. We use senses to relate ourselves with surroundings and other people.

Each area is a metaphor of one of the five human senses and you are constantly called to put yourself in relation with the space. The path is a discovery, and it was designed to leave the spaces to be revealed to a visitor little by little, so to induce and encourage the visitor of continuing the experience. Five Big Devices contain the essence and the poetry of the metaphor. A path is the link between them. The smell is attracted by the support of the essences, hearing, from the game sound amplification, view, from the beautiful rose garden, touch, from feeling the materials of the central cone, and finally, taste stimulated by the fruit trees in the largest support. The balanced blend of the natural essences(trees, shrubs and flowers) and the artificial elements(cement and resin) make the garden not only easy to maintain but also simultaneously durable and mutable.

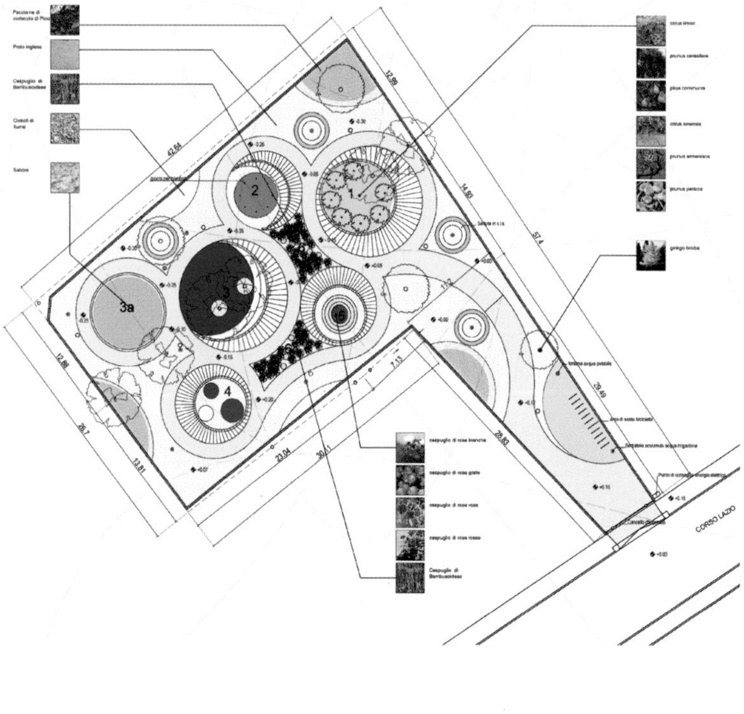
citrus limon
prunus cerasifera
pirus communis
citrus sinensis
prunus armeniaca
prunus persica
ginkgo biloba
cespuglio di rose bianche
cespuglio di rose gialle
cespuglio di rose rosa
Cespuglio di Bambusoideae
1
2
3
3a
4
5
42.64
12.99
14.93
57.4
29.49
28.83
23.04
12.88
26.7
13.81
7.13
CORSO LAZIO

1. GUSTO:
erba +alberi
2.UDITO:
ciottoli
3.TATTO/piazza:
greenfloor
4.: OLFATTO
essenze
profumate
5. VISTA
rosaceae

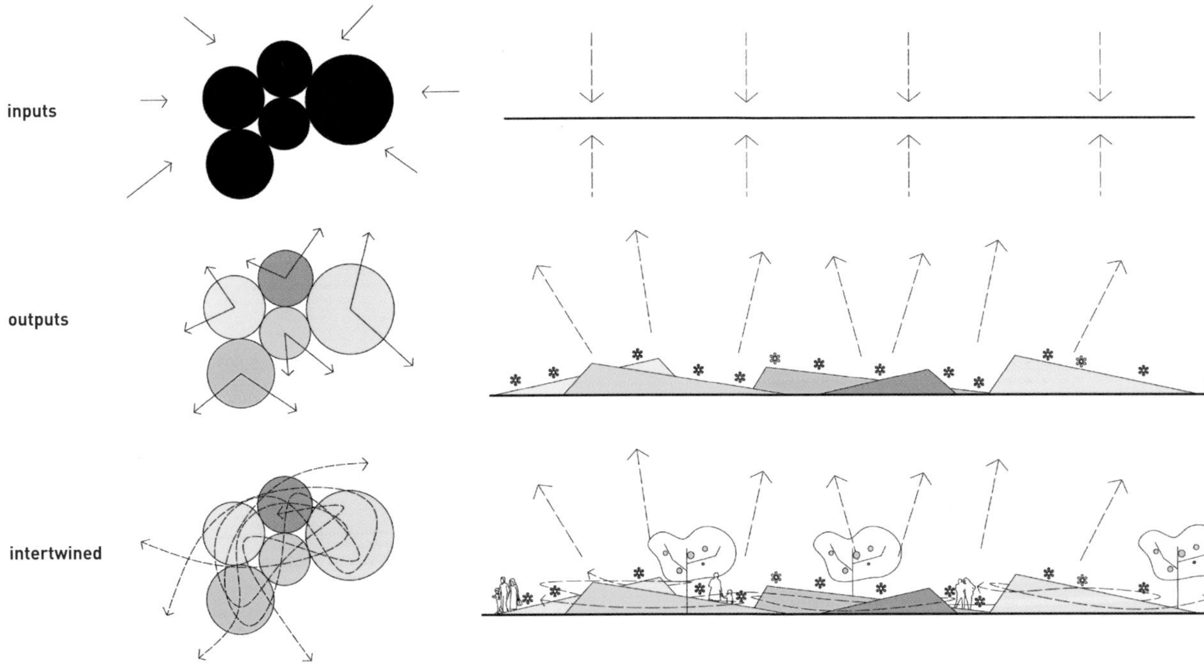

IL TATTO

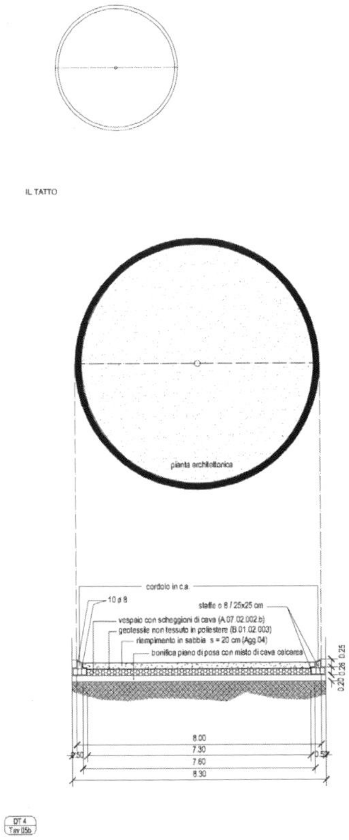

4. L' OLFATTO

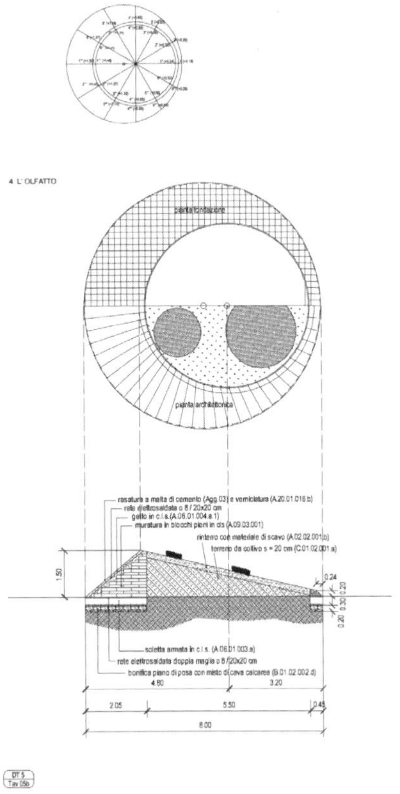

5. LA VISTA

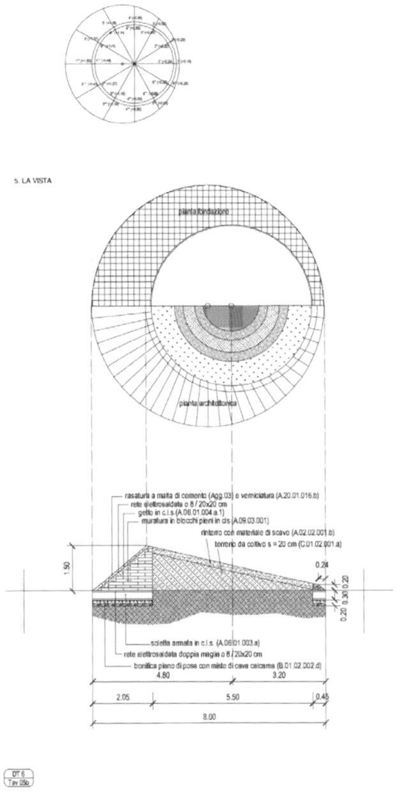

The user will have the sensation of discovering an always different space but with the same kind of characteristic. The five human senses are the main theme of the space; the materials and vegetation will relate to them

The smell is attracted by the support of the essences, hearing, from the game sound amplification, view, from the beautiful rose garden, touch, from feeling the materials of the central cone, and finally, taste stimulated by the fruit trees in the largest support

Each area is a metaphor of one of the five human senses and you are constantly called to put yourself in relation with the space

The balanced blend of the natural essences(trees, shrubs and flowers) and the artificial elements(cement and resin) make the garden not only easy to maintain but also simultaneously durable and mutable.

Plaza

Urban Redevelopment of the Plaza del Milenio

Erie Street Plaza

MediaCityUK Exterior Spaces

Plaza Ricard Viñes

Urban Redevelopment of the Plaza del Milenio

EXP ARCHITECTES and DAD ARQUITECTURA

부지와 프로그램

바야돌리드는 32만여 명이 거주하는 역사적인 도시이다. 스페인 서북부에 위치한 카스티야이레온의 주도로서 피수에르가강과 에스구에바강의 합류부에 위치하고 있다. 피수에르가강의 오른쪽 둑방의 경계를 이루고 있는 델 밀레니오 광장 구역은 이사벨 카톨릭 다리를 통해 역사지구로 연결된다. 이 프로젝트는 공공 공간 개발을 고려하여 계획되었다. 도시 중심부와 이 지역을 다시 연결시켜 피수에르가 강변을 활성화하는 것이 주된 내용으로 주차장, 문화행사를 위한 파빌리온, 거대한 광장, 환경보호구역 등의 요소들로 구성되어 있다. 가로시설물에서부터 주변 경관에 이르기까지 모든 부분을 아우르는 지역을 개발하는 계획이다. 이 프로젝트의 다양한 요소들은 각각의 다른 팀들에 의해 다루어졌는데, DAD건축에서는 400여 대의 차량을 수용할 수 있는 지하주차장과 활성화된 사회기반시설의 설계를, Cloud9는 사라고사의 국제 전시를 위해 설계되었다가 재사용된 다기능 파빌리온의 계획을 담당했다. 또한, EXP건축과 DAD건축은 공공 공간 개발, 도시공원, 교량의 재사용에 대한 계획안을 구성하였으며, Les Petits Fancais는 도심 원근도법을 완성시켰다.

EXP 건축 프로젝트

EXP건축은 지속가능한 개발을 목적으로 하고, 이러한 맥락에서 개발을 진행해 왔다.

이 프로젝트는 도시로 향하는 교량 너머까지 지역을 확장하기 위해, 수변생태계를 공공 공간으로 끌어들임으로써 혁신적인 확장을 이루는 것을 기반으로 한다. 새로 조성된 잔디광장의 중심부에 파빌리온을 배치하고, 잔디광장이 도시 중심부로 연결되도록 하여 이사벨 카톨릭 다리의 개선에 일조했다.

살짝 높여진 광장레벨은 잔디 경사면으로 이루어진 인공적인 지형과 강둑의 지속적인 움직임이 어우러지도록 하여 도시공간으로 뻗어가는 강의 분위기를 연출해준다. 점진적인 흐름에 의해 완만하게 이어지는 동선을 따라 광장과 파빌리온 주변에 이르면 주제 정원, 물의 정원, 두드러진 수목 식재 등을 통해 자연이 익숙하게 다가온다.

물가에 놓인 관찰대, 공공 및 개인이 사용할 수 있는 가로시설물, 상호작용하는 어린아이들의 놀이, 안개분수, 경치 좋은 간헐천, 조각물들과 지형에 따른 레벨을 강조하는 조명들에 의해 강둑은 새로운 자산으로서 도시공원으로 다루어지게 되었다.

Urban Redevelopment of the Plaza del Milenio, Spain, 2011

조명에 반사되는 작은 유리구슬들과 어우러진 콘크리트 벤치는 파빌리온 주변에 배치되어 정원과 연못의 틀을 만들며 진입부분을 강조한다.

휴게를 위해 강둑과 광장에 설치된 앉음 시설은 자율적이며 좀 더 지역적인 색을 띠고 있다. 다양한 동선은 보행자를 위한 편안한 순환동선을 만들고 있을 뿐만 아니라 주변 건물, 강둑, 도시 중심부로의 접근로로서의 역할도 하고 있다.

이사벨 카톨릭 다리는 현대 도시의 요구를 충족하기 위해 조명시스템과 목재데크 마감으로 보행자와 자전거 이용자를 위한 기능을 더 강화하였다. 광장에 적용된 요소들과 공통적인 요소들을 적용하면서 또한, 풍력발전기와 난간에 고정된 광전자 패널을 통해 부분적으로 전기를 공급하였다. 이러한 시설들을 통해 교량이 개선되었고 새로운 도심개발의 요소로 충분하게 작용하였다. 이 다리는 에너지 사회기반시설의 일부로 작용하고, 본 프로젝트에 대한 환경적인 열망을 일관되게 표현하고 있다.

점진적이고 지속가능한 프로젝트

운영은 GBC Espana-VERDE를 통해 이루어지며, 생태적이고 지속가능한 과정들은 대상지 전체에서 표현되고 있다. 이는 정당한 공사과정, 조작과정, 재생물질, 무형의 태양열 패널, LED조명 시스템과 세로형의 도시형 풍력발전기, 우수 재사용, 소박한 자생종 식재, 전기자동차 충전소, 셀프 대여 자전거 등을 통해 드러난다.

또한 이들은 기후, 물, 유지관리, 지형, 지역 자생종, 전망, 재생가능 에너지와 같은 지역자원을 개발하는 맥락에서 지속가능한 간섭들을 나타내는 것이다. 다기능 시스템으로서 이루어지는 이 프로젝트는 지역 정체성을 강화하여 생기발랄하고 고무적인 장소로서 환경의 질을 높이는 점진적인 변화의 가능성을 보여주고 있다.

Design _ EXP ARCHITECTES and DAD ARQUITECTURA

Design Team _ Antoine Chassagnol, Nicolas Moskwa, Maxime Vicens[Concept], Sara Delgado Vaquez, Juan Carlos Delgado[Development]

Client _ Ayuntamiento de Valladolid, Spain

Location _ Valladolid, Spain

Area _ 2.5 Hectares

Completion _ 2011

Text & Material _ EXP ARCHITECTES and DAD ARQUITECTURA

A number of paths allow easy circulation for pedestrians as well as accessibility to the surrounding buildings, to the banks and to the city center

다양한 동선은 보행자를 위한 편안한 순환동선을 만들어 줄 뿐만 아니라 주변건물, 강둑, 도시 중심부로의 접근로로서의 역할도 하고 있다

The project of urban redevelopment by EXP architects consists in renewing the square, with its new pavilion in the immediate environment, and providing for a multiuse structure which a capacity of 1500 persons.

The site and the program

Valladolid, an historic city of 320 000 inhabitants, located in North West Spain, is the capital of the province of Castile and Leon. The city stands at the confluence of the Pisuerga and the Esgueva rivers. The district of the Plaza del Milenio orders the right bank of the Pisuerga and is connected to the historic center by the Isabel the Catholic Bridge.

The project concerns the development of public spaces. It consists in re-connecting the district with the city center and of enhancing the banks of the Pisuerga river.

The project comprises several interlinked components: a car park, a pavilion dedicated to cultural events, a vast square, and an environmental reserve. The project addresses the development of the area at every scale, from the street furniture to the landscape of the river itself. The various components are managed by different teams: the underground car-park containing up to 400 vehicles and energetic infrastructures (DAD arquitectura); the multifunction pavilion - initially conceived for the international exhibition of Saragossa and reused - (Cloud 9); the development of the public spaces, and of the urban park, and the requalification of the bridge (EXP architects & DAD arquitectura); completed with an urban scenography (Les Petits Francais).

The EXP architects project

The team has developed a contextual intervention with objectives of sustainable development.

To extend the district beyond the bridge towards the city, the project is based on a progressive expansion of the ecosystem of the river towards the public space. It places the pavilion at the very heart of a new green space connected to the city center thanks to the renovation of the Isabel the Catholic Bridge.

The ground of the square lifts up slightly, providing an artificial topography of turfed slopes in continuity with the movement of the banks, allowing the atmosphere of the river to migrate towards the urban space. By a gradual passage from the vegetable to the mineral, nature is thus tamed, domesticated on the square and all around the pavilion through the creation of thematic gardens, water gardens, and the planting of remarkable trees.

The banks of the river are treated as an urban park offering new assets: observation platforms at the water's edge, collective and individual street furniture, interactive children's games, mist generators and water fountains, scenic geysers, sculptures, and lighting highlighting contour lines.

Concrete benches incorporating glass microbeads reflecting the light are disposed around the pavilion, framing gardens and ponds, and identifying the access points. Other autonomous, more domestic, seating devices are installed on the banks and on the square for rest and relaxation.

A number of paths allow easy circulation for pedestrians as well as accessibility to the surrounding buildings, to the banks and to the city center.

The role of the Isabel the Catholic Bridge is reinforced by a complete upgrade to provide for modern urban needs. It is equipped with bridges for pedestrians and cyclists, decked in wood, and enhanced by a lighting device system coordinated with that of the square, partly fed by vertical wind turbines and photovoltaic panels fixed to the parapet. Thus retrofitted, the bridge becomes a full element of the new urban development, constituting part of the energy infrastructure, consistent with the environmental aspirations of the project.

The project addresses the development of the area at every scale, from the street furniture to the landscape of the river itself

가로시설물에서부터 주변 경관에 이르기까지 모든 부분을 아우르는 지역을 개발하는 계획이다

An evolutionary and sustainable project

The operation will be certified GBC Espana - VERDE. Aseries of ecological and sustainable processes is featured on the site as a whole: clean construction processes, manufacturing process, recyclable materials, amorphous solar panels, LED lighting system, vertical urban wind turbines, rainwater recycling, planting of rustic native species, recharging terminals for electric vehicles, self-service bikes, etc.

This is a hyper-contextual and sustainable intervention exploiting local resources: climate, water and its management, topography, local plant species, perspectives, energies. The project is conceived as a multifunctional system, a vibrant, inspiring place, drawing people together, strengthening local identity and enhancing the quality of the environment, all the while providing a capacity for evolutionary change.

The district of the Plaza del Milenio is connected to the historic center by the Isabel the Catholic Bridge

델 밀레니오 광장 구역은 이사벨 카톨릭 다리를 통해 역사지구로 연결된다

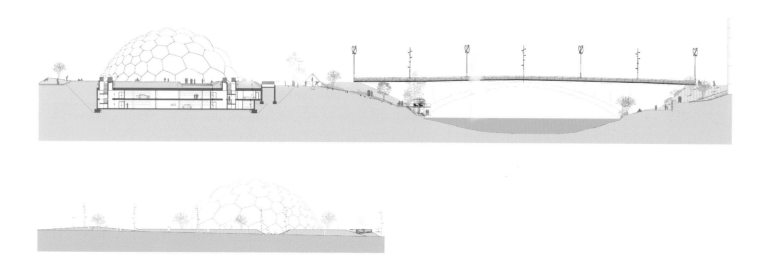

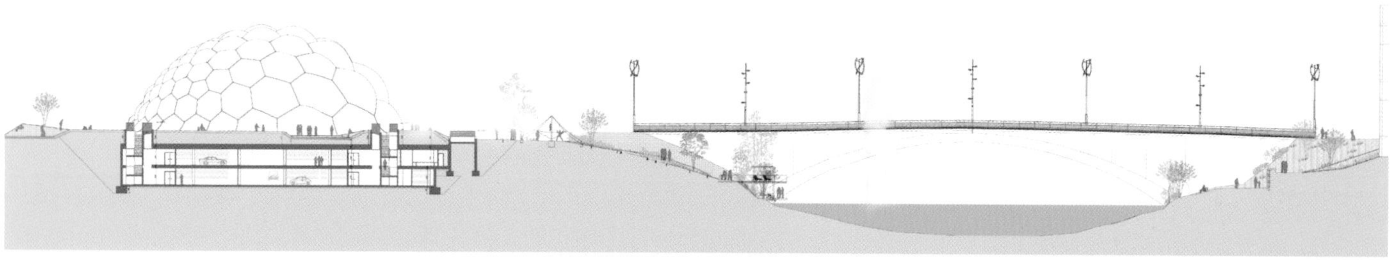

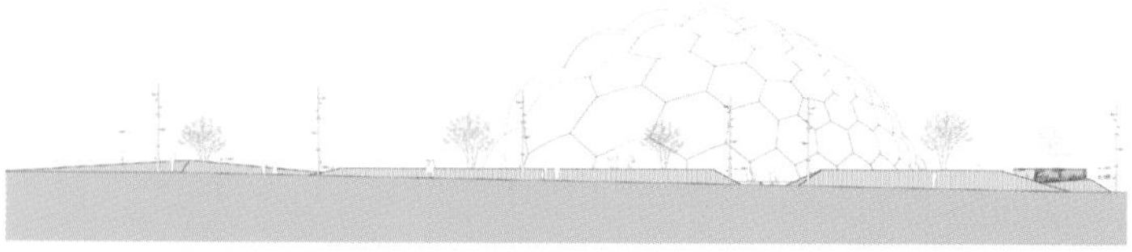

A pavilion dedicated to cultural events, a vast square, and an environmental reserve

문화행사를 위한 파빌리온, 거대한 광장, 환경보호구역 등의 요소들로 구성되어 있다

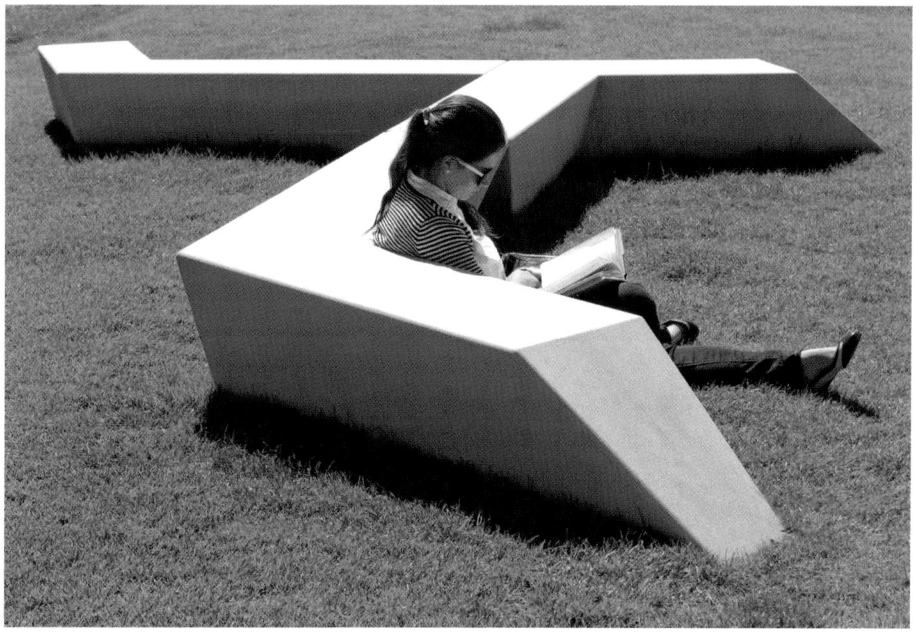

Seating devices are installed on the banks and on the square for rest and relaxation

휴게를 위해 강둑과 광장에 설치된 앉음 시설은 자율적이며, 좀 더 지역적인 색을 띄고 있다

Erie Street Plaza

Stoss Landscape Urbanism

이리 스트리트 플라자는 위스콘신주Wisconsin 밀워키시Milwaukee의 히스토릭 서드 워드Historic Third Ward 지구에 위치한 작은 도시 광장이다. 13,000평방피트 넓이의 이 광장은 밀워키강Milwaukee River이 페더럴 채널Federal Channel을 만나 미시건호Lake Michigan로 흘러들어가는 지점에 위치하고 있다. 밀워키 리버워크Milwaukee Riverwalk는 밀워키 도심과 새롭게 부상하고 있는 서드 워드 지역 및 비어라인 지역Beerline Districts 등을 연결하는 3마일 길이의 보행자 및 자전거 도로인데, 광장은 리버워크를 따라 자리잡은 일련의 공공 공간들 중 마지막 연결 고리이다. 프로젝트의 디자인을 시작하는 단계에서는 이리 스트리트 플라자의 미래, 즉 사용자, 기능, 프로그래밍, 심지어 그 필요성마저 미정인 상태였다. 주변 도시 환경은 주로 기반 시설이나 산업 시설이어서 인근 주민이나 잠재적 이용자를 찾기 어려웠다. 해당 장소는 그 자체로서 주차장으로 쓰이고 있었으며, 호수에서 불어오는 강풍을 비롯한 가혹한 환경 조건 하에 놓여 있었다. 대체 누구를 위한 광장이란 말인가? 어떻게 사용될 수 있을까? 이러한 불확실성, 달리 말해 무한한 가능성이 바로 디자인의 핵심이었다.

유연한 공간: 프로그래밍

정해진 프로그램도 직접적 이해당사자도 없었기 때문에 유연성이 가장 중요한 요소였다. 광장은 일종의 도심 속의 평원처럼 인식되고 있었으며, 사회적, 환경적 활동 및 활용을 가능케 해주리라 기대되었다. 장소 자체가 가진 다채로운 모습은 낚시, 뱃놀이, 일광욕 등 가벼운 일상적 활동에서부터 아트 페스티벌, 집회, 콘서트, 영화 상영, 결혼식, 축제, 직거래 장터, 그리고 겨울의 제전 등에 이르기까지 광범위한 활용 및 활동을 그려볼 수 있게 해준다.

다채로운 모습, 지형학적 전략, 그리고 하이브리드 생태학: 디자인 전략 및 요소

이 광장은 친근하면서도 독특하고 단순한 부분들의 절제된 조합으로 이뤄졌다 할 수 있는데, 서드 워드의 삶, 리버워크, 그리고 생태 시스템의 독특한 결합과 더불어 생동하고 있다. 광장은 도심 리버워크로부터 이어진 목조 보드워크와 미시건호의 철재 격벽bulkhead 등 지역 기반 시설 및 지리적 맥락으로 둘러싸여 있다. 리버워크가 강변을 따라 펼쳐지기 보다는 광장의 안쪽 테두리를 통해 이어지기 때문에 광장과 강이 보다 가깝게 맞닿게 되는 한편, 일시적 범람을 감당해낼 수 있는 역량 또한 증대된다. 프로젝트의 근간은 광장을 관통해 강변으로 이어지는 빛나는 수풀, 유연한 들판, 그리고 강철 습지 등 총 세 종류의 각기 다른 하이브리드 생태계이다. 빛나는 수풀은 식물 경사면의 윗부분, 즉 광장의 도심 쪽 가장자리를 차지하고 있다. 기둥처럼 솟은 수풀은 차가운 겨울바람으로부터 광장을 보호할 수 있도록 배치되었지만, 이와 동시에 전망과 안전을 도모할 수 있도록 속이 들여다보이는 구조로 설계되었다. 수풀은 도로와 평행한 직선 형태를 유지하는 한편, 강변 방향으로 개방되어 있다. 디자인의 핵심 요소인 유연한 들판은 하이브리드 녹색 광장으로서 포장면과 잔디밭으로 구성되어, 집중도가 높은 행사나 보다 여유로운 활용 모두에 적합한 형태이다. 공원에는 블록으로 성형된 포장면을 깔아 가변성과 유연성을 극대화하였다. 불규칙적으로 흩어져있는 벽면 의자나 주변의 빛을 반사하거나 내부에서 빛을 내보내는 발광성 유리 섬유 벤치 등으로 인해 광장이 지닌 불확정성이 더욱 두드러지게 나타난다. 이러한 시설들의 불규칙적인 배치를 통해 다양한 화합이나 개인적 휴식 등이 가능하며, 햇빛과 그늘 모두를 다채롭게 활용할 수 있게 된다. 유리 섬유가 가진 발광성은 밤이 찾아올 때 그 진가를 발하는데, 내부로부터 빛을 내보내는 동시에, 주변을 지나가는 자동차의 불빛을 반사하게 된다. 빛을 내는 벤치는 이 프로젝트의 대표적 특징으로 자리매김하게 되었다. 광장의 다채로운 특성은 광장 경사면의 아래쪽인 강가에 자리잡은 강철 습지로 이어진다. 빗물을 붙잡아 정화하는 역할을 담당하는 강철 습지는 광장의 빗물 관리 전략에 있어 핵심이라 할 수 있다. 기반 시설 및 산업 활동에 자리를 내주었던 습지식물들이 제자리를 찾아, 현재 보호를 받으며 이곳에서 잘 자라나고 있다.

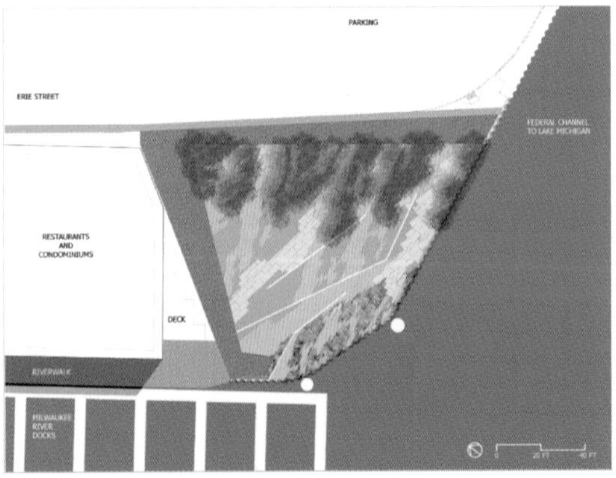

Site Plan

Along the boardwalk the grove opens up intermittently, allowing passage through to the heart of the plaza. The benches glow at night and have become a signature of the project ©John December

지속가능성

이리 스트리트 플라자는 빗물의 환경친화적 순환을 도모하고 있다. 다시 말해 빗물을 모아 새롭게 조성된 습지를 유지하고, 지하수를 확충하는 한편, 강물을 관개에 활용하고 있다. 폭우는 강철 습지가 흡수하게 되므로, 광장 방문객들이 이러한 친환경적 순환에 대해 이해할 수 있게 될 것이다. 현재 20년 주기로 간헐적으로 나타나는 미시건호의 수위 상승으로 인해 광장의 저지대가 침수될 가능성도 존재한다.

새로운 이웃, 새로운 삶:
이리 스트리트 플라자의 현재(그리고 미래)

프로젝트가 불확실성을 안고 시작된 이래로 인근의 새로운 건설 공사로 인해 해당 지역이 활기를 얻게 되었고, 광장에도 활력이 감돌게 되었다. 립 타이드 시푸드 바 앤 그릴Rip Tide Seafood Bar and Grill에는 광장을 내려다볼 수 있는 식사용 야외 데크가 마련되어 있다. 콘도미니엄도 인근 지역에 새롭게 건설되었다. 이러한 새로운 환경과 새로운 광장의 완공으로 인해 주민들이 서드 워드 지역을 바라보는 인식도 달라지게 되었다. 낮 시간대의 여러 운동 수업들과 저녁 시간대의 산책 나온 사람들을 볼 때 현재 광장의 활용이 무난히 이뤄지고 있음을 짐작할 수 있다. 주변 지역에서 일어나게 될 향후의 변화 역시 광장에 영향을 주는 동시에 광장의 유연성에 의해 수용될 것이다. 적극적 방법이든, 보다 소극적 방법이든, 혹은 간헐적 방법이든, 각각의 이용자들은 자신들만의 방식으로 광장을 활용하게 될 것이다. 사회적, 경제적 변화, 또는 환경 조건의 변동 등이 일어남에 따라 광장의 활용 방식이 기존에 비해 보다 급진적이고 극단적인 방향으로 변화할 수도 있을 것이다.

Design _ Stoss Landscape Urbanism
Chris Reed, principal, lead designer
Scott Bishop, project manager
Design Team _ Tim Barner, Adrian Fehrmann, Kristin Malone, Chris Muskopf
Graham Palmer, Megan Studer
Completion _ 2010
Location _ Milwaukee, Wisconsin, USA
Area _ 13,000sf (0.25 acres)
Photograph _ Stoss Landscape Urbanism, John December
Text & Material _ Stoss Landscape Urbanism

Erie Street Plaza is a small urban plaza in the Historic Third Ward district of Milwaukee, Wisconsin. The 13,000-square-foot plaza lies at the point where the Milwaukee River meets the Federal Channel as it empties into Lake Michigan. It is the final link in a series of public space activators along the Milwaukee Riverwalk, a three-mile pedestrian and bicycle corridor that connects downtown Milwaukee to the emerging and redeveloping Third Ward, Beerline Districts, and the lakefront beyond.

At the beginning of the project's design, the future of Erie Street Plaza - its users, its function, its programming, even its necessity - were undecided. The urban context was generally one of infrastructure and industry; the site lacked neighbors and potential users. The site itself was a surface parking lot, subject to harsh environmental conditions, including high winds off the lake. Who is it for? How will it be used? This uncertainty, this open-endedness, was at the core of its design.

FLEXIBLE FIELD: PROGRAMMING

With no set program and no immediate stakeholders, flexibility was key. The plaza was conceived as a civic plain -simply articulated and openended- that would foster social and environmental activity and appropriation. The site's variegated surface accommodates a wide range of potential uses and activities: art festivals, gatherings, concerts, movies, weddings, festivals, farmers' markets, and winter carnivals, as well as less intense, everyday activities like boat-watching, fishing, sunbathing, and simply hanging-out.

VARIGEATED SURFACE, TOPOGRAPHIC STRATEGIES, and HYBRID ECOLOGIES: DESIGN STRATEGY + ELEMENTS

The plaza is an understated assemblage of simple parts, both familiar and exotic, that pulse with the life of the Third Ward, the Riverwalk, and this unique confluence of ecological systems. The plaza is wrapped by local infrastructural and geographical frames - wooden boardwalk from the downtown Riverwalk and steel bulkhead from the Lake. Rather than following the water's edge, the Riverwalk traces the site's inland perimeter, reinforcing the plaza's connection to the river, and its accommodation of ephemeral inundations.

The project grows from three hybrid ecologies that step down across the site towards the water: radiant grove, flexible field, and steel marsh. The radiant grove occupies the upper end of the vegetal gradient, at the plaza's urban edge. The poplar grove is positioned to shelter the rest of the plaza from cold winter winds yet are deliberately transparent to allow for views and safety. The grove maintains a dense straight line parallel to street edge but opens up toward the river.

The primary element -the flexible field- is a hybridized plaza-green, with pavers and lawn surfaces that allow for both intense activity and more passive use. The plaza is articulated as an eroded field of custom pre-cast pavers distributed to maximize variability and flexibility. The plaza's indeterminacy is accentuated by the erratic

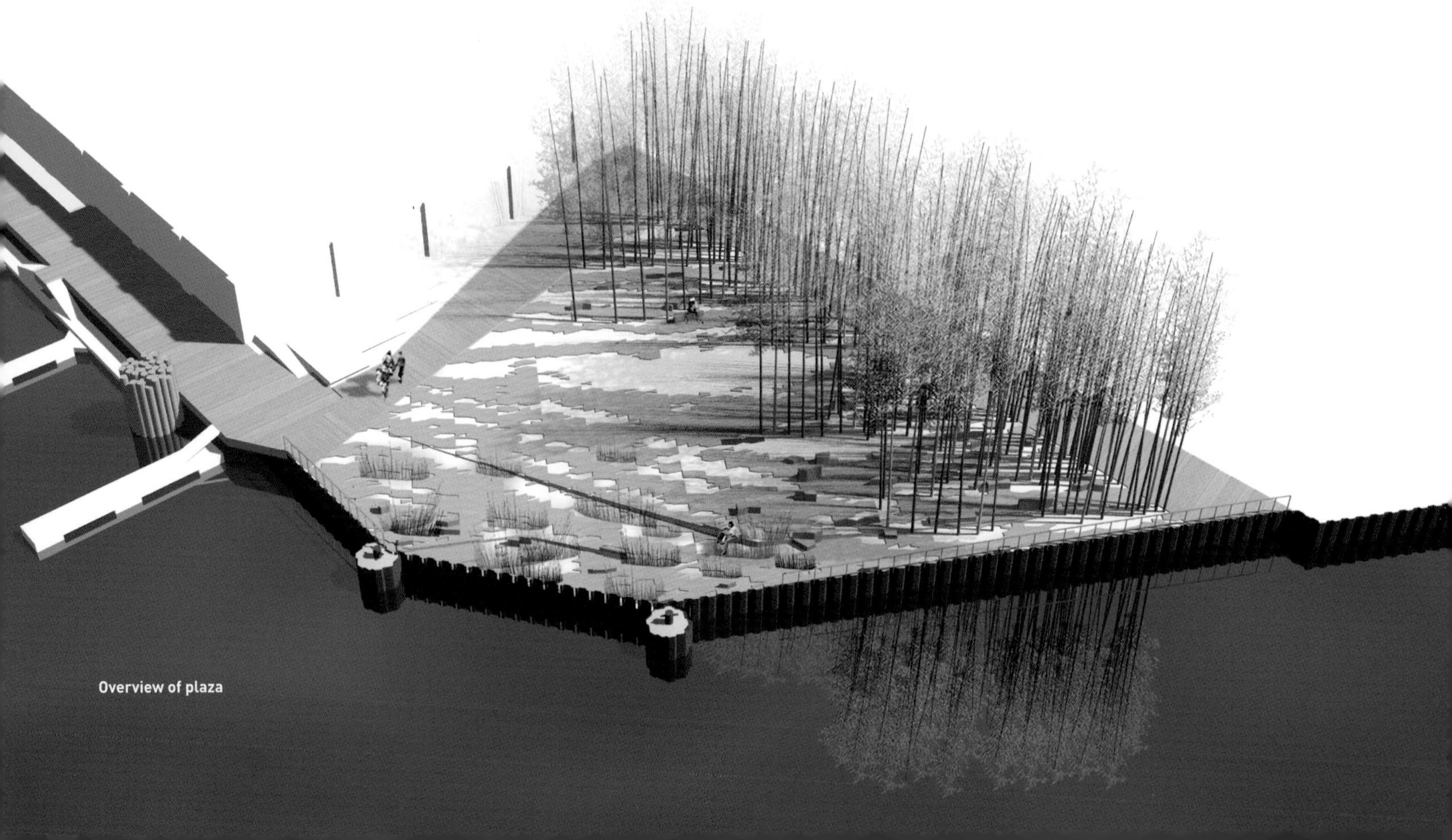

Overview of plaza

scattering of seatwalls and luminous fiberglass benches, which capture and reflect ambient light and project light from within. Their irregular placement allows for multiple and diverse social groupings or solitary retreats, in shade or full sun, protected or exposed. The luminous qualities of the fiberglass are accentuated as night falls, projecting light from within and reflecting the passing headlights of automobiles. The glowing benches have become a signature element of the project.

The variegated surface extends into the steel marsh, which occupies the lower end of the plaza gradient at the river's edge. Capturing and cleaning site stormwater, the steel marsh is key to the site's stormwater management strategy. Lowering the grade behind the bulkhead wall allowed for the collection of site stormwater in a perched position above the river, newly protected from industrial activities and barge wakes. Native marsh grasses of the type displaced by the site's infrastructure and industry thrive in this sheltered location.

SUSTAINABILITY

Erie Street Plaza activates and registers environmental cycles of stormwater by collecting runoff to support a reconstituted marsh/wetland, re-charges the groundwater, and utilizes river water for irrigation. Heavy rainfall will collect in the steel marsh, making legible environmental cycles to plaza visitors. The intermittent high waters of Lake Michigan, present only in twenty-year cycles, may inundate the plaza's lower elevations through slits in the bulkhead wall.

NEW NEIGHBORS, NEW LIFE: ERIE STREET PLAZA TODAY (AND TOMORROW)

Since the projects' uncertain beginnings, adjacent new construction has brought new activity to the area and life to the plaza. Rip Tide Seafood Bar and Grill includes an outdoor dining deck, which overlooks the plaza. Condominiums have also been built nearby. This new fabric and the completion of the plaza are changing local's perceptions of the Third Ward neighborhood. Today mid-day exercise classes and evening loungers testify to group appropriation and informal use of the plaza.

The neighborhood's future change will both impact and be accommodated within the plaza's flexible framework. Passive, active, and occasional uses may alternately occupy the plaza's central field; each may find its own way of uniquely inhabiting and appropriating the space. Such relatively gentle fluctuations in use could also give way to more radical or extreme evolutions as social and market factors change, or as environmental conditions shift.

The variegated surface extends into the steel marsh, which collects and cleans stormwater from the site

Erie Street Plaza ©John December

Art fair /Farmers market

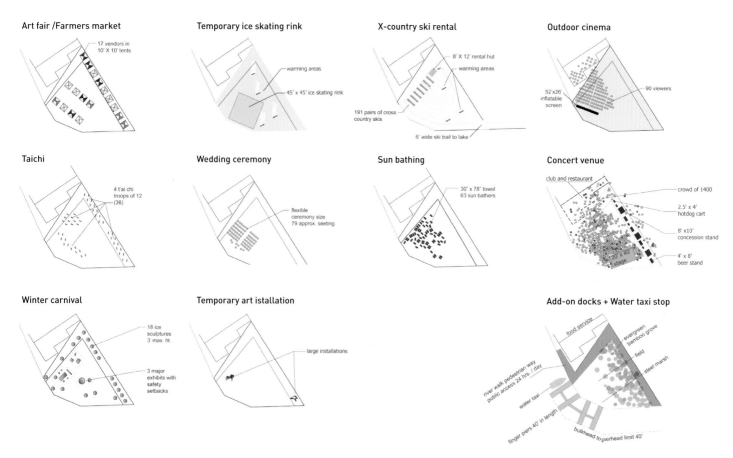

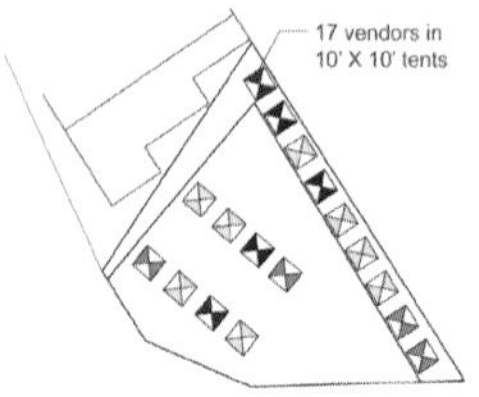

Temporary ice skating rink

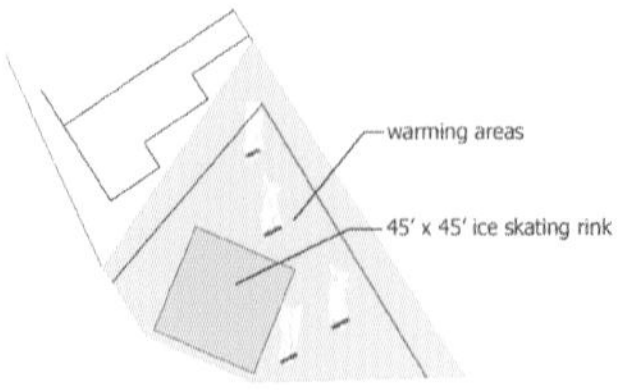

X-country ski rental

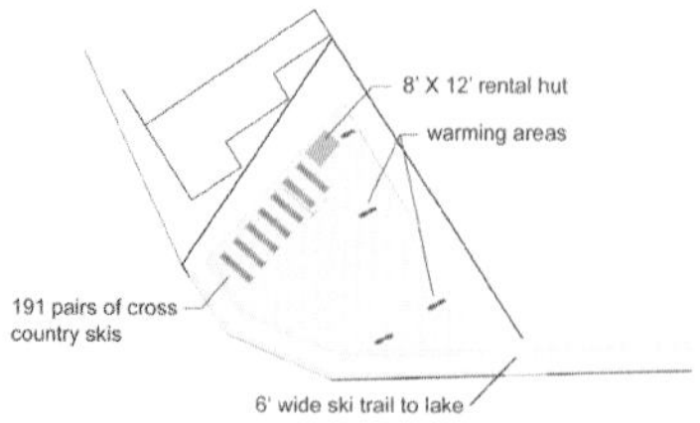

Outdoor cinema

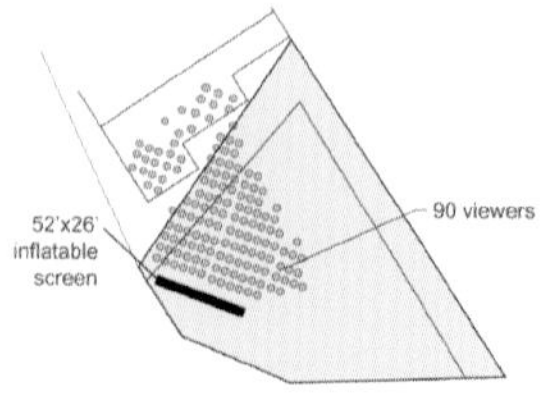

Taichi

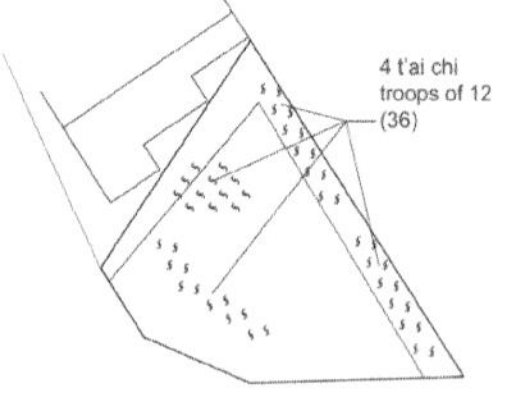

Wedding ceremony

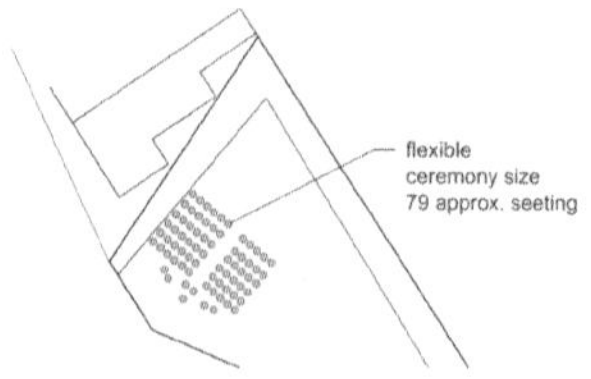

Sun bathing

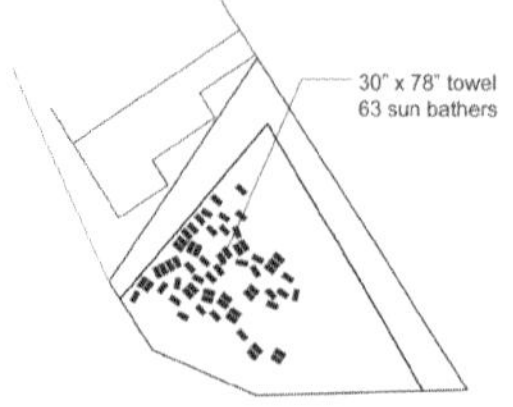

Concert venue

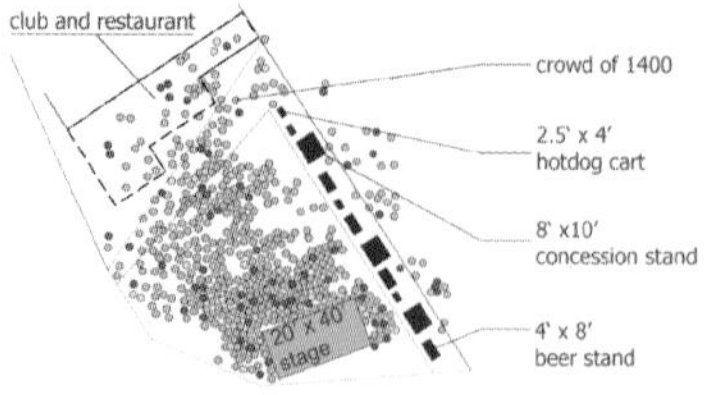

Winter carnival

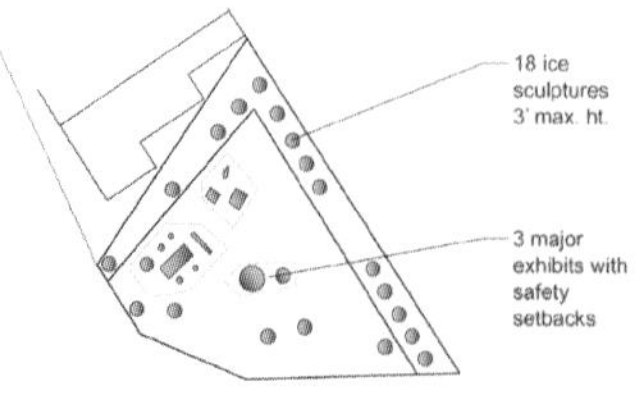

Temporary art istallation

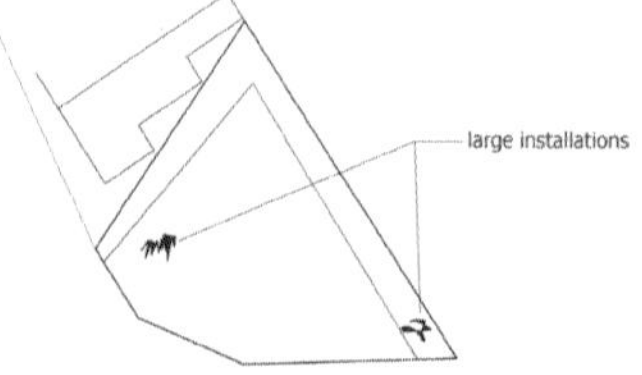

Add-on docks + Water taxi stop

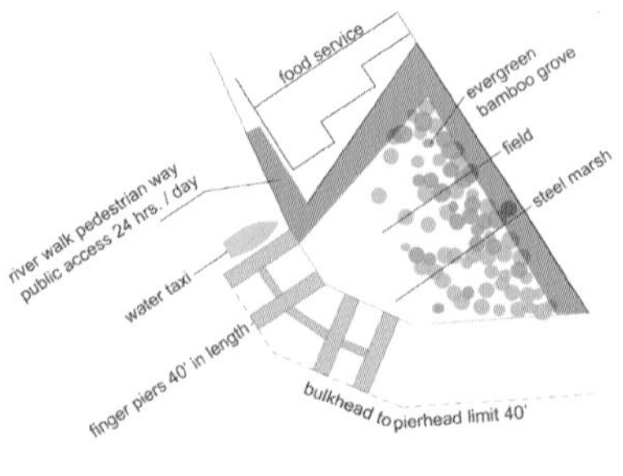

Runoff from the site collects in the marsh, irrigating the wetland plants that live there.

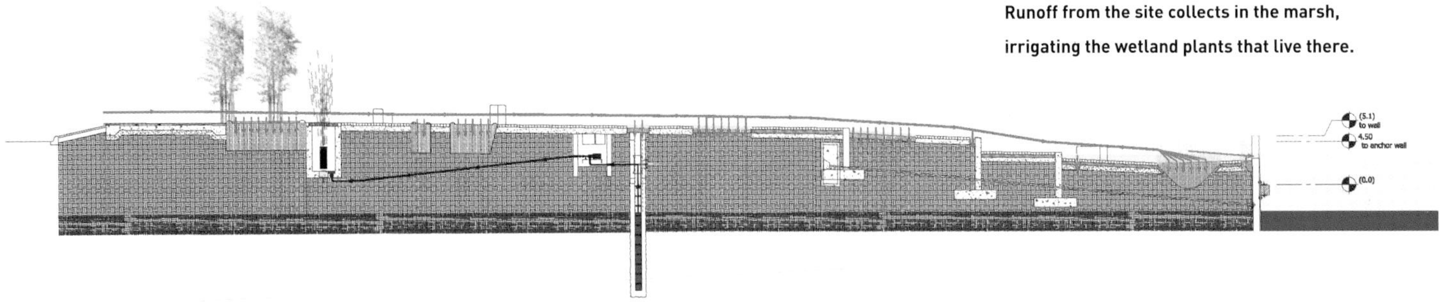

1
2 3

1. View towards the channel; the wetland area is shown in the distance ©John December

2. Detail of the steel marsh and plaza edge. Slots cut into the bulkhead wall allow for intermittent flooding of the wetland at the high point of twentyyear lake level cycles

3. Contrasts in material texture are important: the light bark of young poplars, the synthetic glow of fiberglass, the weathered steel of aged infrastructures

View from Erie Street towards the river. The poplar grove holds a straight line parallel with the street edge, opening up into a looser configuration toward the river

The yellow glow mimics the lights from the industrial buildings across the river ©John December

TheStudios
MediaCityUK

MediaCityUK Exterior Spaces

Gillespies

Public Realm & Landscape Designer & Architecture _ Gillespies

Design Team Leader _ Jim Gibson, Partner, Gillespies

Location _ Salford, England

Client _ The Peel Group

Buildings Architects _ Wilkinson Eyre, Chapman Taylor, Fairhurst Design Group, Sheppard Robson

Masterplan _ Benoy Architects

Main Contractor _ Bovis Lend Lease

Structural and Civil Engineer _ Jacobs UK

M&E Engineers _ AECOM

Quantity Surveyor _ Gleeds

Landscape Contractor _ English Landscapes

Lighting Consultant _ Pinniger & Partners

Completion _ 2011

Photograph _ Darren Hartley Photography and Ben Page Photography

Text & Material _ Gillespies

미디어시티UK로 이전하는 창조적 기업들과 텔레비전 방송국들은 길레스피스Gillespies가 디자인한 신선하고 새로운 공공 공간과 워터프론트 경관에 깊은 인상을 받게 될 것이다. 미디어시티UK의 개발은 필그룹The Peel Group에 의해 이루어졌으며, 국제적으로 주목받는 디지털 미디어의 허브로 탄생하였다. 이는 영국 내 최대 규모의 건축 프로젝트 가운데 하나이며, 과거 산업 생산 용지에 생기를 불어넣었다.

건물 개발과 함께 조성된 고품격의 외부 공간은 새로운 건축물을 통합하고, 정과 인간미가 흐르는 신선하고 창의적인 공공 공간을 가져다 준다. 또한 이러한 외부 공간은 각각의 건물들의 매력과 기능을 향상시키는 한편, 전체적으로 통합된 시각 언어를 만들어낸다.

개발사업 자체의 고밀도와 외부로 노출된 현장이 만들어낸 인공 및 자연 경관에 따른 한계들 속에서 일을 진행하는 것은 길레스피에게도 커다란 도전이었는데, 미기후, 대규모 지하 통신 시설에 따른 제약, 그리고 대테러 보안 규정 등을 모두 감안해야만 했다.

새로운 경관의 중심에는 복합 기능의 Piazza(광장)가 자리잡고 있는데, 방사상 구조와 자연석 포장을 통해 워터프론트와 인접 건물들을 역동적으로 연계시키게 된다. 광장의 넓은 면적 덕분에 다채로운 활동, 방송 이벤트, 그리고 대규모 집회 등이 가능한 기능성 공간이 마련되었다. 또한 야간에는 컴퓨터로 통제되는 350여 개의 LED 조명등과 20미터 높이의 드라마틱한 조형 조명탑이 광장을 돋보이게 만든다.

이번 개발의 핵심인 미디어 파크Media Park는 Piazza(광장) 내 일렬로 늘어선 날렵한 기둥들과 명확한 대조를 이루며 반대편에 위치한다.
미디어 파크 내 풍부한 식물, 목재 데크, 그리고 곡선 형태의 보행로는 야외 방송 촬영에 매력적인 배경이 되어주는 동시에 산책, 휴식, 그리고 창의적인 아이디어를 위한 훌륭한 공간이 된다. 수변이라는 위치적 특징을 살리기 위해 높낮이를 달리해 물결치는 듯한 모습의 녹지 공간을 조성한 것이 덕분에 주변의 방사상 구조와 훌륭한 조화를 이루게 되었다. 또 목재를 새겨 넣어 맞춤 제작된 화강암 벤치는 충분한 앉을 자리를 제공한다.

또한 이 지역의 산업 발전 역사가 묻어나도록 하였다. 철근, 자연석, 시멘트 및 목재 등 개발 프로젝트 전반에 걸쳐 선택, 사용된 건축 자재들은 예전 부둣가 지역이 갖고 있던 성격을 반영하고 있지만, 그 사용에 있어서는 현대적 스타일을 보여준다.

기존의 부지는 건축물이나 기반 시설이 전혀 없는 깨끗한 도화지와 같았다.
길레스피스 건축사무소는 이런 백지와 같은 상태에서 현대적인 동시에 매우 세련된 디자인으로 자신 있게 제안하며 현대적 공간들을 창조해냈다. 특히 뉴미디어 종사자들의 요구를 충족시키는 데 적합하였다.

새로운 공공 공간은 다양한 용도로 활용될 수 있는 동시에 미디어시티UK에서 일하고, 생활하고, 방문하는 사람들이 여가를 즐길 수 있는 장소로도 설계되었다. 예로 도크 테라스Dock Terrace는 전차 승객들에게 멋진 수변 경치를 제공하고 있다. 또한 예전에 사용되던 부두의 높이를 낮추고 폭포 모양의 테라스식 계단을 설치하면서 이곳은 샐포드 퀘이Salford Quay에서 사람들이 물에 가깝게 다가갈 수 있는 몇 안 되는 장소가 되었다.

본 경관은 보행자를 염두에 두고 설계되었으며, 철저한 보안 규정에도 불구하고 영국 내에서 가장 큰 면적의 공공 접근 가능 공간을 만들어냈다.

지속가능한 설계의 모범 사례로서 미디어시티UK 프로젝트는 세계 최초로 BREEAM 기준을 충족시킨 지속가능 커뮤니티로 인증 받게 되었으며, 이를 위해 200그루 이상의 낙엽수 및 상록수를 새롭게 식재하였다.

RANK HOVIS
MediaCityUK
MediaCityUK
3007
Metrolink
3007B

Creative companies and TV channels moving to MediaCityUK will be inspired by its fresh new public spaces and waterside landscape, designed by Gillespies. MediaCityUK has been developed by The Peel Group and creates a globally significant digital media hub. It is one of the UK's largest construction projects and has regenerated a former industrial dock site.

Paralleling the development of the buildings has been the construction of high quality external spaces designed to integrate the new architecture and create a fresh and creative public realm, with heart and human scale. The external spaces enhance the appeal and function of each building individually, and ground them collectively into a holistic visual language.

Gillespies' challenge was how to deliver this given the density of the built development and the constraints to hard and soft landscape created by the exposed site, challenging micro climate and restrictions created by extensive underground communications and anti-terrorism site security restrictions.

At the heart of the new landscape is a multi-functional Piazza, with a radial geometry and elegant arrangement of natural stone paving that establishes a dynamic connection between the waterfront and the adjacent buildings. Its broad expanse serves as a function space for activities, media events and large gatherings and is enhanced at night by over 350 computer controlled LED up-lighters and dramatic 20m high sculptural lighting masts.

Sitting in sharp contrast to the sleek lines of the Piazza is Media Park - the development's green heart. Here, rich naturalistic planting with timber decking and sweeping paths create intimate spaces for strolling, relaxing and creative inspiration as well as attractive backdrops for outdoor broadcasts. Responding to its waterside location, the informality of the park is expressed in the waves of undulating greenery that reflect and juxtapose with the radial geometry of the site. Bespoke designed granite with wood inlay benches offer abundant seating.

Studios

TheStudios

The industrial history of the area is not forgotten. The construction materials selected across the development, including steel, natural stone, cement and wood reflect the former dockside character but are used in a contemporary style.
With no previous architecture or infrastructure, the site was a blank canvas and Gillespies were able to start afresh to create contemporary spaces. The design approach was confident and contemporary and crafted specifically for the creative needs of a new media community.
The new public spaces are designed to fulfil a variety of uses and be a recreational destination for those to live, work and visit MediaCityUK. For example, the Dock Terrace provides tram passengers with beautiful waterside views, but also, because we have reduced the height of the former dock edge and created a cascade of terraced steps, is now one of the few places in Salford Quays where people can get close to the water.

The landscape is designed for the pedestrian and has created one of the UK's largest shared surface environments where, structured within strict security constraints, complete DDA compliance is achieved.
By incorporating exemplary sustainable design principals, MediaCityUK is the first project in the world to become a BREEAM accredited Sustainable Community. The landscape has supported this, including with over 200 new deciduous and evergreen trees having been planted.

Plaza Ricard Viñes

Benedetta Tagliabue(Architect)

Main Partners _ Benedetta Tagliabue(Architect)

Chief Architect _ Josep Ustrell, Daniel Rossell

Client _ Lleida City Hall

Location _ Lleida, Spain

Area _ 9,200m^2

Complete _ 2010. 11

Photograph _ Alex Gaultier, Elena Valles

Text & Material _ Benedetta Tagliabue · EMBT

BALSELLS &
Cansaladeria

Seu Vella 성당을 둘러싸고 있으며 도시 전체에서 가장 두드러진 요소인 드넓은 녹지는 Lleida에서 가장 아름다운 공공 공간이자 우리가 기준으로 삼은 공간이다. 새로 만들어진 Ricard Viñes 광장은 이 녹지의 아름다움을 반영하려 하였다. 우리 제안의 요점은 음악가 Ricard Viñes를 위해 헌정된 조각을 위해 넓은 녹지 공간을 조성하는 것이었다. 이 공간은 도시의 교통과 보행이 모여드는 지점에 0 5 10 횡단도와 녹지 공간으로 이루어진 작은 광장들로 채워졌다.
미로와 복잡하게 얽힌 길들은 고대의 형태를 표현하며, 문화적인 의미와 미로의 상징성에 대한 이해가 깊게 흐르고 있다. 미로labyrinth라는 단어의 앞부분 'labyr'의 어원은 바위와 돌을 의미하며, 'inth'는 기반이라는 뜻을 가진 그리스어에서 유래했다. 정확한 어원은 불분명하지만, 이러한 미로형태, 즉 Path mapping이 오늘날의 안무를 지칭하던 때가 분명 있었다.

우리는 중심 시설을 빙 둘러가며 사람들을 마치 봄의 춤을 추는 듯한 모양의 계단으로 이끄는 미로가 있고, 이 미로와 함께하는 무도회장 같은 오픈 스페이스를 제안했다. 춤 동작을 만들어내고 안내하는 형상의 이 중심 시설은 삶을 표현하며 주변 공간을 채우고 있다. Ricard Viñes 광장에서 사람들과 차량은 별도로 진입하므로, 이 광장에서 보행자들은 그들만의 공공 공간을 가질 수 있다.

사람들은 춤이 기록된 길을 따라간다. 그러나 어느 곳도 겹치지 않는다. 아마도 우리의 설계 아이디어에 가장 가까운 사례는 바르셀로나에서 가장 번화한 지역 중의 한 곳이며 안팎으로 중요한 교통 요지에 위치한 Francesc Maci 광장이다. 유럽의 다른 사례로는 파리의 에뜨와르Etoile나 맨 꼭대기에 천사로 유명한 기둥이 있는 베를린의 티어가르텐Tiergarten처럼 도심지의 멋진 서클로 유명한 곳들이다. 영국의 예로는 건축가 존 우드John Wood가 설계한 배스Bath의 가장 상징적인 형태중의 하나인 로열 크레센트Royal Crescent를 들 수 있다. 이 상징물은 녹지대가 흐름을 조절하며 지속적으로 도시의 이미지를 정의하고 홍보하고 있다. 서클(우리의 로터리와 비슷) 공간들은 통상적으로 접근하지 못하게 설계되어 있다. 따라서 교통의 흐름을 제어하고 운전자들이 자연을 느낄 수 있도록 하기 위해 이러한 공간들은 종종 공원으로 설계된다.

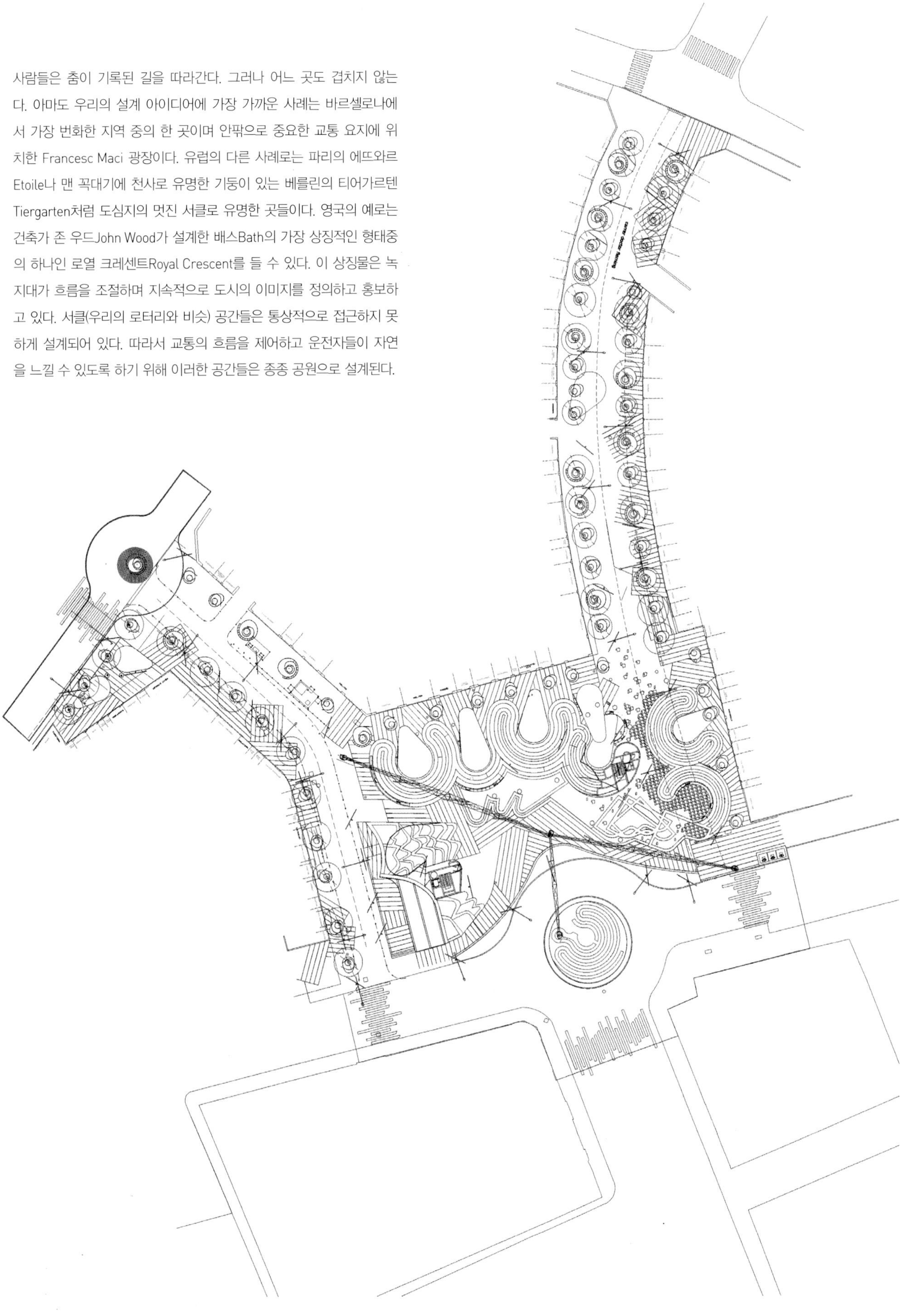

우리는 Calle Roure의 서클 공간을 위한 미로를 설계하였다. 우리는 미로라는 아이디어를 입구에 대한 아이디어로 구현시키고 싶었고, Lleida로 들어오는 도시의 입구는 새로운 녹색 대문이 되었다. 이 프로젝트는 원형으로 구성되어 도시를 위한 새로운 형태의 광장으로 만들어졌다.

이 미로 형태의 서클의 끝 부분은 식재지와 벽돌 포장으로 구성되어있다.

광장은 길에서 보이는 나무와 관목으로 이루어진 미로가 있는 녹지 공간에 의해 분리된다. 이 녹지는 바Bar, 어린이 놀이터, 벤치, 보행자 전용도로에서 이루어지는 지역민들의 여가 활동을 체계화해준다. 광장을 나누고 있는 두 개의 거리는 자연석으로 포장된 보행자 전용도로로 이용되며, 새로 식재된 나무들과 주거용 빌딩으로 들어가는 입구에 생기는 작은 녹지로 인해 유연하게 변모한다. 이 서클 광장에는 공공 광장에 거주하는 커뮤니티를 위한 조명과 공동의 정체성을 위한 거리 파티라는 컨셉을 강조하는 조명이 설치되어 있다. 이 조명들은 서클의 한쪽에서 시작하여, 넓은 조각 같은 조명 요소들이 전체 광장을 비추고 있다. 원형의 중심에 새로 설치된 조각은 도시의 다른 지역에서부터 두드러진 장소를 만들어주는 랜드마크가 되고 있다.

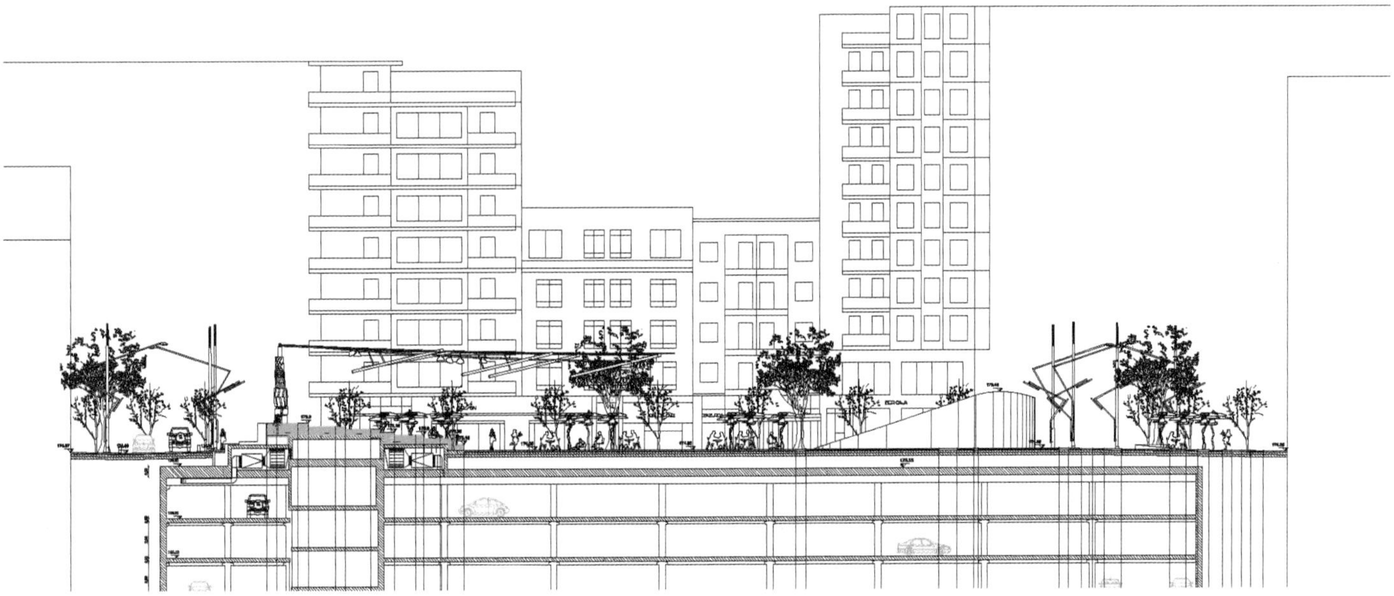

The large green open spaces that surround the Seu Vella Cathedral and dominate the whole city are the most beautiful public areas in Lleida, and are what we chose as our reference point. The designs for the new Ricard Viñes Square must possess some of this beauty. The focus of our proposal is to build a large green open space for a sculpture dedicated to the musician Ricard Viñes. A space full of little squares 0 5 10 cross section and green areas at a point where the city throngs with traffic and pedestrians. The maze or labyrinth provides an ancient model. The cultural meaning and interpretation of the symbol of the labyrinth run deep. The origin of the "labyr" part of the word has to do with rocks and stone, while the "inth"comes from a Greek word meaning foundation site. Even though the precise etymology is unclear, there was a time when path mapping was used to notate dance choreography.

We propose an open space featuring a dance floor with a labyrinthine path guiding the steps of those dancing the spring dance around the central feature - a feature that generates and guides the movement of the dance, filling the surround space with life. People and traffic will move differently in Ricard Viñes Square, where pedestrians will own the public space.

Everyone will follow the paths mapped by the dance notation, but with no overlap. Perhaps the closest reference to our design idea is Francesc Macia Square in Barcelona, in one of the busiest areas of the city, and at a key transit point in and out of the city. Other European cities are famous for the spectacular circles in their metropolises, such as the Etoile in Paris or Berlin's Tiergarten with its famous column topped by an angel. In the UK, the architect John Wood created one of Bath's most iconic features with the Royal Crescent whose circular green spaces control the flow, and substantially contribute to defining and propagating the city's image. Circular spaces are not normally accessible and for this reason are often laid out as parks, regulating traffic flow and giving drivers a glimpse of the natural world.

We have designed a maze for the circular space in Calle Roure. We like incorporating the idea of a labyrinth into the idea of an entrance. The city entrance to Lleida is a new green gate. The project is made up of a circle and new square for the city:

1. The circle ends in a labyrinthine pattern, made up of bands of planting and brick paving.

2. The square is split up by green areas; a maze of trees and low shrubs that are visible from the roadway. This greenery helps organise the neighbourhood's leisure activities with bars, children's play areas, benches and pedestrian pathways. The two streets that feed into the square will be pedestrianised, using natural stone paving, and they will be softened by new tree planting and small green spaces which will punctuate the entrances to residential buildings. From one side of the circle a wide sculptural light source will illuminate the whole square, underlining both the idea of the community that inhabits a public space and the street party concept as a mark of collective identity. A new sculpture installed in the middle of the circle will become the landmark that makes this place stand out from the rest of the city.

Public Space

Burbank Water and Power

Gubei Pedestrian Promenade

D-Cube City

Marina Bay Sands Integrated Resort

Burbank Water and Power

Magnolia Power Plant Campus

AHBE Landscape Architects

캘리포니아를 대표하는 혁신적 공익기업인 버뱅크 워터 앤드 파워BWP의 의뢰를 받은 AHBE는 낡은 산업시설의 외관을 가진 이 회사의 메인 단지를 미국 내에서 손꼽힐만한 지속가능한 모델로 변모시키는 일에 동참하게 되었다. AHBE가 준비한 야심 찬 마스터플랜을 통해 이 산업단지는 그 선례를 찾을 수 없을 만큼 다양한 지속가능한 조경 기술들이 총망라된 재생 녹색 공간으로 탈바꿈하게 된다. 1단계 작업의 완공을 통해 AHBE는 산업과 환경이 공존할 수 있으며, 함께 성장할 수 있다는 사실을 성공적으로 보여주었다.

AHBE was commissioned to help progressive California utility company, Burbank Water and Power (BWP), transform its main campus from an industrial relic into a sustainable model for the rest of the U.S. AHBE created an ambitious master plan for a campus that transforms the industrial complex into a regenerative green space with an unprecedented number of integrated sustainable landscape technologies. With the first phase completed, AHBE has successfully demonstrated that industry and environment can co-exist and thrive together.

Landscape Architecture _ AHBE Landscape Architects
Team **Canopies** _ Leo A Daly (Architect), Mollenhauer Group(Civil)
Courtyard _ Fuscoe Engineering, Inc.(Civil), Tyler/Gonzalez(Architect), Sweeney + Associates(Irrigation)
Green Street _ Insight Structural Engineers(Structural), Kipust Engineering(Electrical), Fuscoe Engineering, Inc.(Civil), Sweeney + Associates(Irrigation)
Green Roof _ The Garland Company
Client _ Burbank Water and Power
Location _ Burbank, California, USA
Area _ 2.8 acres
Completion _ 2011
Photograph _ Heliphoto - Sibylle Allgaier
Text & Material _ AHBE Landscape Architects

Overview of transformed courtyard

변모된 코트야드 전경

Substation converted to employee gathering space
과거의 변전소가 근로자들의 모임장소로 탈바꿈하였다

An abandoned substation is transformed into a garden space

낡고 버려진 변전소가 정원 공간으로 변화되었다

지속가능성과 관련된 특징으로는 물의 여과, 흐름, 역류, 나무의 뿌리세포, 그리고 빗물 집수 등을 기반으로 한 다섯 가지 각기 다른 정화기술을 들 수 있다. 또한 단지에는 캘리포니아 남부에서 가장 긴 '그린 스트리트'가 자리하고 있는데, 인접한 세 개의 도로를 관통해 지나간다. 이러한 '그린 스트리트'는 빗물이 우수처리시스템에 흘러들어 가기 전에 이를 정화하는 역할을 한다. 캘리포니아주 법률에 따르면 모든 프로젝트는 비가 내린 직후 최소 4분의 3인치 이상의 빗물을 정화할 수 있어야 하는데, 이 빗물 속에는 도로나 지붕 같은 도심의 비투수성 표면에 쌓인 각종 먼지, 오염물질 및 기타 독소 등이 축적되어 있기 때문이다. AHBE가 디자인에 접목한 다양한 혁신적 기술 덕분에 이 단지에서는 이미 1인치 이상의 빗물이 처리되고 있다. 향후 시행될 마스터플랜에 따르면 이 단지에서는 모든 빗물을 자체 처리함으로써 법률이 정한 기준을 크게 상회하는 역량을 갖추게 될 것이다. 관리본부(Administration Building)에는 세 곳의 옥상 정원을 마련해 열섬 현상을 완화하고, 빗물의 집수 및 정화를 돕는 한편, 냉방 비용을 경감할 수 있도록 한다. 옥상 정원에는 재활용 유리로 만든 포장재를 활용, 구불구불한 시냇물과 토종 식물들을 보여주도록 한다. 새로운 단지에서 가장 인상적인 요소를 꼽자면 퇴역한 변전소 부지에 자리 잡은 센테니얼 코트야드(Centennial Courtyard)이다. 변전소의 철재 구조물 일부는 여전히 그 자리를 지키고 있는데, 이 거대한 트렐리스(giant super-trellis)는 산업시설과 자연이 더불어 자아내는 통렬한 병치감을 보여준다. 모든 경관 요소들은 두 가지 목표를 동시에 지향하고 있다. 첫째, 직원 및 일반인들에게 녹색 공간을 제공한다는 미학적 목표를 들 수 있고, 둘째, 대규모 지속가능한 조경 기술의 실체는 드러내지 않으면서 단지 전체가 하나의 거대한 정수시설로 탈바꿈해, 물을 정화하고 독성물질을 제거하도록 하는 기능적 목표라 할 수 있을 것이다. 끝으로 단지에는 태양광발전설비가 가동되고 있다. 태양전지판 건설에는 관리본부 건물의 디자인 요소들을 적극 반영함으로써, 건물이 지닌 전통적 아르 데코(Art Deco) 양식을 계승하는 한편, 도시가 지닌 항공산업과의 역사적 연관성이 드러나도록 한다. 태양광발전시스템을 통해 현재 건설 중인 LEED 신규 인증건물에 대한 거의 완벽한 전력공급이 가능할 것으로 예상된다.

버뱅크 워터 앤드 파워의 매그놀리아 발전소 단지는 SITES(Sustainable Sites Initiative) 파일럿 프로그램에 포함된 150개의 미국 국내 및 국제 프로젝트들 가운데 유일한 산업 프로젝트이다. 주로 건물에 적용되는 LEED 평가 시스템과 마찬가지로, SITES를 통해 경관 전반의 효율 및 효용을 측정할 수 있는 유용한 평가 시스템의 근간을 마련할 수 있게 될 것이다.

Sustainable features include five different types of water filtration technologies: infiltration, flow-through, detention, tree root cells, and rainwater capture. The campus also features one of the longest "green streets" in Southern California, running across three contiguous city streets. The "green street" acts as a filter before runoff enters the storm water system. By California law, all projects are required to mitigate at least the first ¾ inches of rainfall, the water that collects all the dust, pollution and other toxins that accumulate on non-permeable urban surfaces such as streets and roofs. Thanks to the combination of innovative technologies that AHBE has integrated into the design, the campus is already mitigating the first full inch. In the future, the master plan would see the campus become a zero-runoff site, far exceeding what state law requires. The Administration Building features three rooftop gardens that serve to reduce the heat island effect, help channel and filter storm water, and reduce the building's air conditioning requirements. The roof gardens are covered with recycled glass pavers that depict a meandering stream and native plants. The most striking feature of the new campus is Centennial Courtyard, a green space located within the footprint of a decommissioned electrical substation. Part of the industrial structure still stands, serving as a giant super-trellis and creating a poignant juxtaposition of industry and nature. All of the landscape serves a dual purpose: aesthetically, providing green space for employees and the public; functionally, hiding extensive sustainable landscape technologies and making the entire campus function as a water filtration system, cleaning water and removing toxins before the water returns to the watershed. Lastly, solar power is also being generated on the campus. The architectural solar array emulates design elements of the BWP Administrative Building, paying homage to both the Art Deco heritage of the building and the City's historical ties to aviation. The solar system will also almost completely power the new LEED-certified building that is currently under construction.

The Burbank Water and Power Magnolia Power Plant Campus is the only industrial project out of 150 national and international projects to be included in the Sustainable Sites Initiative (SITES) pilot program. Similar to the LEED rating system for buildings, SITES is the first step toward creating a rating system that would measure the efficiency and effectiveness of landscapes that tie our urban environments together.

Paving design at salvaged substation structure

재생된 변전소 구조물 아래의 포장면 디자인

Night Illumination of transformed substation

변화된 변전소의 야간 조명

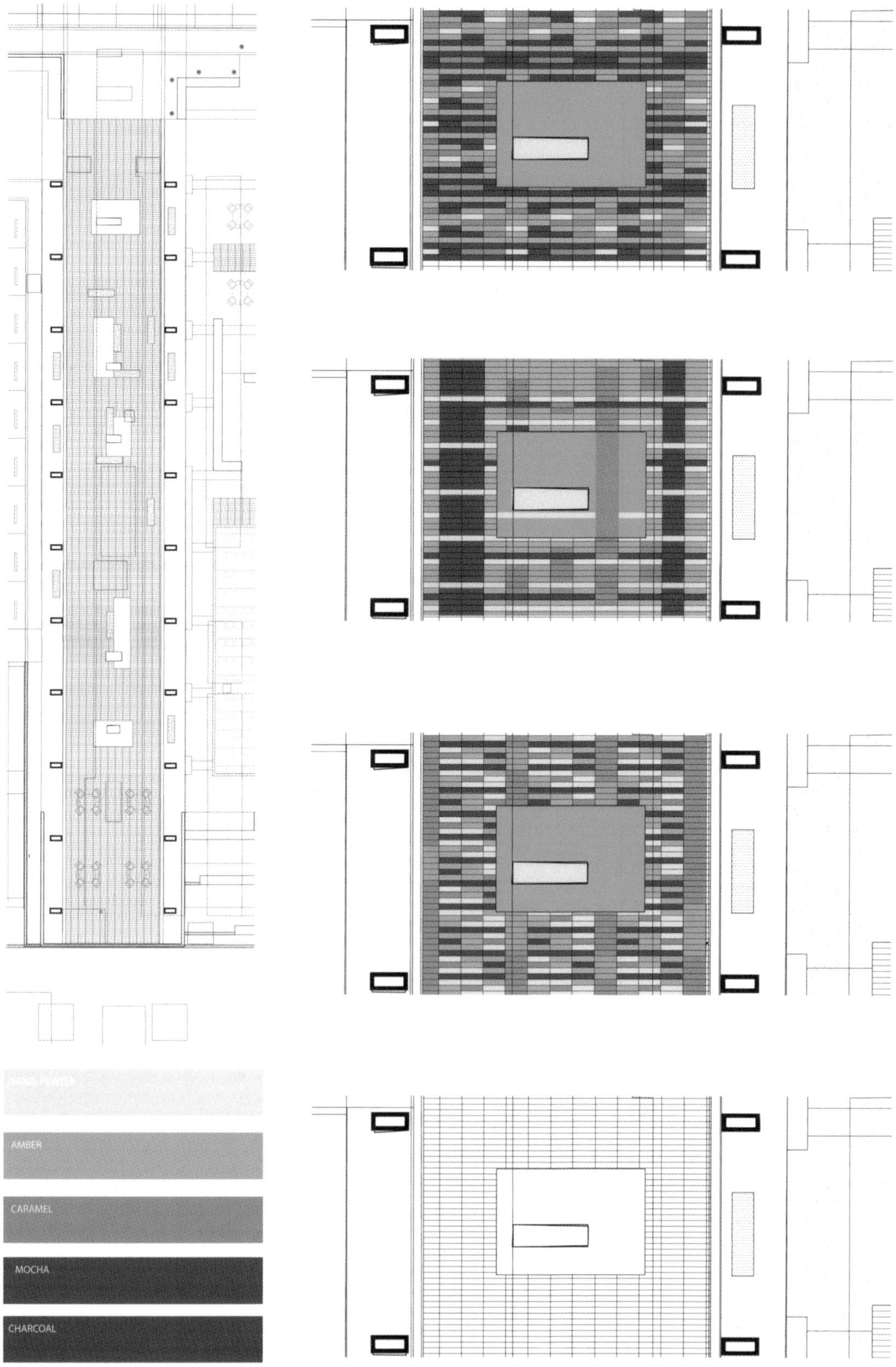

Paving Plan 포장계획

Rock fountain with a mini waterfall

돌을 활용하여 작은 폭포를 만든 수경시설

Outdoor gathering space for employees

근로자들을 위한 야외 모임장소

Community pocket park

커뮤니티 쌈지 공원

"Green street" with permeable paving, LED lights and "tree pod" biofilters

투수성 포장과 LED 조명, "트리 포드"라 불리는 자연정화기능을 가진 "그린 스트리트"

Vegetated rooftop garden at Administration building

초목 식생이 가능한 관리본부의 옥상 정원

Photographic timeline 사진으로 보는 프로젝트 진행과정

Link-Belt

Gubei Gold Street Aerial

Gubei Pedestrian Promenade

SWA Los Angeles Office

Landscape Architecture _ SWA Los Angeles Office
Designer _ Ying-Yu Hung
Client _ Shanghai Gubei (Group) Co. LTD
Location _ Shanghai, China
Area _ 34 square kilometers
Cost _ $90,000
Completion _ 2010
Photograph _ Tom Fox
Text & Material _ SWA Los Angeles Office

구베이 보행자 전용 도로는 도심지의 차량 전용 도로를 700미터에 이르는 안전 지대인 보행자 전용 도로로 탈바꿈시킨 귀중한 사례이다. 이 프로젝트는 대규모 개발 압력 속에서 공공을 위한 오픈 스페이스 간의 균형은 불가능하다고 생각하는 사람들에게 좋은 영감을 불어넣어 주고 있다. 급속한 개발로 인해 지속가능한 도시 구조가 공공연하게 묵과되는 것이 습관이 되어가고는 있지만, 공공 오픈스페이는 도시 열섬 효과를 저감하고, 24시간 내내 벌어질 수 있는 행태들에 대해 유연하게 대처하며, 외부 활동과 스트레스를 풀어 주는 활동 및 사회적 교류를 통해 건강한 삶을 고취시키는 기능을 하고 있기 때문이다.

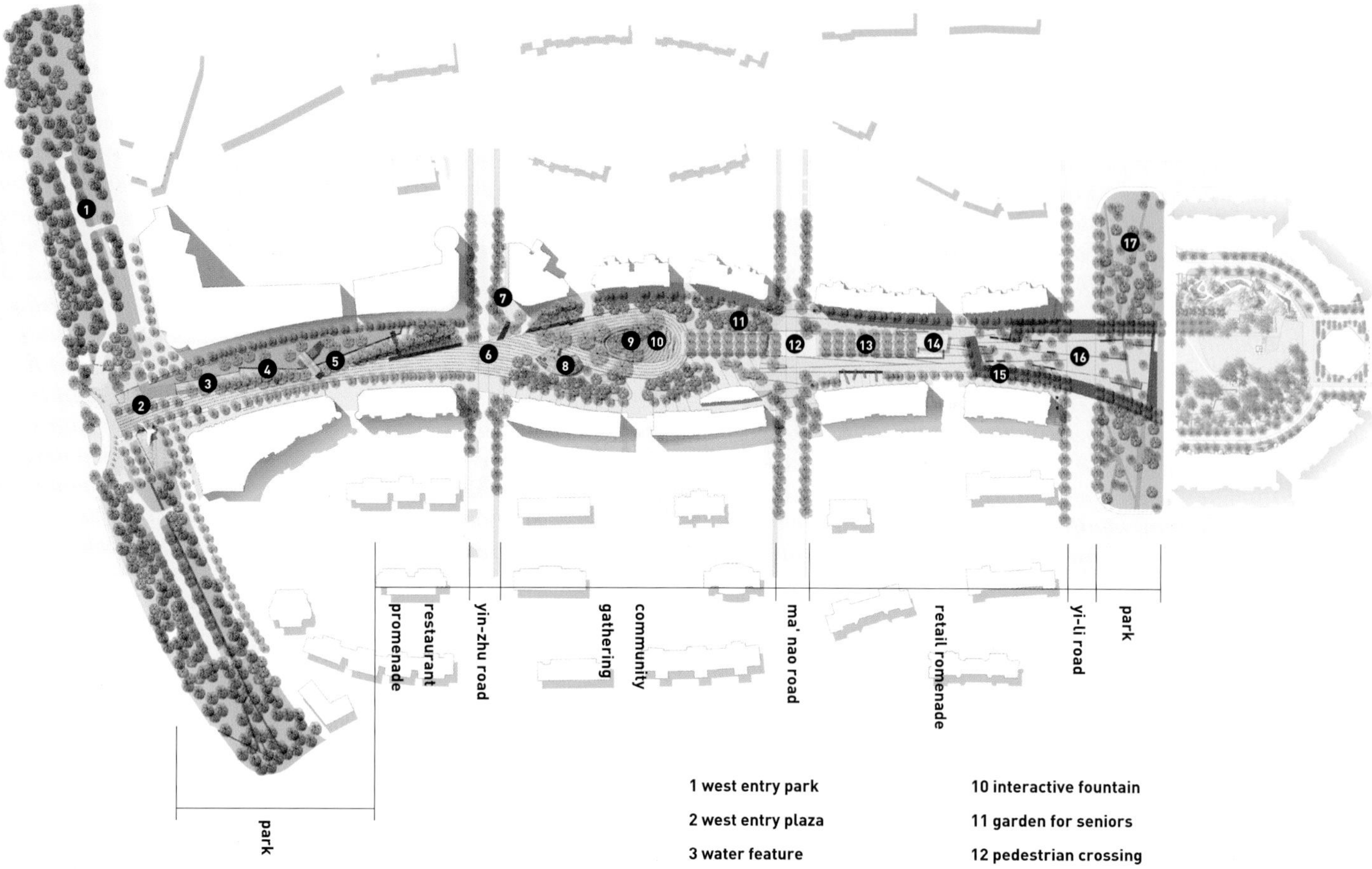

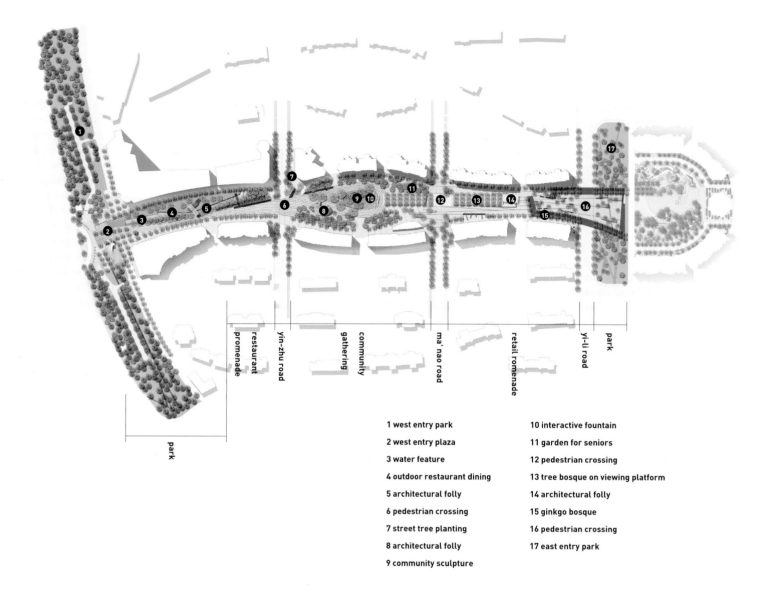

1 west entry park
2 west entry plaza
3 water feature
4 outdoor restaurant dining
5 architectural folly
6 pedestrian crossing
7 street tree planting
8 architectural folly
9 community sculpture
10 interactive fountain
11 garden for seniors
12 pedestrian crossing
13 tree bosque on viewing platform
14 architectural folly
15 ginkgo bosque
16 pedestrian crossing
17 east entry park

프로젝트 설명

상하이 서쪽 창닝지구에 자리한 구베이는 다국적 가정(가구)들과 젊은 전문직들의 인구가 늘고 있는 활기 넘치고 분주한 도심 지역이다. SWA는 북적거리는 상하이에서 귀중한 가치가 되는 개념을 찾아내어, 이를 설계, 구현한 보행자 전용 공간 – '골드스트리트'의 설계사가 되었다. 총 길이는 700미터에 이르고 평균 폭원이 60m에 달하는 보행로와 the East-West Entry Park은 35.6헥타르에 이르는 복합 주거 단지 프로젝트의 핵심이 된다. 선형의 대상지는 북서로 뻗은 가로로 인해 세 블록으로 나뉘어져 있는데, 지상부 2개층을 상업용으로 이용하는 15층에서 28층까지 다양한 높이의 고층 주거용 타워 개발 계획이 진행되고 있는 지역이다.

조경 설계는 고전적인 프랑스식과 현대적 요소의 결합을 바탕으로 진행되었다. 키가 큰 은행나무는 소매 단지를 따라 늘어서서 주변의 터널 같은 타워들에서 부터 중심몰 내의 분위기 있는 정원까지 시각적인 전이 공간을 연출하고 있다. 도시의 현실적이고 차가운 환경과는 반대로 상록수인 녹나무가 일년 내내 우거져 반갑게 맞이해 주고, 낙엽수인 벚나무가 계절감을 느끼게 해 준다. 모든 감각을 사로잡을 수 있는 방법을 모색하면서, 조경가들은 설계안에 방향 식물들을 도입하여 설계하였다. 이러한 방향 식물들은 작고 노란 꽃을 피우는 금목서 같은 식물을 예로 들 수 있는데 이 꽃은 잘 익은 복숭아와 살구향이 난다.

Gubei East Park

디자인 전략

안전한 다목적 공간이면서, 지속가능하고 모든 연령대가 재미있고 흥미롭게 여길 수 있는 연속적인 보행자 전용 오픈 스페이스를 제공하기 위해 다섯 가지 요소의 배열과 통합의 디자인적 전략을 가졌다. 이 다섯 가지의 고려 사항이란 문화 인프라, 환경적 지속가능성, 건강한 삶, 해석상의 자연과 창의적인 디자인을 말한다. 이 고려 사항들은 인위적 형태 위에 생명을 불어넣고 복잡한 도시의 삶을 성공적으로 만들 수 있다는 기대치를 높여 활기찬 도심 환경을 만들어 냈다.

1. 문화 인프라

문화 인프라의 하나로서 보행자 전용 도로는 오픈 스페이스에 적용된 설계적 요소들을 활용하여 과거의 일부를 재해석함으로써 도시의 역사를 상기시킨다. 전통적인 지붕의 점토 기와의 미학을 모방한 다공성 포장 시스템은 형태적으로 점토 기와의 곡선 모양을 본 떠 설계되었다. 또한 각각의 포장 단위별 안정성을 확보하기 위해 사개물림 기법을 반영하였다. 다공질 포장 시스템은 우수 침투에 용이할 뿐만 아니라 기능적인 보행면을 형성하게 해준다.

2. 환경적 지속가능성

지속가능성은 다양한 형태를 가지고 있다. 보행자 전용 도로에 있어서 지속가능성은 초기에 형성이 되었는데, 대규모의 부지는 도시 근교림을 강화할 수 있는 잠재력을 가지고 있었으며 이에 따라 도시 열섬 효과를 줄일 수 있는 가능성을 내포하게 되었다. 1,100그루 이상의 나무들이 보행자 도로에 식재되었고 매년 탄소배출량을 5,456톤 줄이는 효과를 가져왔는데, 이는 두 달 동안 1,100대의 자동차가 배출하는 탄소량과 맞먹는다. 수목의 캐노피로 인해 생기는 그늘과 증발산은 이 지역 기온을 주변 온도 보다 5~10도 정도 낮춰 준다. 은행나무, 녹나무, 느티나무, 대만풍나무, 스위트 아카시아, 목서는 다양한 관목들 및 지피류와 어우러져 계절적인 특성 및 다양한 규모와 생물학적 다양성을 형성하고 있다.

3. 건강한 삶

프로젝트의 단계를 조정하면서 건강과 안전한 삶을 영위하기 위한 기반을 조성하는 것은 아주 기본적인 고려 사항이었다. 17,000여 거주민들을 위한 보행자 전용 도로 내에 융통성을 가진 오픈 스페이스를 설치하는 것은 운동, 사회적 교류, 태극권, 독서, 저녁 식사, 사람들 구경 같은 수동적이고 스트레스 저감을 위한 활동 공간을 제공해 준다. 매주마다 사람들은 커뮤니티 이벤트에 참여할 수 있고 아이들이 롤러블레이드를 타거나 자전거를 타는 모습을 관찰할 수 있다. 또한 다른 사람들과 어울리며 즐거워하는 가족들도 만나 볼 수 있다.

4. 해석 상의 자연

과도하게 도시화된 지역에 살고 있는 아이들에게 자연 결핍 장애가 증가하고 있다. 이 장애는 주변 자연 환경에 대해 한정된 경외심이 발달될 수 있는 어린 시절에 자연 환경에 대한 탐구가 부재하면서 생기게 되는데, 한정된 경외심이란 예를 들어 자연 경관이 무엇인가에 대한 배려나 관심이 없는 것을 들 수 있다. 보행자 전용 도로에서는 공원 안에 자연을 재도입하는 시도를 하였다. 우수를 모아 두는 생태적 습지와 수풀이 무성한 식재지를 도입하였는데 이들은 새들과 곤충, 양서류를 위한 도심 야생 서식처를 제공하는 재생적 생태계를 이루게 한다. 생태적 계획으로서 보행자 전용 도로를 설계함에 있어 자연의 작용을 통합시키는 것은 커뮤니티를 위한 교육적 선례로 작용한다.

5. 설계의 독창성

보행자 전용 도로 설계는 앉을 곳, 소매상점, 분수와 같은 외부 프로그램을 체험하기 위한 물리적 재료의 창의적 이용을 보여 주고 있다. 이 보행자 전용 도로는 고효율이고 이중적이며 예술적이기도 한 반투명의 열가소성 재료로 만들어진 벤치에 대한 창의적인 시스템을 적용하고 있다. 근처의 분수와 상호보완적으로 어우러지는 벤치는 시원한 여름밤에 커뮤니티 이벤트에 사람들의 참여를 유도하는 매혹적인 상징 조명 조형물이 되었다. 소매상점들은 건축적 장식물로 설계되어 모양, 기능, 재료의 물성에 있어 각각 정체성을 가진다. 유리 타일로 만든 거대한 분수는 물이 나오지 않을 때는 그 자체로서 시각적 즐거움을 제공하는 조각물의 기능을 하고 있다. 목재 재질의 포장면은 대규모의 앉음벽이 되고, 유리 분수를 따라 장벽처럼 보이도록 수직적으로 솟아올라 있고 궁극적으로는 건축적인 장식물을 향해 지붕면을 향해 올라간다.

Gubei West Block

미래를 향해

구베이 보행자 전용 도로는 더 큰 완전체를 위한 촉매제로서의 가능성을 가지고 있다. 프로젝트의 성공이 기타 개발업자들과 공공 기관에 공공의 이익을 가져다 줄 뿐만 아니라 전 구역의 부동산 가치를 상승키시는 도시적인 어메니티로서의 가치를 보여 주며 영감을 주고 있는 것이다. 소수의 작은 포켓 파크가 쉽게 결정되고 사적인 개발 사업의 요구만를 채우는 프로그램으로 대체되는 상하이의 일반적인 추세와는 반대로, 이 프로젝트는 빠르게 현대화를 이뤄가는 도시를 위한 성공적인 사례가 되고 있다. 계속적으로 증가하는 도심 건물 밀도에 대한 대위법으로서 공공 오픈 스페이스를 확보하고, 도시 계획과 도시 구조 조정의 미래에 대한 새로운 방향을 제시하는 사례인 것이다.

Gubei Central Block

Project Statement

The Gubei Pedestrian Promenade is a rare example in which a city decided to rezone a vehicular road into a 700-meter long pedestrian-only sanctuary. The sheer scale of the project serves as an inspiration for those who believe in the impossible—a balance of the "development frenzy" (characterized by rampant disregard for a sustainable urban fabric) with public open spaces that reduce the urban heat-island effect, allow for flexible around the clock activities, and promote healthy living through outdoor exercise, stress relieving activities and social interaction.

Project Narrative

Set within the Changning District in western Shanghai, Gubei is a bustling urban community with growing groups of international families and young professionals. SWA was selected to conceptualize, design and realize a rare find in bustling Shanghai—a pedestrian mall (Gold Street). 700 meters in length and averaging 60m in width, the Promenade and the East-West Entry Parks are the centerpiece of a 35.6 hectare mixed-use residential project.

The linear site is divided into 3 blocks separated by two north-south neighborhood streets, with a development program of high-rise residential towers, varying from 15-28 stories in height with 2-story ground floor commercial uses. The project maintains an open space ratio of over 60% with an FAR of 2.9.

The landscape design merges modern elements with classical French. Tall gingko trees line the retail promenade, creating a visual transition from the surrounding tunnel-like towers to the mall's intimate gardens. Contrasting the city's hard-edged environment, evergreen camphor trees ensure a welcoming canopy year-round, while deciduous cherry trees provide seasonal interest. Seeking to engage all the senses, the landscape architects also included fragrant plants in their design, such as sweet olive trees with their tiny yellow flowers that exude the scent of ripe peaches and apricots.

Gubei East Park

Design Strategy

Providing a contiguous pedestrian open space that is safe, multi-functional, sustainable, fun and exciting for all ages involved the layering and integration of 5 distinct considerations: cultural infrastructure, environmental sus-tainability, healthy living, interpretive nature, and inventive design. These considerations, brought to life in built form, created a dynamic urban environment that raises the bar for successful dense urban living.

1. Cultural Infrastructure

Acting as a piece of cultural infrastructure, the promenade recalls the city's history by re-interpreting pieces of the past into design elements that are incorporated into the open space. By mimicking the aesthetic of traditional clay roof tiles, the promenade's porous paving system takes on the curving shape of the clay tile and incorporates the tongue-and-groove locking mechanism to ensure the stability of the units. The porous paving system also provides for storm water infiltration and creates a functional walking surface.

2. Environmental Sustainability

Sustainability takes many forms. For the promenade, it became obvious early on that this large tract of land had the potential to strengthen the urban forest and thus reduce the urban heat-island effect. Over 1,100 trees were planted in the promenade, resulting in the ability to sequester 5,465 metric tons of carbon dioxide per year, equivalent to the amount of carbon dioxide emitted by 1,100 cars for two months. The shade created by the tree canopy, along with evapo-transpiration, lowers the ambient temperature by 5-10 degrees in the immediate context. Ginkgo biloba, Cinnamomum camphora, Zelkova serrulata, Liquiambar formosana, Acacia farnesiana, and Osmanthus fragrans, coupled with diverse shrubs and groundcovers serve both the goals of sustainability while also creating seasonal character, varied scale and biological diversity.

3. Healthy Living

Creating a platform to promote health and well-being was a prime consideration during the programming phase of the project. With an estimated 17,000 residents, the flexible open spaces of the promenade provide public space for outdoor exercise, social interaction and passive, stress-relieving activities such as Tai-Chi, reading, dining and people watching. On any given weekend, one can participate in community events, see children roller-blading and riding bicycles, and observe families enjoying the company of others.

4. Interpretive Nature

Nature deficit disorder is on the rise with children living in highly urbanized areas. This disorder is caused by a lack of exposure to nature during childhood that develops into a limited respect to their immediate natural surroundings (e.g. no concern or care for what is natural landscape). The promenade reintroduces "nature" into the park by incorporating bioswales and lush vegetation to capture and treat storm water while nurturing a regenerative ecology that could support urban wildlife habitat for birds, insects and amphibians. As an ecological initiative, the integration of natural processes within the design of the promenade serves as an educational precedent for the community.

5. Design Invention

The promenade's design features a creative use of materials to explore common outdoor programs such as seating, retail kiosks and fountains. The promenade contains an inventive system of benches made of a translucent polycarbonate material that is highly functional, durable, and artistic. Coupled with an interactive fountain nearby, the seating becomes an iconic light sculpture attracting people to participate in community events during cool summer nights. The retail kiosks are designed as architectural follies that have individual identity via their shape, function and materiality; a grand fountain made of glass tiles becomes a sculpture in its own right, providing visual interest when the water is turned off. Wood paving surfaces rise vertically to become large-scale seat walls, barriers along the glass fountain, and finally ascending as roof surface for the architecturally folly.

Toward the Future

Gubei Pedestrian Promenade has the potential to become a catalyst for the greater whole, where the success of the project can inspire other developers and public agencies to see the value of such an urban amenity, which not only benefits the public, but elevates the real estate value of the entire district. Contrary to the common trend in Shanghai where handfuls of small pocket parks have become quickly appropriated and replaced with programs catered to the needs of private development, this project serves as a successful case study for cities undergoing rapid modernization: to be mindful of setting aside public open space as a counterpoint to continually increasing urban building density, and to steer the future of city planning and urban restructuring into a new direction.

Gubei West Block

D-Cube City

Oikosdesign landscape + architecture

3D Design Model of D-CUBE CITY
디큐브씨티 3D 이미지

Landscape Architect _ Oikosdesign landscape + architecture
Construction _ DAESUNG Engineering & Construction
Landscape Construction _ CORYO Landscape Architecture Co., Ltd, DAESAN L&C, HANSEL GREEN Co., Ltd, JSBinc, DONG SEO CORPORATION
Location _ Sindorim-dong, Guro-gu, Seoul, Korea
Site Area _ 25,756m²
Landscape Area _ 9,260m²
Completion _ 2011
Photograph _ Oikos design, DAESUNG E&C, Park, Sang Baek
Text & Material _ Oikosdesign landscape + architecture

MILLEFLEUR PARK - Completed 준공사진

디큐브시티

디큐브시티는 대성산업(주)가 30년 동안 대규모의 연탄공장을 운영하던 서울시 구로구 신도림동 일대의 공장부지 위에 새로운 Life Style의 생활화와 지속적인 도시의 변화를 이루고자 하는 노력의 일환으로 최첨단 기술력을 바탕으로한 복합문화시설을 유치함으로써 탄생하게 되었다. 네덜란드의 조경설계회사인 Oikosdesign landscape + architecture대표 아네모네가 디자인한 디큐브시티는 외부광장과 실내공간을 "자연과 문화의 연계"라는 핵심컨셉으로 조경을 포함한 조형적인 조화와 표현으로 Landscape, Lighting, Art work, Water feature, Construction 및 Interior design 등을 통합하는 창의적인 환경 디자인 설계로 완성되었다. 특히 디큐브시티가 많은 조경가들과 디자이너들에게 주목받고 있는 이유는 최초의 설계계획안을 설계변경 없이 100% 완벽하게 구현하였다는 점과 준공 후에도 소재와 식재, 시민들의 공간 이용행태 등을 꾸준히 모니터링하여 조경가의 설계 의도가 지속적으로 유지될 수 있도록 하는 사후 관리 과정이 체계적으로 잘 되어있다는 점이다. 또한 디큐브시티를 계획한 대성산업(주)는 전체 면적의 30%를 서울시에 기부하여 지역주민들을 위한 기업의 사회적 책임을 실천하였으며 준공 이후에도 광장 관련구역을 지속적으로 유지관리하여 시민들에게 서비스 편의를 제공하고 있다.

MILLEFLEUR PARK - 3D 설계계획안

SECTRET GARDENS - Completed 준공사진

D-CUBE CITY

D-Cube City, where there used to be home to a large coal processing plant owned by Daesung Corporation for last 30 years, sets a new standard in mixed-use cultural complex. High-end technologies are introduced to lead new life style and sustainable urban changes. Designed by the Netherlands-based landscape design studio Oikosdesign landscape + architecture with its founding partner Anemone Beck Koh, this place formulates a co-existence of nature and culture. It integrates outdoor plaza and indoor space by creative environment design embracing landscape, lighting, artworks, water features, architecture as well as interior design.

What attracts the attention of many landscape architects and designers is that it fully realized its original design concepts without significant changes and provides constant design maintenance system by monitering materials, plantation, and user behavior patterns. Futhermore, Daesung D-Cube City donated 30% of the space to the Seoul Metropolitan Government to practice corporate social responsibility for the community. It also constantly maintains square area for the convenience of the citizens.

SECTRET GARDENS - 3D 설계계획안

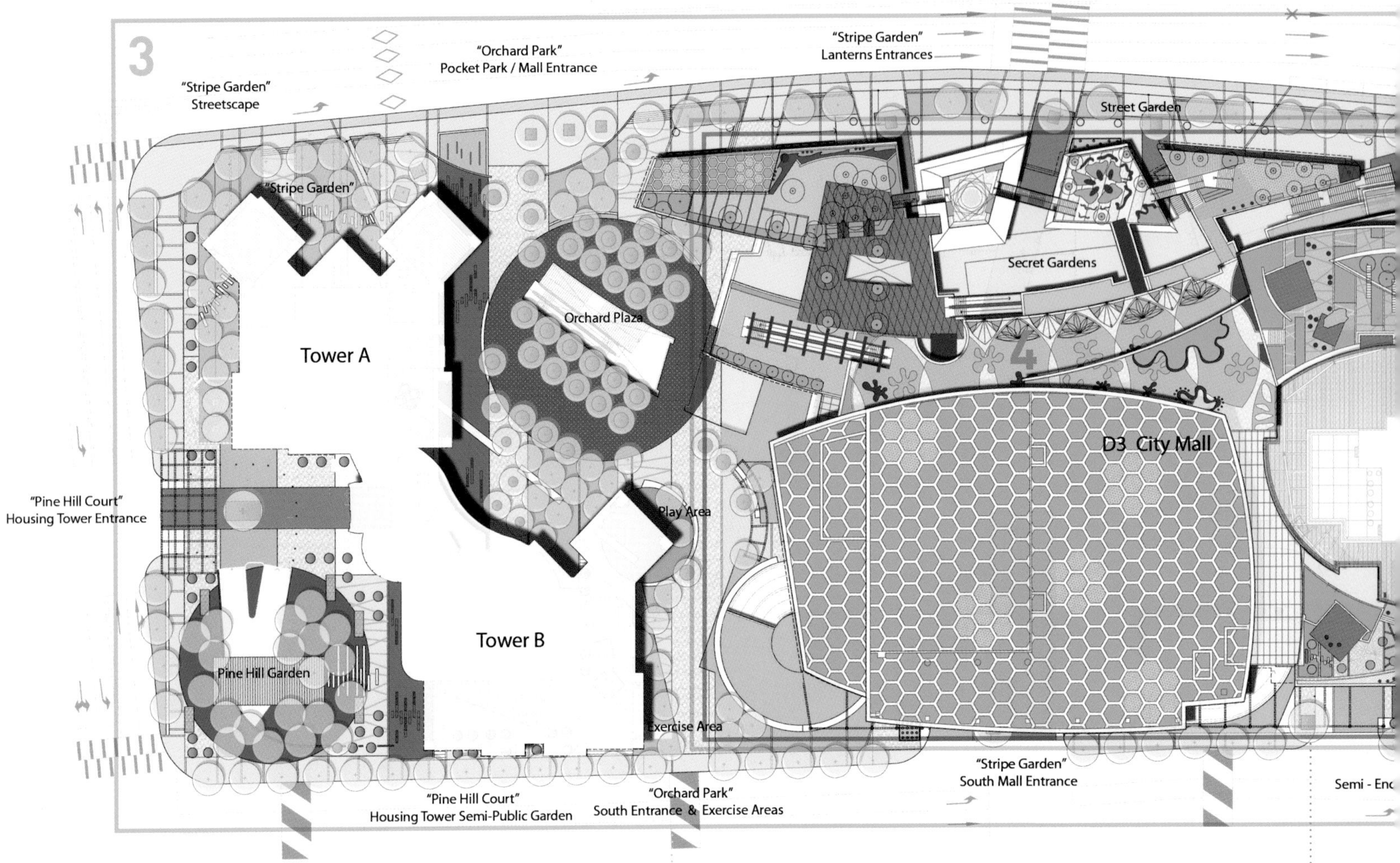

디큐브시티 조경설계 컨셉

디큐브시티 부지는 신도림 부지의 역사를 기억하고, 현대적인 다양한 환경예술작품과 다문화적인 이벤트를 연결하는 장소로 자연과 문화를 연계하는 조경설계 컨셉을 기본으로 한다. 또한, 신도림의 새로운 랜드마크가 될 녹지공간을 제공하고 공용 및 개인적인 공간과 중간 영역들의 특징적인 조경공간들을 연계시키므로써 다양한 사람들의 경험 및 공간성들을 통합하는 조경설계를 접목하였다. 조경면적을 최대한으로 넓게 설계하는 방식으로, 광장 공원에서 이어지는 지하철 연결통로까지도 조경 및 예술공간으로 확장 · 구성하고, 옥상정원을 최대한 비상업적인 이미지들로 설계하여, 친근한 공공지역 조경으로 시민들에게 편의와 휴게장소를 제공하고자 하였다.

D-CUBE LANDSCAPE PLANNING CONCEPT

Intended to remember the Shindorim district's industrial past and to link contemporary environmental artworks and multi-cultural events, landscape planning of the D-Cube City formulates a co-existence of nature and culture. Furthermore, as a new landmark green space for the district, and as a integrated landscape of public, private and liminal spaces, its landscape design embraces a variety of user experiences and spatiality. In order to maximized landscape area, subway passageway connected to plaza garden is designed as a green and artistic space. Rooftop garden, designed to give an impression of non-commercial place, aims to provide friendly and comfortable resting place.

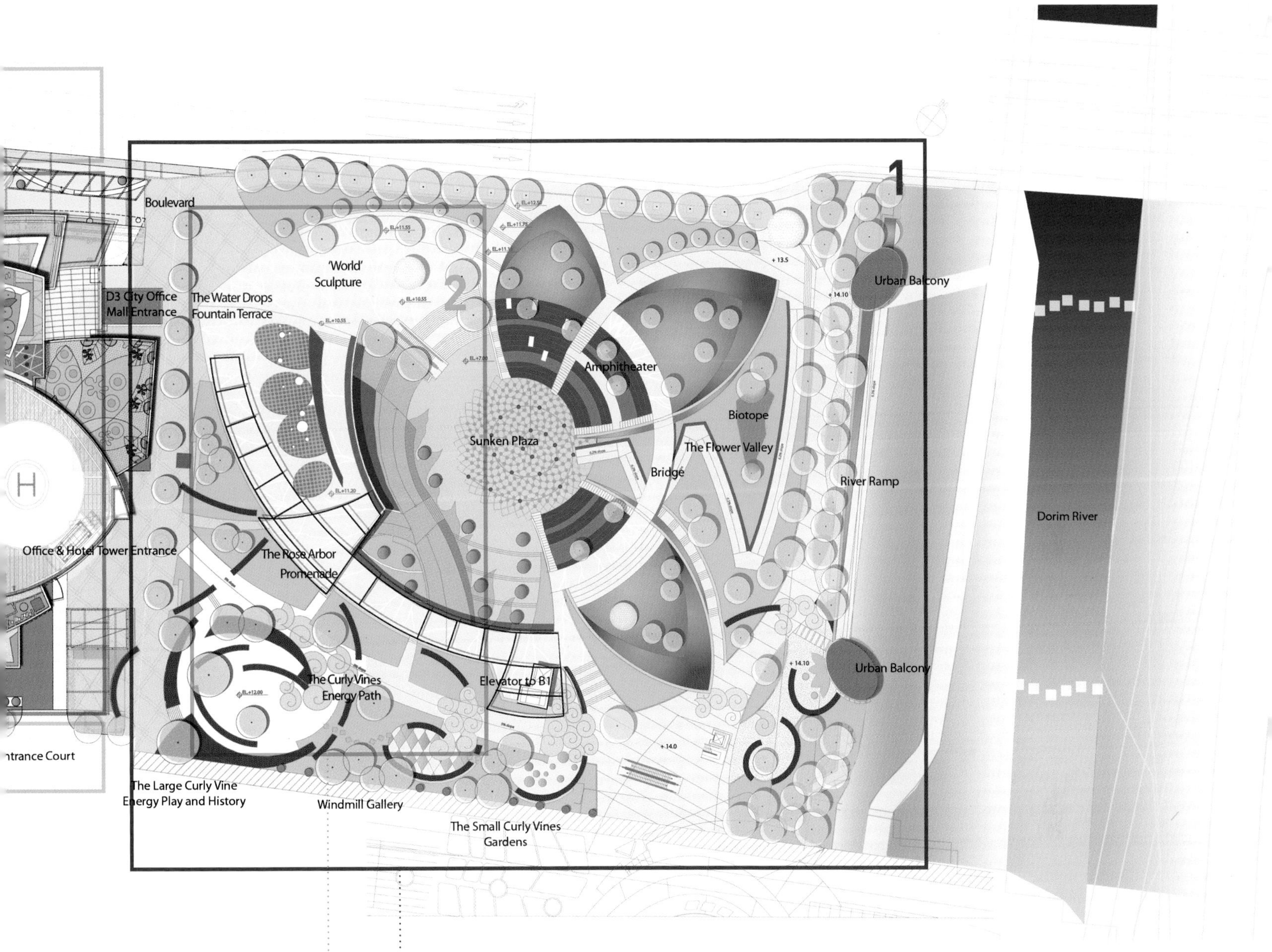

1 **'MILLEFLEUR PARK'** D-CUBU PARK **천 송이 꽃 광장**

2 **UNDERGROUND CONCOURSE 지하 광장**

3 **'CULTURED FIELDS'** D-CUBE CITY GROUND-LEVEL LANDSCAPE **경작지 패턴의 필드**

4 **'SECRET GARDENS'** ROOF LANDSCAPE **비밀의 정원**

D-Cube City Mster Plan

MILLEFLEUR PARK
천 송이 꽃 광장

어떤 시간이든, 누구에게나 활력을 제공하는 장소로 태양에너지가 만들어 내는 풍부한 꽃과 식물로 계절을 즐길 수 있는 중심 광장이다. 자연 에너지를 상징하는 규칙성을 사용한 공간 구성과 공원 시설계획을 볼 수 있다.

Millefleur Park (Park of a 1000 flowers) is a central plaza, where large diversity of flowers and plants which exuberate with solar energy, and seasonal changes vitalize everyone at any time. Regular patterns symbolize energy in nature and are used to organize space and the park facilities.

1. Sunken Plaza 중앙 광장

공원 중심부로 일반인들을 위한 이벤트 무대 장소로 사용(바닥 분수 연출 가능)

2. Amphitheater 꽃잎 모양의 원형극장

계단식 원형스탠드(700여 명 착석 가능)

3. Fountain terrace 분수테라스

강렬한 색채의 해바라기 꽃잎 모양의 분수

4. Rose Arbor 장미 넝쿨 통로

인상적인 강렬함과 함께 개별적인 대화와

분위기를 연출하는 공간

5. Flower Valley 야생화계곡

야생화가 피어있는 계곡의 분위기 연출로

맹꽁이의 이동과 서식을 위한 수생생태공간

Sunken Plaza 중앙 광장

CULTURED FIELDS
경작지 패턴의 필드

자연과 문화가 연계된 공간으로 경작 형태의 라인과 곡선, 격자모양의 패턴을 컨셉으로 한다.

Nature and culture are connected in this space. Several patterns including line, circle and grid shape the cultured fields.

STRIPE GARDEN 줄무늬 패턴 가든

Street Park
거리공원

Hotel Entrance Court
호텔입구 천장

ORCHARD PARK 과수 공원

Cherry Tree Grove in Orchard Plaza
벚나무 숲

2 Pavilion on the water
제2 파빌리온

SECRET GARDENS
비밀의 정원

Music Hall Entrance Terrace
콘서트 홀 입구 정원

Green Roofs on Music Hall
콘서트 홀 옥상 정원

Roof Garden on Plaza
백화점 옥상 가든

UNDERGROUND CONCOURSE
지하 광장

기본적인 콘크리트 기둥을 최소한의 경제적인 마감처리로 예술작품으로 나타내었다. 지하 1층/지하 2층의 보행통로 지역을 빛이 투과되도록 조도를 연출함으로써 생동감 넘치는 환경으로 만들었다. 지하 1층 지하 2층 가장자리 벽면을 시각적으로 잘 보이는 강한 색깔로 처리하였으며, 방향 제시 및 어두운 보행 통로지역을 팽창되는 느낌으로 연출하기 위해 슈퍼그래픽 아트작품을 배치하고 특별히 기둥들을 시적인 스타일과 예술적 처리를 하여 시각적인 일관성을 갖도록 표현하였다.

Minimal and economic finishing touches on concrete pillars gives an impression of artwork. Glowing light filtering through the exterior in the pedestrian corridor on level B01 and B02 enlivens the environment. Vivid walls occupy the corner walls on level B01 and B02 to give direction, while super-graphic artworks give an impression of expanded space to dark pedestrian corridor. Poetic and artistic treatment on the pillars aim to visual consistency.

Water Leaf Fountain
물잎 분수

Enlightened Eaves
문명화된 처마

B1/B2 Intergration by Art Work
지하 1층/2층 예술 작품을 통한 통합

Green Leaf Access Ramp
푸른잎 접근 램프

Marina Bay Sands Integrated Resort

PWP Landscape Architecture

싱가포르섬까지 이어진 인공 간척지인 마리나 베이 반도 Marina Bay Peninsula에 위치한 마리나 베이 샌즈 인테그레이티드 리조트는 해당 지역 개발사업 전체를 아우르는 핵심적 프로젝트로서, 향후 반도 전역에 걸쳐 진행될 모든 프로젝트를 위한 도심 경관 전략의 기준을 제시하게 될 것이다. 빌딩과 오픈 스페이스 등으로 구성된 방대한 규모의 이 콤플렉스는 싱가포르의 동남부 지역에 자리하고 있는데, 싱가포르만으로 접어드는 바다에서 바라봤을 때 마치 등대와 같은 구실을 할 뿐만 아니라 신규 개발지와의 연결고리로서의 역할을 담당하게 될 것이다. PWP는 싱가포르 최초의 종합 리조트 및 카지노 시설인 마리나 베이 샌즈에 대한 개발과 더불어 이 지역을 도시 전역과 연결해줄 공공 공간에 대한 개발을 동시에 진행하였다. 전체 프로젝트는 Singapore Garden City Framework 및 Singapore Green Plan의 기조를 적극 반영했는데, 이를 통해 지속가능성과 도시 녹화라는 싱가포르 정부의 두 가지 커다란 목표에 기여하게 된다. 2011년 본 프로젝트의 완성을 통해 30여 년 전 간척사업으로 시작된 싱가포르의 영토확장 사업이 첫 결실을 맺게 되었다. 향후 이 지역이 보다 활기를 띄게 되면 싱가포르 정부는 더 많은 건설 부지를 민간에 할당해 마리나 베이 샌즈와 기존 도심지역 사이의 공간에 활발한 개발이 이루어지도록 할 것이다. 조경은 일시적인 제약 요건 및 신규 건축물을 위한 구조적 장치로서 매우 중요한 역할을 담당해왔다.

마리나 베이 샌즈는 디자인 공모전의 결과물로서, 그 속에는 카지노를 통해 관광산업의 발전을 도모하려는 싱가포르 정부의 열망이 담겨있다. 약 40에이커 크기의 부지 가운데 75% 가량이 활용가능한 옥외 환경을 갖고 있으며, 이들 대부분이 공공 공간으로 활용되며, 소규모 부지들이 리조트 숙박객들을 위한 사적 공간으로 할당된다. 1.5킬로미터의 수변 산책로Waterfront Promenade, 호텔 로비를 관통해 두 개의 주요 도로와 메인 빌딩을 이어주는 경관 데크Landscape Deck, 공중 산책로Sky Promenade 및 옥상 광장Rooftop Piazza, 3동의 호텔 건물을 에워싸고 있는 호텔 정원Hotel Garden, 그리고 가로 경관Streetscapes 등이 대표적인 공공 공간이다. 이러한 모든 요소들을 한데 아우르는 것과 더불어 마리나 베이 샌즈의 마스터플랜이 추구하는 바는 싱가포르만 주변에 끊기지 않는 수변 산책로를 만들어 기존의 도시 공간과 신규 개발지를 연결하는 것이다. 이와 함께 싱가포르 도심을 향한 시야를 확보함으로써 싱가포르가 지닌 도회적, 사교적 특성을 그대로 유지하고자 하였다.
마리나 베이 샌즈 리조트의 원예 및 생태 디자인은 싱가포르의 고온다습한 열대성 기후와 도서 지역의 지형적 특성을 바탕으로 보행자의 편의와 수자원 이용에 있어서의 한계를 최대한 반영하는 방향으로 이루어졌다. 수변 산책로에는 대왕야자가 심어진 3열의 가로수 길이 조성되어 물가를 따라 서늘한 산책로를 제공하는 한편, 보행자들이 나무 아래 만들어진 그늘에서 쉴 수 있도록 했다. 산책로에 떨어지는 빗물은 돌로 만들어진 포장면을 통과해 토양 속으로 흘러들어가 나무에 충분한 물을 공급하는 데 도움을 주고, 바다로 흘러들어가기에 앞서 토양층을 통과함으로써 충분한 여과, 정수 과정을 거치게 된다.

이와 마찬가지로 가로경관 역시 보행자의 편의와 수자원 이용에 있어서의 한계를 최대한 반영하여 설계하였고, 이를 통해 지속가능한 환경적 장치들을 이용한 탄탄한 공공 공간을 확보하게 되었다. 인도에 떨어지는 모든 빗물은 식물이 자라나는 지역으로 흘러들어가도록 했으며, 가로수 주변에는 모두 투수성 포장재가 사용되었다.

싱가포르만과 도심을 향해 270도의 멋진 조망을 제공하는 스카이 데크Sky Deck는 57층의 호텔건물 3개동에 걸쳐 자리 잡고 있다. 이곳에 위치한 전망데크는 관광객들에게 큰 인기를 얻고 있어 싱가포르의 관광수입 증대에 기여하고 있다. 스카이 파크Sky Park에는 올림픽 공인 규격의 세 배 길이에 달하는 수영장과 두 곳의 레스토랑, 바 등이 들어서 있다. 다른 곳들과 마찬가지로 이곳에도 투과성의 포장재가 사용되어 표면에 떨어지는 빗물이 식물의 성장에 도움을 주고 있다.

공학, 건축, 그리고 비지니스 전문가들과의 긴밀한 협조와 더불어 PWP는 싱가포르 현지의 조경가 및 원예가들과의 협업을 통해 개장 당일부터 완결된 경관을 선보이기 위해 힘썼다. 싱가포르는 작은 도시 국가이기 때문에 묘포장의 규모가 작고 묘목의 수량 역시 극히 제한되어 있었다. 프로젝트의 디자인 목표를 실현시키기 위해 PWP는 묘포장의 임시 확충 방안뿐만 아니라 선행적 나무 확보 전략을 구상하였다.
이러한 전략을 통해 인접 국가 및 해외로부터 우리에게 필요한 수량과 품질을 충족시킬 수 있는 다양한 수종의 나무를 조달할 수 있게 되었다. 싱가포르에 임시 묘포장을 이른 시기에 마련함으로써 양질의 나무를 적절한 시기에 확보할 수 있었고, 운반이 어려운 다수의 대형 나무들을 프로젝트 진행 지역 인근에서 확보한 덕분에 산책로와 스카이 파크에 강렬한 조경적 특성을 즉각적으로 부여하게 되었다.

Landscape Architecture _ PWP Landscape Architecture

Lansdcape Design Team _ Peter Walker/FASLA, Adam Greenspan, Julie Canter, Su-Jung Park, Conway Chang

Architecture _ Safdie Architects

Landscape Architect of Record _ Peridian Asia

Architect of Record _ Aedas Pte Ltd

Engineers _ Ove Arup & Partners

Lighting _ Project Lighting Design

Client _ Las Vegas Sands

Location _ Singapore

Completion _ 2011

Photograph _ PWP Landscape Architecture, Timothy Hursley

Text & Material _ PWP Landscape Architecture

Marina Bay Sands-View from downtown singapore ©PWP, Photo by Timothy Hursley

싱가포르 시내에서 바라본 마리나 베이 샌즈

Hotel garden greenwall | 호텔정원의 입면녹화 ©PWP

Located on the Marina Bay Peninsula, a man-made land-fill expansion to the island of Singapore, the Marina Bay Sands Integrated Resort is the keystone project, defining and setting standards for the urban landscape strategy of all future projects on the Peninsula. The remarkable complex of buildings and open spaces designed for the southeastern edge of the city of Singapore act as an anchor to the new territory as well as a beacon from the sea at the entrance into Singapore Bay. PWP worked on both the Marina Bay Sands, Singapore's first integrated resort and casino, and on the simultaneous development of the public open spaces that will both define and connect this new district to the entire city. The entire project is within the Singapore Garden City Framework and the Singapore Green Plan, which support the city wide goals of both sustainability and greening. The completion of this project in 2011 represents the first built project in a planned expansion of the city of Singapore that began over 30 years ago through landfill efforts. As the area becomes more active over the coming years the government plans to release additional building sites, allowing further development to infill between the Marina Bay Sands and existing downtown Singapore. Landscape has played a critical role as both a temporary condition and a structuring device for new buildings.

The Marina Bay Sands was constructed as the result of a design competition motivated by Singapore's desire for a casino, which would increase the tourism economy. Safdie Architects, the design architect for the Marina Bay Sands, invited PWP to collaborate on this great project. Of the nearly 40 acre site, 75% has outdoor inhabitable environments, most of which are public space, while a smaller portion is private for resort guests. The public landscapes include: a 1.5km long public Waterfront Promenade; a Landscape Deck which bridges across two major city streets from the main building through the hotel's atrium lobby; a Sky Promenade and Rooftop Piazza, an elevated promenade and outdoor plaza at the top of the main building; a Hotel Garden that surrounds the three hotel towers, the 50 story living facade of the three hotel towers, and the Streetscapes. Combining these elements, the overall landscape master plan for Marina Bay Sands aims to connect the existing city to the new site through a continuous public waterfront promenade around Singapore Bay while maintaining view corridors toward downtown in order to sustain the urban and social character of Singapore.

Given the hot and humid tropical climate and island geography of Singapore, the horticultural and ecological design of all elements at the Marina Bay Sands IR has been guided by pedestrian comfort and limited water resources. At the Waterfront Promenade, triple allees of Roystonia palms are interrupted with informal groupings of large canopy trees providing a cooler walk along the water and places to sit below the trees. All of the run-off from the promenade drains through the stone paving and infiltrates into the soil to help irrigate the trees, while also being filtered and cleansed by passing through the soil prior to entering the Bay. All of the palms and canopy trees are located within generous continuous planting trenches below grade to support a long life span and root structure.

Likewise, the streetscape planting palettes were also guided heavily by pedestrian comfort and limited water resources in order to have strong public spaces through sustainable environmental means. Storm runoff from all of the sidewalk areas flows into the planting areas and permeable paving is used around all of the street trees.

Offering two hundred and seventy degree views of the sea, the bay, and the downtown the unique, three acre Sky Park, which spans three 57 story hotel towers, contains a public viewing deck, which has become a significant tourist destination contributing to Singapore's economic development. Elements within the Sky Park include a linear swimming pool that is longer than three Olympic swimming pools, two restaurants, a bar, and a series of flagstone garden rooms containing mature trees and soaking tubs. The garden rooms are intimate in scale providing a truly private experience in contrast to that of the Promenade. As incorporated everywhere else, the permeable paving adds to the environmental value in which surface water is directed to the planting areas.

In addition to engaging in elaborate coordination between engineering, architectural, and business professionals, PWP worked with local landscape architects and horticulturalists to help create a mature landscape, on-structure, on this new development site from opening day. Because Singapore is a small island city, tree nurseries are few and carry minimal stock. To help realize the design goals of the project PWP conceived of an early tree procurement strategy as well as a temporary nursery plan. This strategy allowed for plants to be sourced from adjacent countries as well as from over-seas in order to reach the overall number and quality of specimens required. The early establishment of a temporary nursery within Singapore enabled the Owner to purchase quality trees to be grown to larger matched sizes significantly closer the site. At installation, large quantities of huge trees that could never have been transported through border check points gave the waterfront Promenade and the Sky Park a strong and immediate landscape character.

Hotel-56 story east facade with bougainvillea planting | 분꽃과에 속하는 덩굴성 관목인 부겐빌레아가 식재된 56층 호텔의 동쪽 입면 ©PWP, Photo by Timothy Hursley

Streetscape | 가로경관 ©PWP

Podium roof garden walk | 포디움 옥상 정원의 보행로 ©PWP

Skypark pool terrace with view to downtown | 싱가포르 도심이 바라보이는 스카이파크의 수영장 테라스 ©PWP, Photo by William Cho

Skypark infinity pool | 스카이파크의 인피니티 풀 ©PWP

Skypark jacuzzi | 스카이파크의 야외 욕조 ©PWP

Skypark garden room | 스카이파크의 가든 룸 ©PWP

Waterfront promenade | 워터프론트 프롬나드 ©PWP

Sky promenade | 스카이 프롬나드 ©PWP, Photo by Timothy Hursley

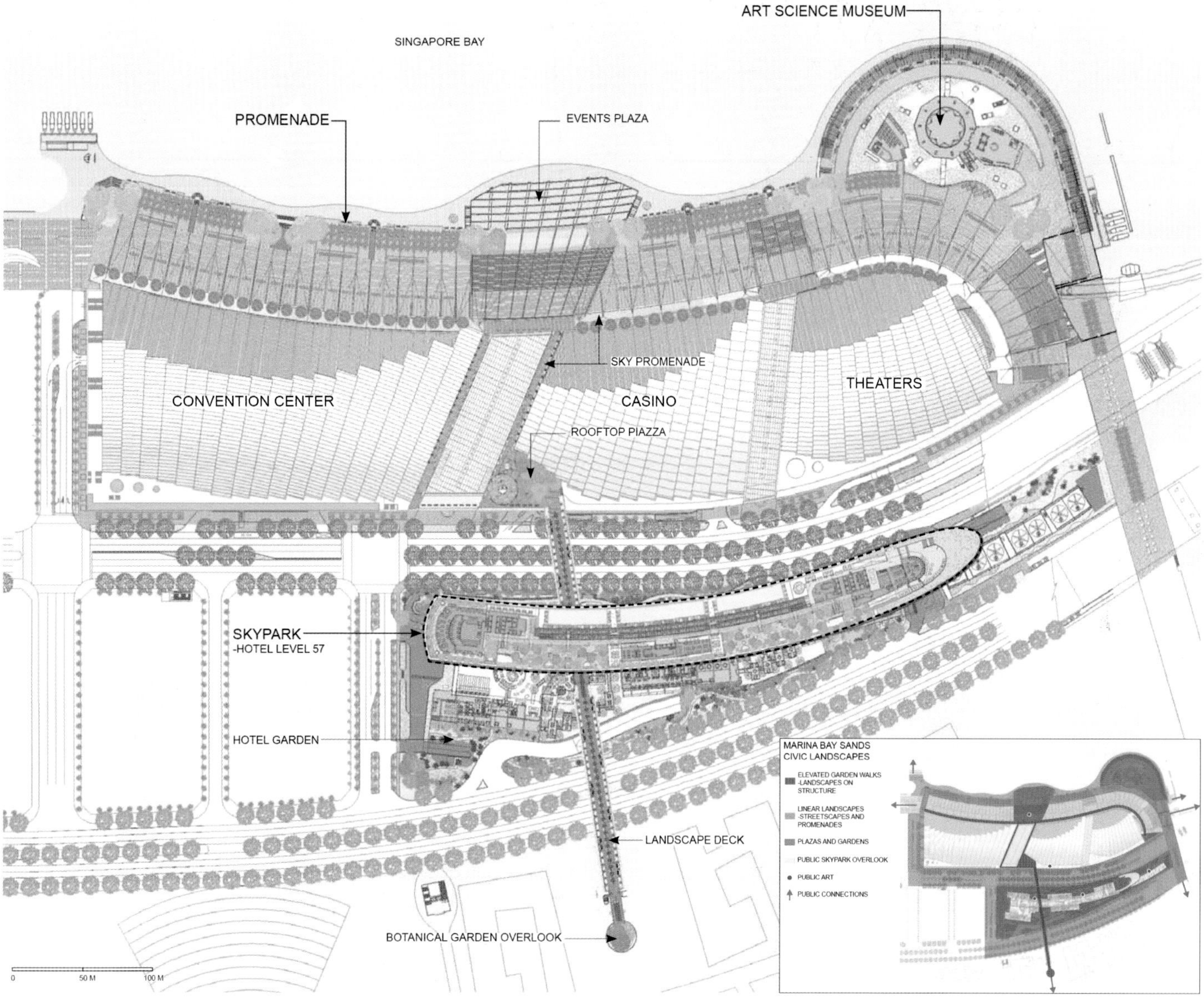
ART SCIENCE MUSEUM
SINGAPORE BAY
PROMENADE
EVENTS PLAZA
SKY PROMENADE
CONVENTION CENTER
CASINO
THEATERS
ROOFTOP PIAZZA
SKYPARK
-HOTEL LEVEL 57
HOTEL GARDEN
LANDSCAPE DECK
BOTANICAL GARDEN OVERLOOK
0
50 M
100 M
MARINA BAY SANDS
CIVIC LANDSCAPES
ELEVATED GARDEN WALKS
-LANDSCAPES ON
STRUCTURE
LINEAR LANDSCAPES
-STREETSCAPES AND
PROMENADES
PLAZAS AND GARDENS
PUBLIC SKYPARK OVERLOOK
PUBLIC ART
PUBLIC CONNECTIONS

Site Plan

Marina Bay Sands night overview | 마리나 베이 샌즈의 야간 전경 ©PWP, Photo by Timothy Hursley

2012 ASLA Pro Aw

GENERAL DESIGN

AWARD OF EXCELLENCE

A Green Sponge for a Water-Resilient City: Qunli Stormwater Park
Turenscape and Peking University, Beijing

HONOR AWARD

Canada's Sugar Beach
Claude Cormier + Associés Inc., Montréal

Lafayette Greens: Urban Agriculture, Urban Fabric, Urban Sustainability
Kenneth Weikal Landscape Architecture, Farmington Hills, Michigan

Quarry Garden in Shanghai Botanical Garden
THUPDI and Tsinghua University, Beijing

Arizona State University Polytechnic Campus: New Academic Complex
Ten Eyck Landscape Architects, Inc., Phoenix

200 5th Avenue
Landworks Studio, Inc., Boston

Powell Street Promenade
Hood Design, Oakland, California

Tudela-Culip (Club Med) Restoration Project in 'Cap de Creus' Cape
EMF Landscape Architecture and Ardévols Associates Consultants

Shangri La Botanical Garden
Jeffrey Carbo Landscape Architects, Alexandria, Louisiana

Winnipeg Skating Shelters
Patkau Architects, Inc. Vancouver, British Columbia, Canada

National 9/11 Memorial
PWP Landscape Architecture, Berkeley, California

Sunnylands Center & Gardens
The Office of James Burnett, Solana Beach, California

RESIDENTIAL DESIGN

AWARD OF EXCELLENCE

Drs. Julian and Raye Richardson Apartments
Andrea Cochran Landscape Architecture, San Francisco

HONOR AWARD

Quaker Smith Point Residence
H. Keith Wagner Partnership, Burlington, Vermont

Quattro by Sansiri
TROP Company Limited, Ladprao, Thailand

New Century Garden: A Garden of Water and Light
Steve Martino and Associates, Phoenix

Malinalco Private Residence
Grupo De Diseño Urbano, S. C., Mexico City

Maple Hill Residence
Stephen Stimson Associates Landscape Architects, Cambridge, Massachusetts

Reordering Old Quarry
Reed Hilderbrand LLC, Watertown, Massachusetts

Urban Spring
Bionic, San Francisco

ANALYSIS AND PLANNING

AWARD OF EXCELLENCE

The One Ohio State Framework Plan
Sasaki Associates, Inc., Watertown, Massachusetts

HONOR AWARD

Governors Island Park and Public Space Master Plan
West 8 Urban Design & Landscape Architecture, P. C., New York City

Wusong Riverfront: Landscape Infrastructure Pilot Project
SWA Group, Sausalito, California

Core Area of Lotus Lake National Wetland Park Landscape Planning
Beijing Tsinghua Urban Planning & Design Institute, Beijing, China

Coastal Roulette: Planning Resilient Communities for Galveston Bay
SWA Group, Houston

Nanhu: Farm Town in the Big City
SWA Group, San Francisco

A Strategic Master Plan for the Dead Sea
Sasaki Associates, Inc., Watertown, Massachusetts

SW Montgomery Green Street: Connecting the West Hills to the Willamette River
Nevue Ngan Associates, Portland, Oregon

Red Mountain / Green Ribbon — The Master Plan for Red Mountain Park
WRT, Philadelphia

fessional

ards

COMMUNICATIONS

AWARD OF EXCELLENCE

Digital Drawing for Landscape Architecture: Contemporary Techniques and Tools for Digital Representation in Site Design
Bradley Cantrell and Wes Michaels

HONOR AWARD

Asphalt to Ecosystems: Design Ideas for Schoolyard Transformation
Sharon Gamson Danks, Bay Tree Design, Inc.

Landscape Infrastructure: Case Studies by SWA
SWA Group, Los Angeles

Landscape Urbanism Website and Journal
Sarah Peck

What's Out There
The Cultural Landscape Foundation

RESEARCH

HONOR AWARD

Arizona Department of Transportation Ironwood Tree Salvage and Saguaro Transplant Survivability Studies
Logan Simpson Design Inc. and Arizona Department of Transportation

Productive Neighborhoods: A Case Study Based Exploration of Seattle Urban Agriculture Projects
Berger Partnership, Seattle

LANDMARK AWARD

AWARD OF EXCELLENCE

Village of Yorkville Park
Ken Smith Landscape Architect, Landscape Architect of Record: Schwartz Smith Meyer Landscape Architects, Inc.

General Design

AWARD OF EXCELLENCE

A Green Sponge for a Water-Resilient City: Qunli Stormwater Park

Turenscape and Peking University, Beijing

©Kongjian Yu

현대의 도시들은 지표수가 범람할 시 이에 대한 대처가 매우 취약하다. 조경은 이 문제를 해결하는 데 있어서 핵심적 역할을 수행할 수 있다. 이 프로젝트를 통해 일종의 녹색 스펀지로서 도시의 빗물을 정화 · 저장하는 한편, 자연 서식지 보존, 대수층 확충, 여가 목적에의 활용, 그리고 심미적 경험 제공 등 다양한 생태적 서비스 등과 결합될 수 있는 빗물처리 공원의 특성을 엿볼 수 있다.

Contemporary cities are not resilient when faced with inundations of surface water. Landscape architecture can play a key role in addressing this problem. This project demonstrates a Stormwater park that acts as a green sponge, cleansing and storing urban stormwater and can be integrated with other ecosystem services including the protection of native habitats, aquifer recharge, recreational use, and aesthetic experience, in all these ways fostering urban development.

대상지가 위치한 곳은 중국 북부 하얼빈시 동쪽 외곽에 2,733헥타르 규모로 조성되고 있는 춘리신도시Qunli New Town이다. 2009년 중반 신도시 한복판에 습지생태 보존구역으로 지정된 이곳에 34헥타르 규모의 공원을 조성하기 위해 조경가가 초빙되었다. 당초 의뢰인이 제시한 목표는 이 습지를 보존하는 것이었으나 조경가가 제안한 내용은 한걸음 더 나아가 이 지역을 도심 빗물처리 공원으로 탈바꿈시켜 다양한 생태적 서비스를 제공할 수 있게 하는 것이었다. 이를 위해 조경가는 생태적, 생물학적 과정들이 중단된 상태로 도심 한복판에서 점차 소멸되고 있는 습지를 어떻게 지켜낼 것인가, 이러한 도심 습지 생태계를 통해 도시에 적합한 다층적 생태계를 조성하려면 어떤 디자인을 채택해야 하는가, 이처럼 거대한 경관을 관리할 수 있는 경제적인 방법은 무엇인가를 생각하게 되었다.

디자인 전략

1. 자연 서식지의 지속적 성장을 돕기 위해 기존 습지의 중앙부는 그대로 두기로 한다.
2. 외곽 지역에 둔덕과 연못을 조성할 수 있도록 '잘라내기-채우기' 전략을 채용한다. 토사를 채취해 활용함으로써 둔덕과 연못을 공원 주변부에 목걸이 형태로 조성할 수 있다. 이러한 원형 구조를 통해 빗물을 정화 · 정수하는 일종의 완충 지역을 만들어 중앙 습지 주변을 둘러싸고 도시와 자연이 부드럽게 서로 연결될 수 있도록 한다. 새롭게 형성된 도심 지역에서 흘러들어오는 빗물은 습지 주변부에서 취합된 뒤 연못을 통해 정화된 후 균등하게 습지로 흘러들어간다. 토종 습지 식물들은 다양한 깊이의 연못에서 자라나며, 자연의 생육 · 순환 과정이 다시 시작된다. 토종 자작나무 숲이 각기 다른 높이의 언덕 위에서 자라나 빽빽하게 우거진 삼림을 만든다. 촘촘히 이어진 산책로가 원형으로 배치된 둔덕과 연못을 연결해 방문객들에게 숲속을 거니는 듯한 경험을 선사한다.
3. 스카이워크를 통해 곳곳에 흩어져있는 둔덕들을 연결하여 주민들에게 캐노피에서 아래쪽 습지를 내려다볼 수 있는 기회를 제공한다. 플랫폼, 다섯 개의 파빌리온대나무, 나무, 벽돌, 돌, 금속, 그리고 두 곳의 전망대를 둔덕 위에 만들어 스카이워크로 연결한다. 이를 통해 방문객들은 먼 곳까지 조망할 수 있으며, 공원 중심부의 자연환경을 관찰할 수 있다.

Location _ Haerbin City, Heilongjiang Province, China
Client _ Qunli New Town Government
Photograph _ Kongjian Yu

Beginning in 2006, a 2,733 hectare (6,753 acres) new urban district, Qunli New Town, was planned for the eastern outskirts of Haerbin in northern China. In mid-2009, the landscape architect was commissioned to design a park of 34 hectares (84 acres) right in the middle of this new town, which is listed as a protected regional wetland. The original task given by the client was to preserve this wetland. Going beyond the original task of preserving the wetland, the landscape architect proposed to transform the area into an urban stormwater park that will provide multiple ecosystems services.
The challenges are obvious: How can a disappearing wetland be preserved in the middle of the city when its ecological and biological processes have been cut off by the urban context? How such an urban wetland ecosystem can be designed to provide multiple ecosystems for the city? And what is the economic way to deal with such a big landscape?

Design Strategy

1. The central part of the existing wetland is left along to allow the natural habitats to continue to evolve.
2. Cut-and-fill strategy to create an outer ring of mounds and ponds. Earth is excavated and used to build up a necklace of ponds and mounds around the perimeter of the park. This ring acts as a stormwater filtrating and cleansing buffer zone for the core wetland, and a transition between nature and city. Stormwater from the newly built urban area is collected around the perimeter of the wetland and then released evenly into the wetland after having being filtered through the ponds. Native wetland grasses and meadows are grown on ponds of various depths, and natural processes are initiated. Groves of native silver Birch trees (Betula pendula) grow on mounds of various heights and create a dense woodland. A network of paths links the ring of ponds and mounds, allowing visitors to have a walking-through-forest experience.
3. A skywalk links the scattered mounds allowing residents to have an above-the-wetland and in-the-canopy experience. Platforms, five pavilions (Bamboo, Wood, Brick, Stone, and Metal), and two viewing towers (one made of steel and located at the east corner, the other one made of wood and looking like a tree at the north-west corner) are set on the mounds and connected by the skywalk, allowing visitors to have views into the distance and observation of nature in the center of the park.

©Kongjian Yu

A Green Sponge for a Water-Resilient City: Qunli Stormwater Park

Turenscape and Peking University, Beijing

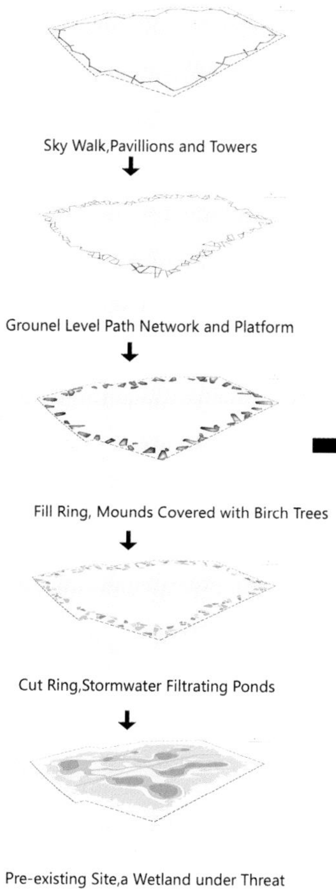

©Kongjian Yu

©Kongjian Yu

General Design

HONOR AWARD

Canada's Sugar Beach

Claude Cormier + Associés Inc., Montréal

Location _ Montreal, Toronto, Canada
Client _ Waterfront Toronto
Photograph _ Claude Cormier + Associés, Jesse Colin Jackson, Nicola Betts

캐나다의 슈가 비치는 각기 다른 세 가지 컨셉의 공원으로 구성되었는데, 해변 경사로를 가로질러 있는 설탕 정제공장에서 아이디어를 얻어 세 공원을 통합해 'Sugar Beach'로 명명하였다. 도시의 고층건물로 형성된 스카이라인이 갖고 있는 수직적인 특성과 온타리오 호수Lake Ontario의 수평적인 특성 사이를 연결시키는 슈가 비치는, 주변 환경이 가진 고유한 느낌을 느낄 수 있는 장소이다. 미묘한 차이를 통해 의도적으로 세세함을 나타내고자한 설계자의 노력으로 주변 환경에 집중하게 하며, 다양한 공간들을 통합한 것 이상으로 장소를 더욱 돋보이게 만들었다.

Canada's Sugar Beach is three parks in one, united by a singular reference borrowed from the sugar refinery across the slip. Poised between the extreme verticality of the City skyline and the superlative horizontality of Lake Ontario, Sugar Beach is a space to experience the unique phenomena of the surrounding context. A deliberate effort of detail through nuance draws focus to the surroundings so the space becomes greater than the sum of its diverse parts.

쇠퇴한 산업도시의 주차장으로 사용되던 이 장소에 도시 중심부의 해안선을 따라 토론토Toronto의 두 번째 도심 해변을 조성하게 되었고, 2010년 8월에 슈가 비치가 개장하였다. 공원에 설치된 밝은 핑크색의 파라솔과 줄무늬 사탕 같은 형태의 기반암이 가장 먼저 방문객들의 눈길을 끌며, 동쪽 만灣 근교의 새로이 조성된 이 해안가로 자연스럽게 발걸음을 옮기게 한다.

슈가 비치의 설계는, 지역의 산업유산을 이용하여 근처의 레드패스 설탕공장Redpath Sugar factory, 1854년 몬트리올에 설립과의 협력으로 완성되었다. 비스듬한 해안선을 따라 조성된 8,500㎡의 공원은 해변, 광장, 산책로 세 가지 요소로 뚜렷이 구분된다. 공기 중에 퍼져있는 설탕의 달콤한 향을 공원의 컨셉에 반영하여 방문자가 그 모습과 냄새를 느낄 수 있도록 설계하였다. '설탕'이라는 기본 컨셉은 공원 전반에 걸쳐 많은 요소들에 반영되어 표현되었다. 두 곳의 기반암에는 빨간색과 하얀색의 줄무늬를 그리고, 파라솔에는 사탕같이 부드러운 핑크색을 칠했으며, 산책로 하부에 묻혀있는 분수 기계실의 스테인리스 스틸 통풍 파이프에는 심지어 막대사탕 무늬를 그려 넣었다.

해변가의 역동적인 수경시설은 단풍나무 잎 모양이 새겨진 화강석으로 만들어져 어른들과 아이들이 재미있게 이용할 수 있도록 하였다. 또한 이 수경시설은 움직이는 조명을 설치하여 밤에는 색다른 볼거리를 제공한다.

토론토 워터프론트 전체를 가로지르는 해변 산책로는 West 8과 DTAH에서 제안했는데, 마스터플랜에는 단풍잎이 새겨진 모자이크 무늬의 화강석 포장과 제작한 벤치, 목재 조명과 같은 요소가 속해있다. 이 요소들은 슈가 비치 산책로에 통합적으로 적용되었다.

Formerly a surface parking lot in a faded industrial area, Canada's Sugar Beach opened in August 2010 to become Toronto's second urban beach along the City's downtown shoreline. The park's brightly colored pink beach umbrellas and iconic candy-striped bedrock welcome visitors to the new and emerging waterfront neighbourhood of East Bayfront.

The design for Canada's Sugar Beach draws upon the industrial heritage of the area and its relationship to the neighboring Redpath Sugar factory. The 8,500㎡ (2 acre) park features three distinct components-an urban beach, a plaza space, and a tree-lined promenade running diagonally through the park. With the fragrance of sugar in the air, the park's conceptual reference is experienced in both sight and smell. Sugar as concept was used to establish a language for many of the elements throughout the park, from the red and white bedrock candy stripes on the park's two outcroppings, the soft confection-like pink of the umbrellas, and even the candy cane pattern on the stainless steel ventilation pipes for the fountain mechanical room buried under the promenade.

A dynamic water feature set into a granite maple leaf beside the beach makes cooling off fun for adults and children. It also becomes a spectacle of illuminated choreography at night.

Promenade is a continuation of the proposal by West 8 and DTAH for a continuous waterfront promenade across the entire Toronto waterfront. Elements of their masterplan, - such as the maple leaf granite mosaic paving pattern, custom benches, and wooden light poles – have been adapted to seamlessly integrate the promenade at Sugar Beach.

©Nicola Betts

©Nicola Betts

©Nicola Betts

©Jesse Colin Jackson

©Claude Cormier + Associés

Canada's Sugar Beach

Claude Cormier + Associés Inc., Montréal

©Jesse Colin Jackson

General Design

HONOR AWARD

Lafayette Greens:
Urban Agriculture, Urban Fabric, Urban Sustainability

Kenneth Weikal Landscape Architecture, Farmington Hills, Michigan

Location _ Detroit, Michigan, USA
Client _ Compuware Corporation
Photograph _ Beth Hagenbuch BLA

Lafayette Greens:

Urban Agriculture, Urban Fabric, Urban Sustainability

Kenneth Weikal Landscape Architecture, Farmington Hills, Michigan

도시농업에 대한 호기심과 관심에 가속이 붙는 듯하다. 기업의 후원을 받는 도시 정원은 디트로이트Detroit 중심부에 도시농업, 커뮤니티가든, 생산적인 경관과 식량관련 운동에 대한 화제를 이끌어 냈다. '매력적인 공공공간'의 기능을 하는 생산적인 채소정원은, 도시농업을 통해 아름답고 생산적인 공간과 도시적인 삶이 공존할 수 있다는 가능성을 실제적으로 보여준다.

Interest and excitement about urban farming is gaining momentum. This corporate sponsored urban garden brings urban agriculture, community gardening, productive landscapes and the entire conversation about the food movement into the heart of downtown Detroit. A productive vegetable garden that also functions as an engaging public space, it is a tangible expression of the possibilities for integrating urban agriculture into city spaces and city life in a way that is participatory, beautiful and productive.

설계안이 진행되면서 라피엣 그린에 대한 프로그램은, 지속가능한 자재의 활용, 어디서도 가능한 활동, 공공의 이용과 즐거움을 위한 공간, 미래지향적이며 현재 진행되는 공공예술 프로젝트 및 교육적인 어린이 정원을 포함시키는 방향으로 발전하였다. 설계가들은 정원과 주변 도시구조 사이의 관계를 깊게 조사했다. 최근 도시농업에 대한 열정이 주목받고 있는데도 불구하고 '이런 활동이 도시에서, 도시적인 삶의 경험에 있어 과연 적절한 현상인가'에 대한 많은 의구심과 질문이 쏟아지고 있다. 때문에 도시농업은 미학, 환경에 대한 고려, 생산성과 경제성을 모두 다루어야 한다. 조경설계가들은 어떻게 도시농업을 표현할지, 대상지에서 어떻게 특별하게 작용해야 하는가를 재구성하는데 여념이 없었다. 라피엣 그린의 경우, 수준 높은 도시공간으로서 커뮤니티 정원은 공공공간이자, 공공녹지 및 커뮤니티 공간으로서 생산적이며 다기능적이다.

라피엣 그린의 전반적인 설계안은 대상지 분석을 통해 이루어졌다. '돌출된 화분' 형태의 채소원은, 높은 건물로 뒤덮인 도시환경에서는 불리하기 때문에 태양각도를 고려해 빛을 받을 수 있는 최적의 상태로 방향을 틀어 설치하였다. 이러한 독특한 모양 때문에 보행자들은 이 지역을 지나거나 가로질러갈 때 가던 길을 멈추고 돌아오게 된다. 라벤더가 식재된 넓은 가로는 사람들에게 인기 있는 길이 되었다. 보행자들은 이 공간을 빠르게 지나갈 수도 있지만 벤치에 앉아 쉬거나 정원에 들어가 보고 200여 종의 채소, 과일, 허브와 초화류를 감상할 수도 있다. 정원 곳곳에는 다양한 의자를 놓아두고 공공적으로 이용할 수 있도록 하여, 사실상 앉을 곳이 없는 혼잡한 도시에서 잠시 쉬어갈 수 있는 공간이 되도록 조성하였다.

As design development progressed, the program for Lafayette Greens evolved to include the use of sustainable materials and practices wherever possible, spaces for public use and enjoyment, future and ongoing public art projects and a fun educational Children's Garden. The designer looked closely at the relationships between the garden and the surrounding urban context. In spite of the current enthusiasm for urban agriculture, there are also many reservations and questions about whether this type of activity is appropriate in the city and urban living experience. Aesthetics, environmental concerns, productivity and economics all need to be addressed. The landscape architects were intent on re-imagining how urban agriculture could look and function in a site specific way; in this case, the community garden as a sophisticated urban space, productive and multi-functional as public space, green space and community space.

The overall design of Lafayette Greens was shaped by the site analysis. Raised vegetable beds were oriented for optimal sun exposure based on sun angle studies, especially critical in an environment of tall buildings. Due to its unusual shape, pedestrians had to go out of their way when passing through the area or cut across the vacant site. A wide Lavender Promenade now carries people along this desire line. Pedestrians can move through the space quickly, rest on a bench or enter the garden and explore over 200 types of vegetables, fruits, herbs and flowers. A variety of seating is provided throughout the garden to encourage public use of the space and provide respite from the surrounding busy city streets which offer virtually no outdoor seating.

©Beth Hagenbuch BLA

©Beth Hagenbuch BLA

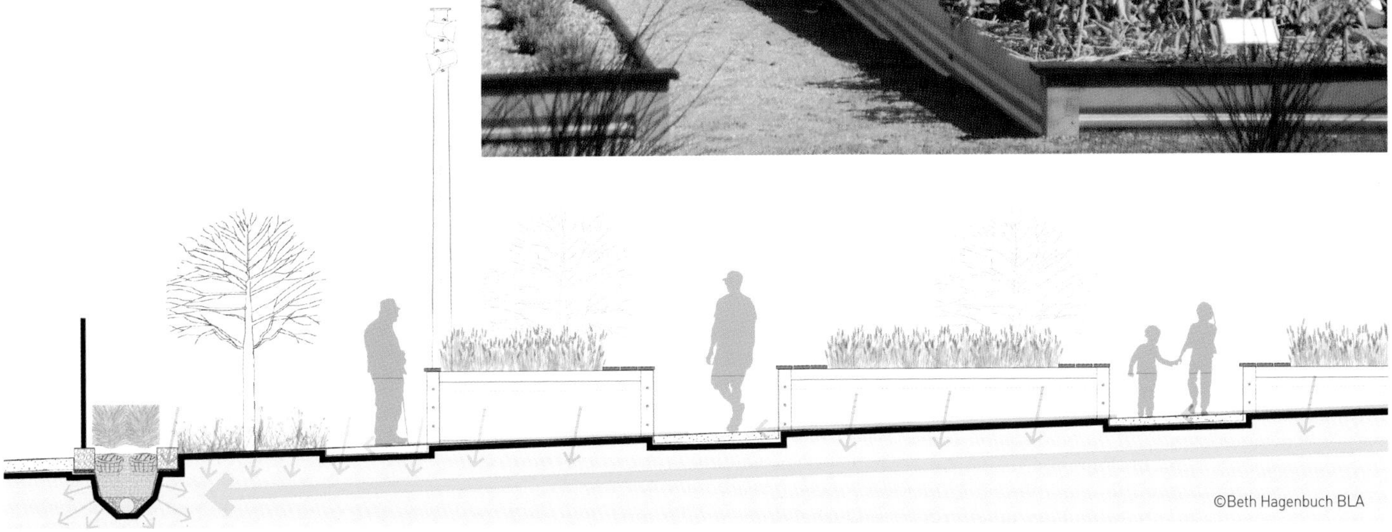
©Beth Hagenbuch BLA

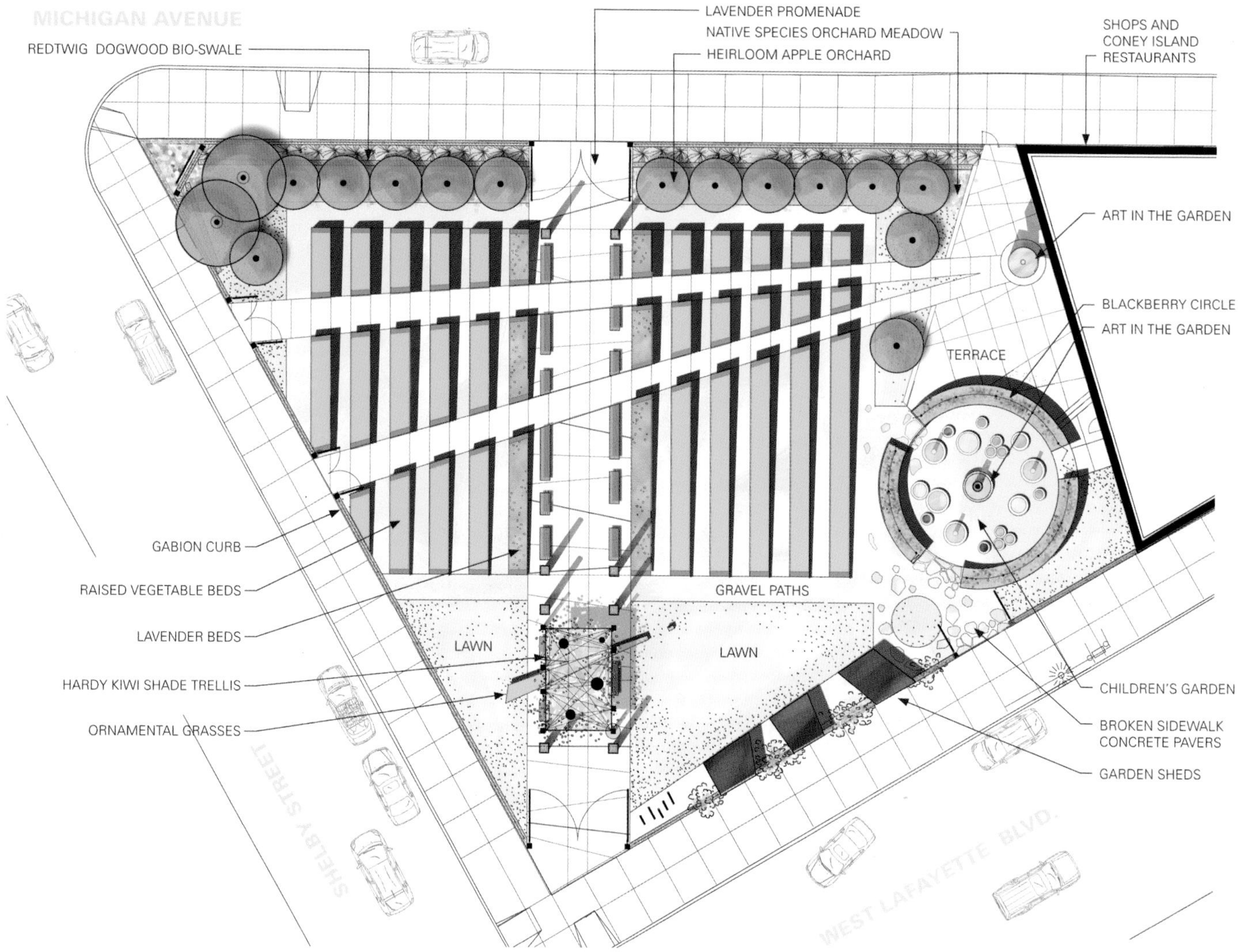
MICHIGAN AVENUE
REDTWIG DOGWOOD BIO-SWALE
LAVENDER PROMENADE
NATIVE SPECIES ORCHARD MEADOW
HEIRLOOM APPLE ORCHARD
SHOPS AND CONEY ISLAND RESTAURANTS
ART IN THE GARDEN
BLACKBERRY CIRCLE
ART IN THE GARDEN
TERRACE
GABION CURB
RAISED VEGETABLE BEDS
GRAVEL PATHS
LAVENDER BEDS
LAWN
LAWN
HARDY KIWI SHADE TRELLIS
ORNAMENTAL GRASSES
CHILDREN'S GARDEN
BROKEN SIDEWALK CONCRETE PAVERS
GARDEN SHEDS
SHELBY STREET
WEST LAFAYETTE BLVD.

Lafayette Greens:

Urban Agriculture, Urban Fabric, Urban Sustainability

Kenneth Weikal Landscape Architecture, Farmington Hills, Michigan

General Design

HONOR AWARD

Quarry Garden in Shanghai Botanical Garden

THUPDI and Tsinghua University, Beijing

©Yao Chen

Location _ Shanghai, China
Client _ Shanghai Chenshan Botanical Garden
Photograph _ Yao Chen

방치되어 있던 채석장 부지를 개조해서 조성한 채석장 정원은 상하이의 새로운 랜드마크이자 상징이 되었다. 이 정원은 생태적인 복원과 문화적인 재건 전략을 바탕으로 한 매력적인 장소로 평가받고 있다. 위험하고 사람의 접근이 불가하여 버려졌던 이 땅은, 방문객이 자연적인 경관과 채석산업에 대한 문화체험을 할 수 있는 관광지가 되었다. 또한 고차원적인 건설기술을 활용한 역동적이고 미적인 공간 조성에 대한 시도는 이 프로젝트에서 가장 주목받는 부분이 되었다.

Renovated from abandoned quarry yard, Quarry Garden has become one new landmark and name card of Shanghai. Its capabilities are fully displayed based on ecological restoration and culture reconstruction strategies. One dangerous inaccessible abandoned land has been built into one attractive tourist resort for visitors approaching natural landscape and experiencing the culture of quarrying industry. And the challenge of constructing dramatic aesthetical space on highly-difficult construction techniques also becomes one highlight of this project.

설계가들은 절 · 성토작업을 통해 지형을 복원하고 '거울연못'과 '꽃을 감상할 수 있는 단'을 조성하였다. 깊은 웅덩이와 호수 표면에 비치는 전경이 조화를 이루며, 관광센터 역할을 하는 '거울연못'은 언덕의 수직적인 평면이 주는 단조로운 느낌을 상쇄시키도록 조성되었다. '꽃을 감상할 수 있는 단'이 있는 남쪽 언덕은, 대상지 외부의 경관 저해요소로부터 분리되어 있으며 초화류의 식재와 전시를 위한 이상적인 장소로 활용된다.

우선 설계가들은 돌담을 자유롭게 활용하였고, 녹슨 철판을 변형시켜 리듬감 있는 연속적 파사드facade로 조성했다. 다양한 등산로들은 방문객들이 '단' 정상에 가기 위한 탐험로이자 다양한 식물들이 식재되어있는 '비밀의 정원'을 찾는 길이 된다. 급수탑은 기존 터널시설을 이용하여 '비밀의 정원' 내부에 설치하였다.

이 깊은 웅덩이는 면적이 약 1헥타르 정도며 물 바닥부터 테라스 사이의 높이 차는 20~30m 정도다. 독특한 지형 때문에 이 지역은 프로젝트의 핵심공간이 되었다. 깊은 웅덩이는 석재를 운반하는 경사로 조성에도 영향을 받았기 때문에 남쪽 돌담 공간에는 심각한 고저차가 생겨났다. 남쪽 돌담중 비교적 덜 심각한 수준의 풍화암 구간을 안전한 구조물이 될 수 있도록 다듬어 방문객이 아래쪽 웅덩이로 접근할 수 있게 설계했다. 설계가들은 강철통, 물 빠짐이 좋은 캠버camber강철버팀대, 구불구불한 목재 부교floating bridge로 구성된 관광 루트를 만들었다.

Designers reconstruct the landform by digging and land filling and form the new 'Mirror Lake' and 'Flower-seeing Platform'. 'Mirror Lake' forms another touring center balancing with the Deep Pool and the reflecting of the lake surface reduces the dull sense of the hill's vertical plane; the south hill on which the 'Flower-seeing Platform' is built not only isolates the interference outside the site, but also provides ideal place for flower planting and displaying.

First, the designer utilizes the free stone wall and the rusty steel plate to reshape facade sequence with rhythmic changes; then, a variety of mountain-climbing routes are explored for people to reach the top of the Platform and to visit the 'secret garden' of diverse plants. A water tower has been built inside the 'secret garden' based on the existing facilities tunnels.

The deep pool has a water area of about 1 hectare (2.47 acres); both the water depth and the height difference between the water surface and the terrace area is between 20-30m (65.6-98.4 feet).Due to its unique space form, this area is doomed to make the core zone of this project. Since the deep pool has been affected by the rampway for transporting stones, the rock wall on its south side is much more abundant in space level. Meanwhile, considering less serious rock weathering, the rock wall on the south side boasts of stable structure for visitors to access the bottom pool. The designer has created a sightseeing route composed of pourable steel barrel, freely-cambered steel trestle, artificial "the strip of sky" landscape and winding wood floating bridge.

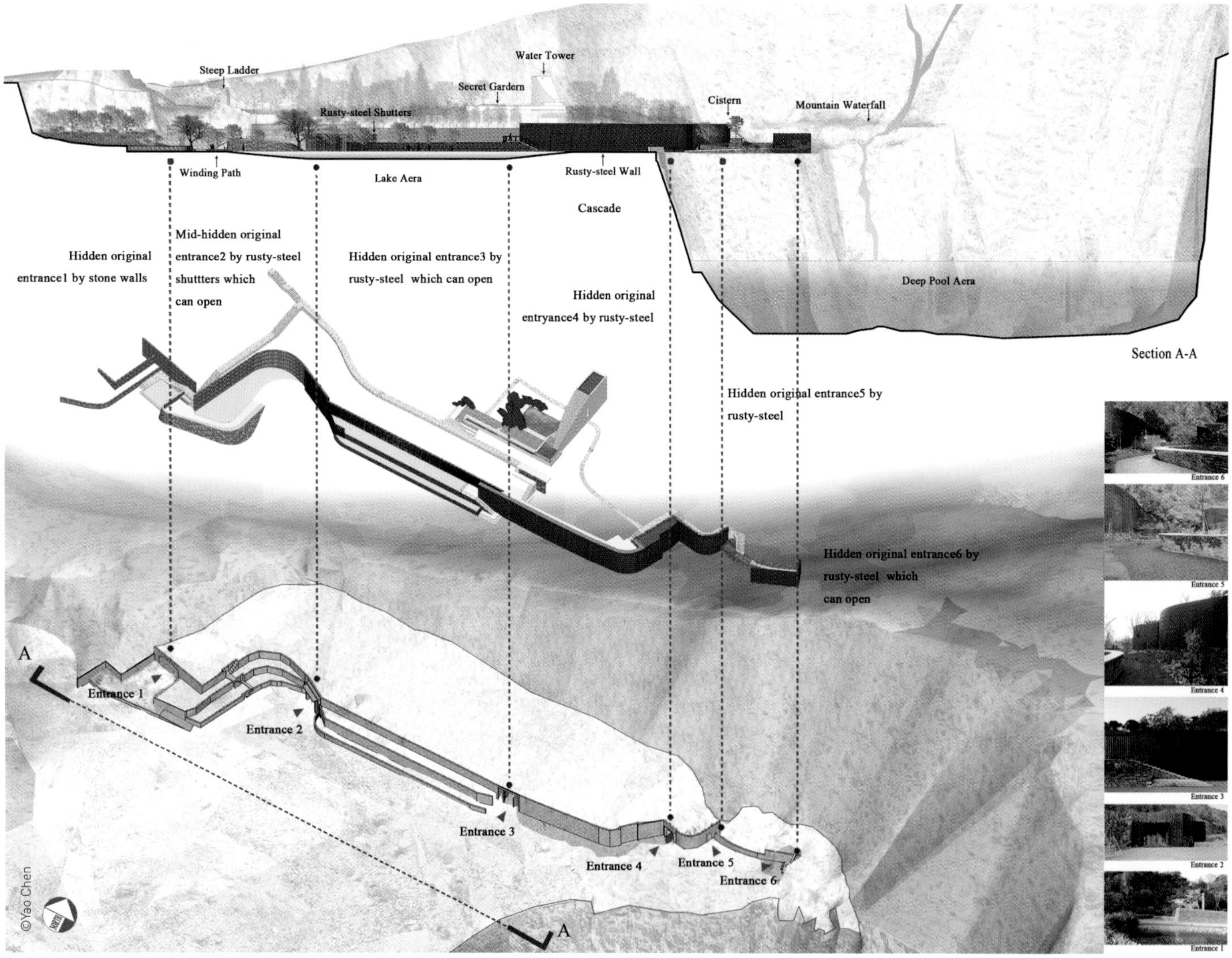
Water Tower
Steep Ladder
Secret Gardern
Rusty-steel Shutters
Cistern
Mountain Waterfall
Winding Path
Lake Aera
Rusty-steel Wall
Cascade
Deep Pool Aera
Section A-A
Hidden original entrance1 by stone walls
Mid-hidden original entrance2 by rusty-steel shuttters which can open
Hidden original entrance3 by rusty-steel which can open
Hidden original entryance4 by rusty-steel
Hidden original entrance5 by rusty-steel
Hidden original entrance6 by rusty-steel which can open
A
Entrance 1
Entrance 2
Entrance 3
Entrance 4
Entrance 5
Entrance 6
A
©Yao Chen
Entrance 6
Entrance 5
Entrance 4
Entrance 3
Entrance 2
Entrance 1

Quarry Garden in Shanghai Botanical Garden

THUPDI and Tsinghua University, Beijing

©Yao Chen

©Yao Chen

©Yao Chen

©Yao Chen

©Yao Chen

General Design

HONOR AWARD

Arizona State University Polytechnic Campus:
New Academic Complex

Ten Eyck Landscape Architects, Inc., Phoenix

Location _ Mesa, Arizona
Client _ Arizona State University
Photograph _ Bill Timmerman

이 프로젝트는 21에이커 부지에 5개의 강의동을 포함하는 캠퍼스를 신축한 사례이다. 교육을 활성화하기 위해 공군기지로 사용되었던 척박한 부지를 애리조나주립대의 소노라 사막 캠퍼스로 조성하였는데, 넓은 면적의 아스팔트 포장 도로는 우기 시 범람이 잦았기 때문에 포장을 걷어내고 중정과 캠퍼스단지 주변으로 아로요에 빗물이 저장될 수 있도록 설계하였다. 학생들과 교직원들은 우기가 짧은 이 지역에 소중한 빗물길을 감상하며 자연과의 교류를 맺게 되었다.

The Arizona State University^ASU Polytechnic Academic Campus project consists of 21 acres of site work in association with five new classroom building complexes. The goal was to transform the barren site of the former Air Force base into a thriving Sonoran Desert campus for learning. A major large asphalt street that formerly flooded during rains was transformed into a permeable, water harvesting arroyo adjacent to new campus malls and courtyards, giving students and faculty a daily connection to nature and each other while celebrating the path of precious, ephemeral rain water on campus.

클라이언트는 우수문제를 해결하면서 소노란 사막의 아로요arroyo, 사막지역 소협곡를 배려할 것을 요구하였으며, 이는 캠퍼스몰 설계에서 잘 구현되었다. 캠퍼스 지역에서 배수되는 빗물은 캠퍼스 동서축을 연결하는 보행로를 따라 조성된 식재지역으로 유입되도록 설계되었고 빗물 오염원을 정화시키는 기능을 하는 자생식물들을 선정하였다. 흙다짐 포장 보행로와 녹음수 식재는 도시열섬 효과를 줄일 수 있게 설계되었으며, 콘크리트 포장은 장애인과 긴급용 비상차량의 접근성 확보 요구사항에 맞게 조성하였다.

개별 건물동의 중정은 미기후의 이점을 최대한 살려 설계되었다. 농업비즈니스의 모리슨 스쿨the Morrison School of Agribusiness에 조성된 중정의 관개용 수로는 과수원지역 관수에 사용되며, 이스트벨리의 농업유산과 관개를 연상케 한다.
과학기술대학The School of Science and Technology의 중정에는 벽을 따라 자생식물들을 식재하였으며, 관개수로가 연결되어 있어 애리조나 캐니언에서 나타나는 것과 유사하게 주기적으로 수경이벤트를 보여준다. 인문교육학과 예술학the Education Humanities and Art 건물 중정은 원형극장의 형태를 띠고 있으며, 퍼포먼스를 관람할 수 있는 잔디광장이 마련되었다.
원형극장의 무대는 사이트 근처에 있는 자갈들로 채워진 개비온 옹벽gabion wall으로 조성되었다. 행정동과 보행로를 연결하는 워너서튼 수로와 중정에는 덩굴식물로 덮인 터널모양의 쉘터 구조물이 조성되어 학생들이 이곳을 통과하도록 설계되었다. 중정에 식재된 수변에서 자생하는 수목들과 식물은 건물 주변에서 유출되는 우수들을 저장하는 기능도 한다.

Inspired by our client's need for storm water solutions and the Sonoran Desert's arroyos, the design of the desert mall allows campus drainage to meander through a new, high performance, water cleansing native landscape adjacent to new major east west pedestrian circulation through the campus. Stabilized decomposed granite walkways in combination with desert shade trees help to reduce the urban heat island effect while the judicious use of textured concrete paving ensures ADA accessibility and proper emergency access required for a campus setting.

Each individual building courtyard is designed to relate to the schools program housed within and to take advantage of the microclimates created by the buildings. The Morrison School of Agribusiness courtyard includes a series of irrigation canals that feed an orchard court recalling the agricultural heritage and irrigation of the East Valley.
The School of Science and Technology courtyard is shaped by a living wall planted with native vegetation adjacent to an irrigation seep, creating a periodic water event similar to those found in Arizona canyons. In addition, outdoor classrooms are designed into the space. Shaped by an amphitheater built from recycled sidewalks, the Education Humanities and Art courtyard includes a lawn gathering space to view performances.

Arizona State University Polytechnic Campus: New Academic Complex

Ten Eyck Landscape Architects, Inc., Phoenix

©Bill Timmerman

©Bill Timmerman

©Bill Timmerman

©Bill Timmerman

©Bill Timmerman

©Bill Timmerman

General Design

HONOR AWARD

200 5th Avenue

Landworks Studio, Inc., Boston

뉴욕 맨해튼 메디슨 스퀘어 파크 근처 200 5번가에 위치한 역사적 랜드마크 건물이 리노베이션되었다. 장엄한 공간에 새로운 생명을 불어넣어 현존성을 드러낸 이곳의 핵심이 되는 공간은 중정이다. 오래된 것과 새로운 것의 대비가 중정을 바라보는 건물의 입면에 표출되었다. 유동적인 트레이와 풍성한 식물소재가 돋보이며, 모임장소와 정원 분위기를 연출한다.

The renovation of 200 5th Avenue, a historic landmark building adjacent to New York's Madison Square Park, breathed new life into its grand spaces and re-activated its civic presence. The contemporary courtyard is the centerpiece of this transformation, which contrasts old and new by leaving historic facades of the courtyard intact. The floating tray and lush plantings add brightness and texture to this landscape insertion and create a range of gathering areas and garden views.

디자이너와 개발사가 추구한 주요 컨셉 중의 하나는 초기 설계단계에서 브로드웨이와 5번가 교차점에 위치한 메디슨 스퀘어 파크와 건물 중정을 시각적으로 연결시키는 것이었다. 보존전략대로 5번가로 진출입하는 입구를 그대로 유지하였으며 내부 벽은 15층 유리 커튼월로 마감했다. 건물 리노베이션을 통해 메디슨 스퀘어 파크의 그린 이미지를 로비로 끌어와 시각적으로 연결시켰으며 건물 중정까지 그 연결범위를 확장시켰다.

중정에서 중요한 요소는 흰색의 트레이로 로비층에서 중정의 2층부터 5층까지 연결되는 것이다. 이 트레이는 기성품 콘크리트 포장으로, 폴리머로 강화되고 자갈층 베이스로 받치고 있으며, 중량감이 적어서 건물 콘크리트 슬라브 하중에 크게 부담이 가지 않는다. 또한 2인치 정도의 두께여서 강도도 충분하다. 흰색 트레이 포장은 건물의 입면 가까이에서 한번 꺾여 올라가 벤치와 플랜터로 마무리 된다. 중정의 플랜터는 콘크리트 기성품으로, 지면에서 우뚝 솟아 나온 모양을 하고 있다. 중정에서 바라보는 시야를 최대한 확보하기 위해 대나무*Phyllostachys bissetii*가 식재되었으며, 중정의 콘크리트 재질과 식물의 질감이 대비를 이루는 효과를 준다.

2010년 'LEED친환경 인증제도' 골드 등급 인증을 받았으며, 뉴욕시에서 유일하게 Core & Shell 건물로서 높은 위상을 얻은 이곳은 환경적으로도 성공적인 사례로, LEED 인증을 받는데 조경기술이 한 몫 하였다. 예를 들어 참신한 우수저장 및 지붕우수저장 시스템을 통해 식물 관수용 수원을 우수로 대체했으며, 관수량을 70퍼센트 줄일 수 있었다. 또한 뉴욕시 연간 총우수량을 줄이는데 일조하고 옥상녹화를 통해 에어컨 비용을 줄였으며, 녹색식물은 심리적 안정 등의 긍정적 효과를 가져왔다.

Location _ New York City, USA
Client _ L & L Holding Company, LLC
Photograph _ Andrea Varutti, L&L Holding Company, LLC, Landworks Studio, Inc.

One of the main concepts the designer-developer team seized upon early in the design process was to visually connect the courtyard with Madison Square Park, located at the intersection of Broadway and 5th Avenue. Employing a strategy of preservation augmented by a localized surgical intervention, the architect brought back the original 5th Avenue entry and replaced a solid interior wall with a fifteen-story glass curtain wall. These architectural renovations set the stage for visual connectivity to Madison Square Park throughout the lobby and extending into the interior courtyard.

The courtyard's signature element is a floating white tray that steps up from the lobby level to the second, third, fourth, and fifth floors of the courtyard. Constructed of polymer-reinforced, pedestal supported, precast concrete pavers that are lightweight enough to lower the loads on the building slab yet strong enough to be only 2" thick, the tray folds along the historic facade, peeling up to form benches and planters at its edges. In the center of the courtyard, a sculptural planter — also made of lightweight precast concrete — rises out of the groundplane, hosting a stand of Bissett Bamboo and providing vegetal contrast to the concrete areas while not obstructing views across the courtyard.

While social and experiential aims were core drivers of this project, the renovation at 200 5th Avenue was also widely successful environmentally. In 2010 the USGBC awarded the project LEED Gold — New York City's only landmarked Core & Shell building to achieve such a high designation. Landscape technologies complemented to help achieve this LEED status. For instance, an innovative rainwater capture and roof water harvesting system supplies water for the plantings, helping to reduce the amount of potable water needed for irrigation by over 70percent and reducing load on the city's storm drainage system. Planting on the walls reduces heat buildup on the facades, thus reducing air conditioning costs, but it also has a qualitative benefit as viewing plants is proven to speed physiological healing and enhance psychological well-being in humans.

©Landworks Studio, Inc.

©Andrea Varutti

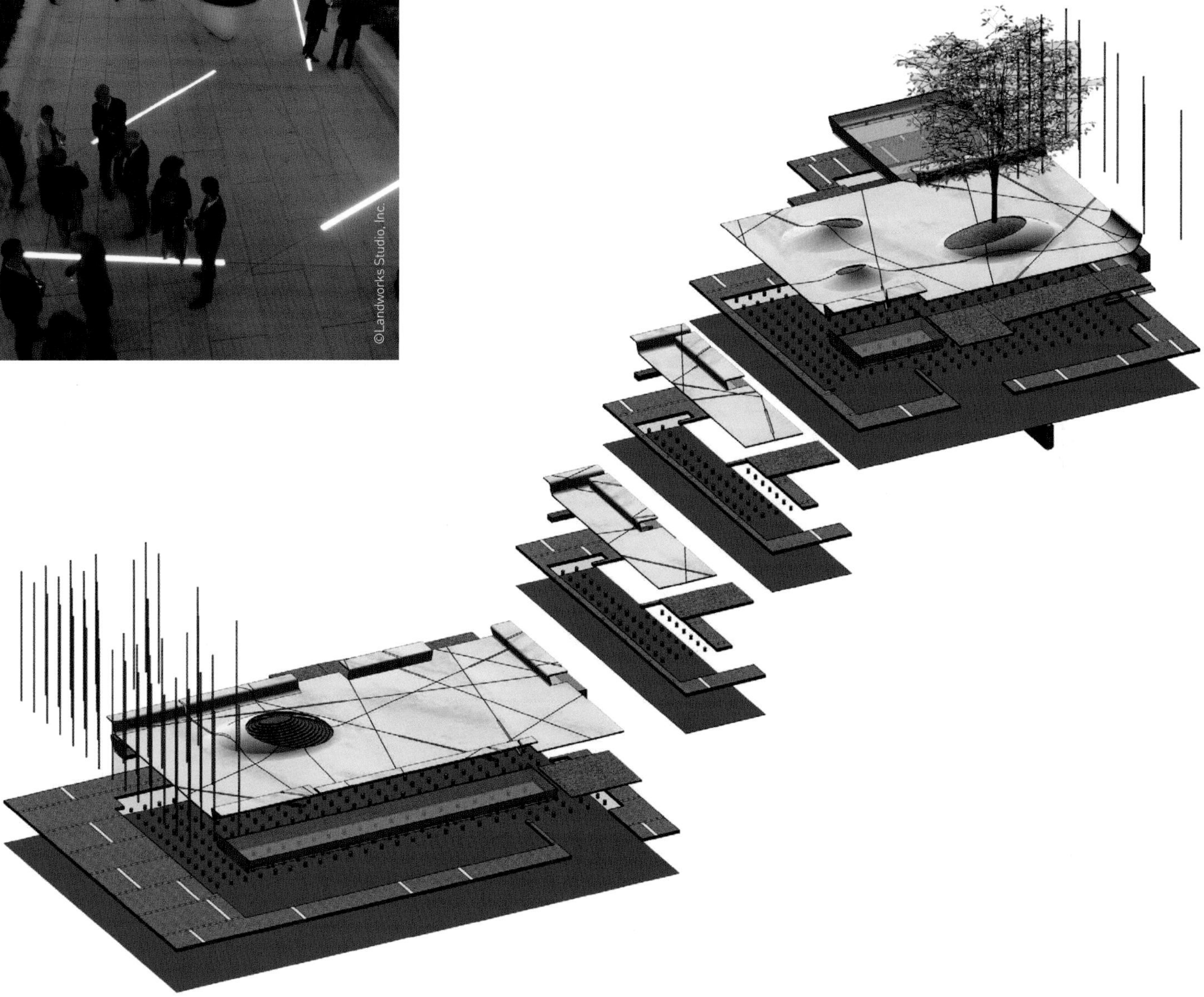

©Landworks Studio, Inc.

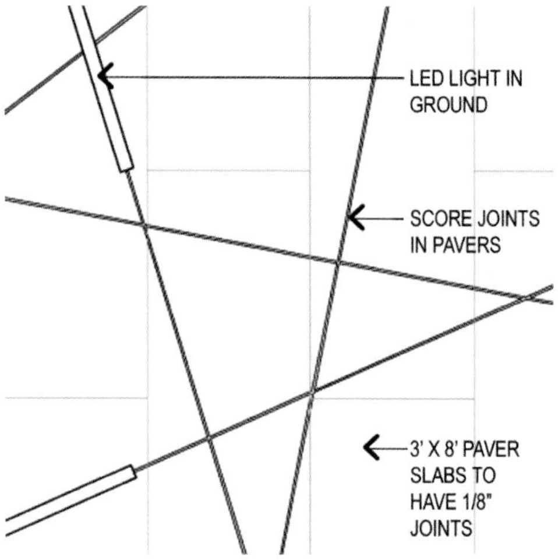

©Andrea Varutti

©Andrea Varutti

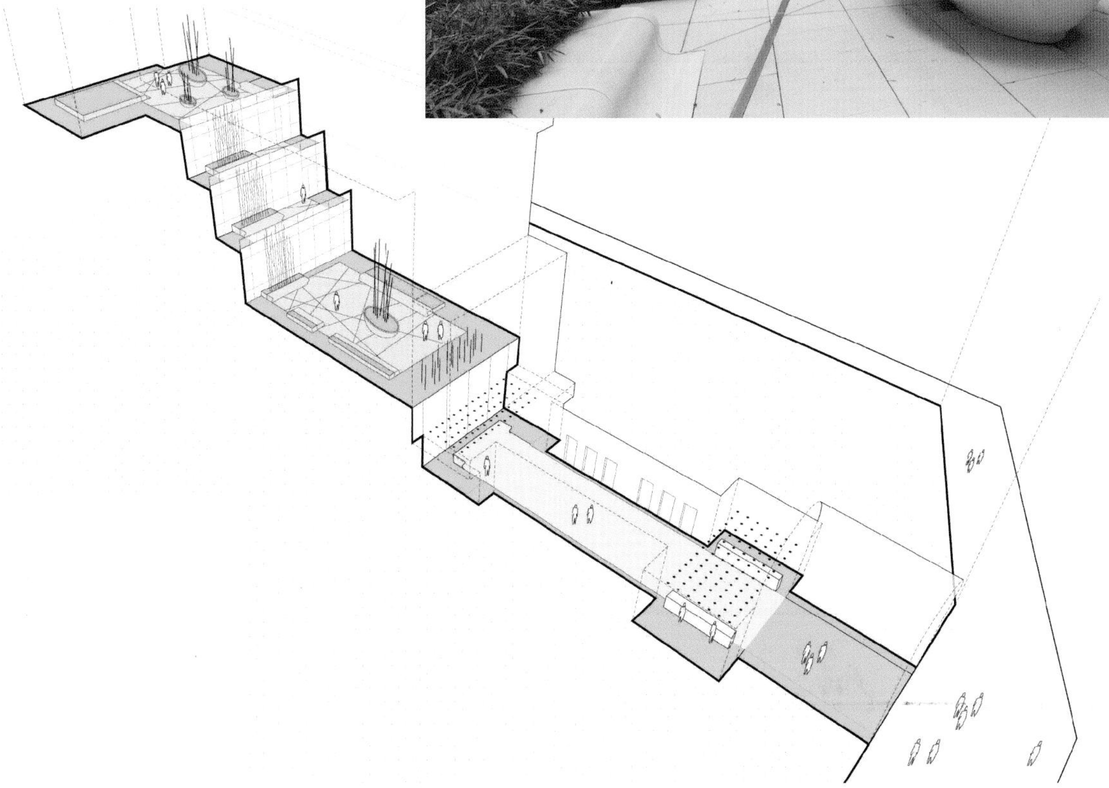
©Studios Architecture and Landworks Studio, Inc.

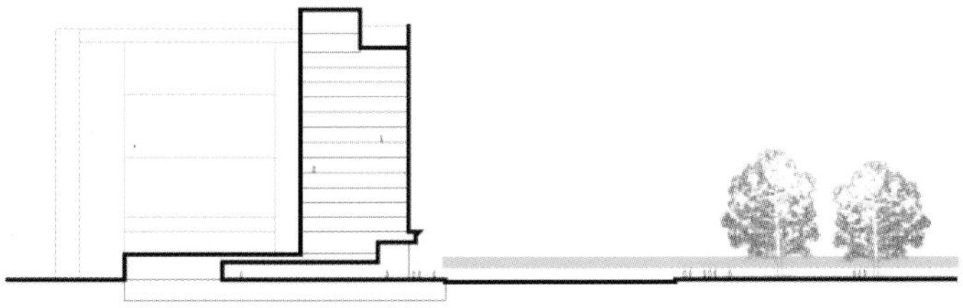
200 5TH AVENUE EXISTING
MADISON SQUARE PARK

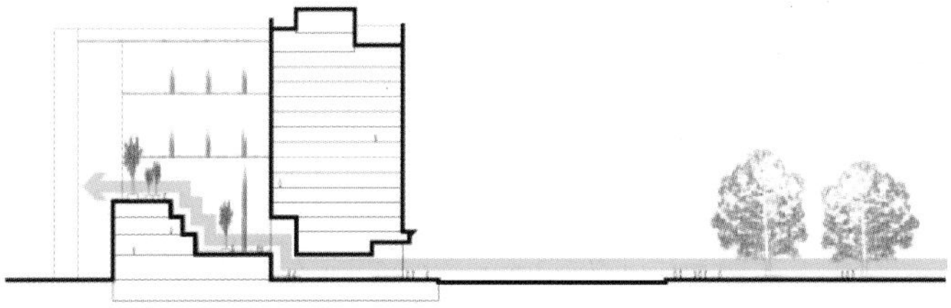
200 5TH AVENUE NEW
MADISON SQUARE PARK

General Design

HONOR AWARD

Powell Street Promenade

Hood Design, Oakland, California

Location _ San Francisco, California, USA
Client _ Union Square Business Improvement District
Photograph _ Marion Brenner and Beth Amann, Hood Design Studio, LLC

샌프란시스코San Francisco에서 가장 혼잡한 간선도로 중 하나이자, 네 블록에 걸쳐 평행주차공간이 있었던 도로가 보행자 전용도로로 새롭게 변모하였다. 파웰거리 보행로는 기존 보도를 약 74 인치 확장하여 조성했는데, 혁신적인 자재와 기술, 도시설계가 통합적으로 어우러진 공간이 되었다. 이러한 기술과 새로운 경관이 결합되어, 교통체증과 역사상 오래된 전차들 사이의 거리에서 보행자를 위한 공간을 제공하고 있다. 이는 보행자의 쾌적함을 위해 도시 공간의 자투리땅을 되찾고자 하는 프로그램 '보도를 공원으로Pavement to Parks'의 대표적인 사례로 꼽힌다. 이 프로젝트는 미국 아우디Audi가 참여해 민관협력을 통한 기금으로 진행되었고 '대담하게 설계된 세상A Boldly Designed World'에 대한 개념을 반영하고자 하였다.

On one of the busiest thoroughfares in San Francisco, four city blocks of parallel parking are replaced with a new pedestrian promenade. The Powell Street Promenade provides a 6'2" extension of the existing sidewalk, combining material innovation, technology and urban design into a new landscape that offers refuges for pedestrians amid the street's busy vehicular and historic cable car traffic. It is the largest example of the city's "Pavement to Parks" program, which seeks to reclaim swathes of urban land for pedestrian amenities. The project was funded in a public-private partnership with Audi USA and was intended to reflect their notion of 'A Boldly Designed World'.

이 디자인은, 파웰거리를 단순히 사람들이 지나다니는 통로가 아닌 그 자체로 목적지가 되도록 변화시켰다. 기존에 갖고 있던 상징적인 존재감을 유지하면서도, 완전히 새로운 도시환경 속에서 보행환경을 향상시키며 사람들이 모여들게 하는 장소로 변모된 것이다.

새로 조성된 보도는 1/8인치에서 3/16인치 폭의 알루미늄 격자망으로 설치되었다. 이 촘촘한 규격들은 ADA의 공인을 받은 보도포장으로 표면의 배수가 가능하게끔 한다. 또한 이 구조는 벤치, 화분, 레일, 태양광 발전타워를 연결하고 있는데 이 설치물들은 거리에 놓인 조각물처럼 예술성을 띤 형태로 배치되어 있다.

벤치, 테이블과 레일, 144인치에 이르는 태양광 발전타워는 모두 알루미늄으로 제작되었다. 이 탑형 구조물 꼭대기에 설치된 태양광발전 패널은 하루 종일 에너지를 발생시켜 저장하고, 대상지의 무료 무선인터넷 공급과 LED 조명을 위한 에너지로 활용되도록 하였다. 조명은 격자망 하부의 바닥조명과 통합적으로 설치하여, 저녁시간동안 보도 아래에서 은은히 빛나는 효과를 내도록하였다. 보행로 전 구간에 걸쳐 지수위와 자생식물을 활용한 공간을 조성하여 보행자들이 오래 머무를 수 있는 장소를 제공하였다. 패스트트랙fast-track, 신속처리 절차을 통해 두 달 동안 시공되었다.

The Promenade transforms Powell Street from a corridor that people pass through into a destination in itself; engaging, enhancing, and immersing pedestrians in an urban environment that is distinctly new, while retaining its existing iconic presence.

The new walking surface is constructed of aluminum grating with spacing between 1/8" and 3/16." This narrow dimension allows for ADA approved pedestrian surface while accommodating surface drainage. This structure also connects benches, planters, rails and photovoltaic towers so that they emerge from the walking surface skeuomorphically in one sculptural gesture along the street.

Benches, tables, rails and 12-foot tall towers are also constructed of aluminum. Photovoltaic panels atop these towers generate energy throughout the day, which is then stored and used to power free Wifi access along with LED lighting on site. The lighting is integrated beneath the grating, providing a glow effect from underneath the promenade during the busy nighttime hours. Low-water and native plantings are employed throughout the promenade to frame spaces for pedestrians to linger. The fast-track installation took place over the course of two months.

©Marion Brenner and Beth Amato

General Design
HONOR AWARD

Powell Street Promenade
Hood Design, Oakland, California

©Marion Brenner and Beth Amann

THE SMURFS
JULY 29
Lori's DINER
Breakfast
Lunch
Dinner
THE FABULOUS 50's
HOE
AREHOUSE
Clearance
DINER
CHANCELLOR HOTEL

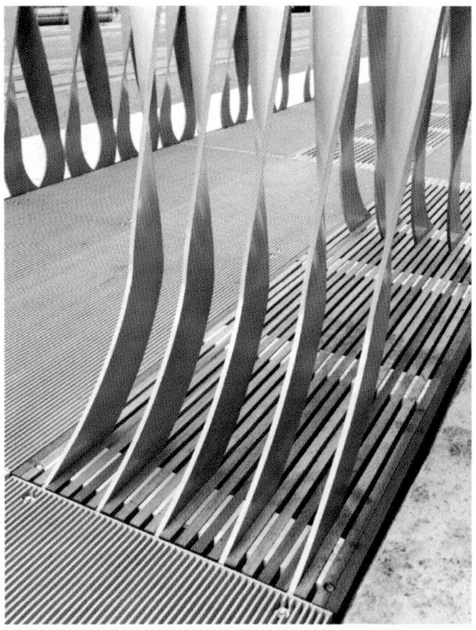

©Marion Brenner and Beth Amann

Small Table

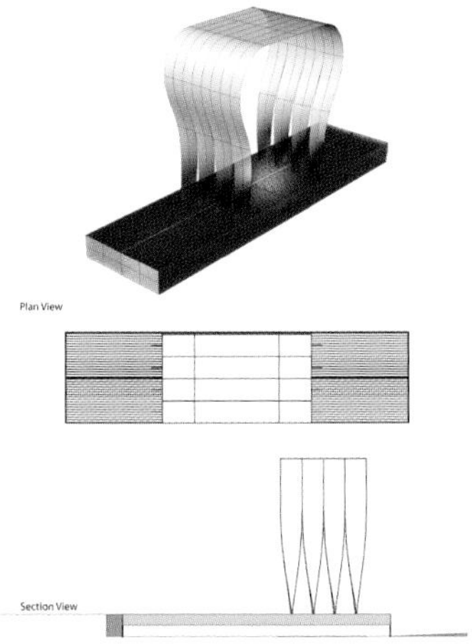

Long Table

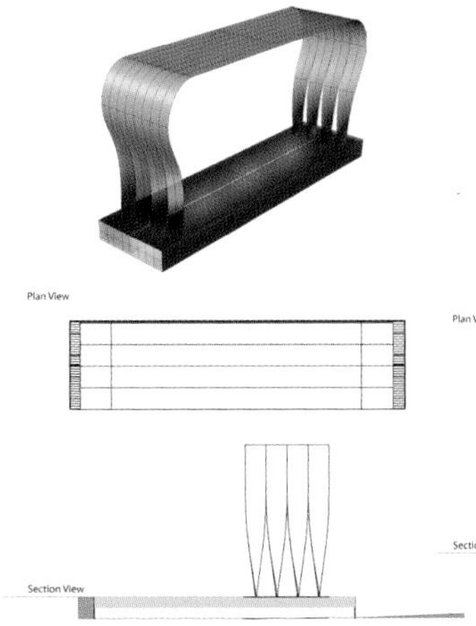

Rall Type 1

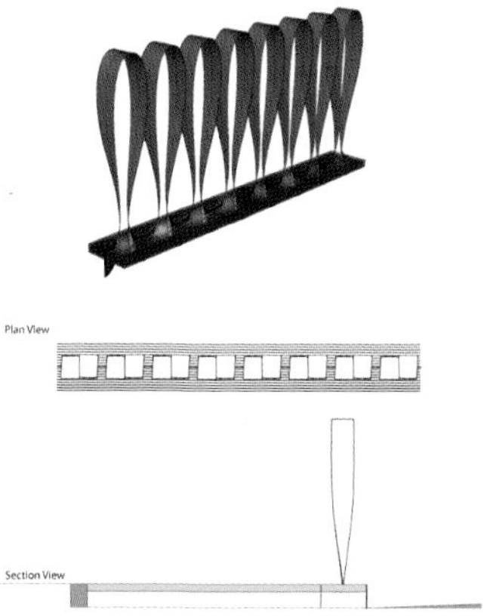

Rall Type 2

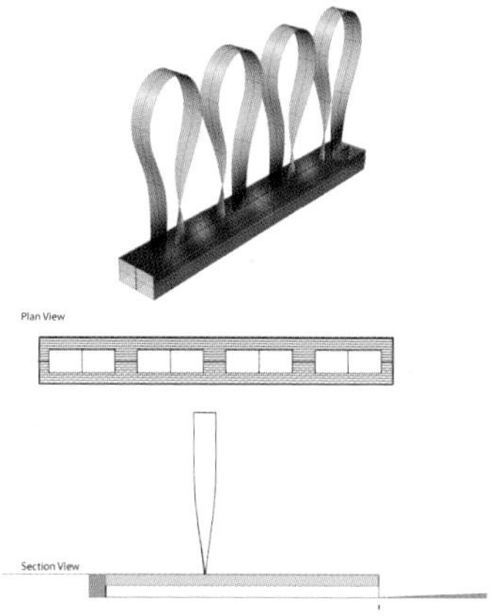

Bench A: Diagonal

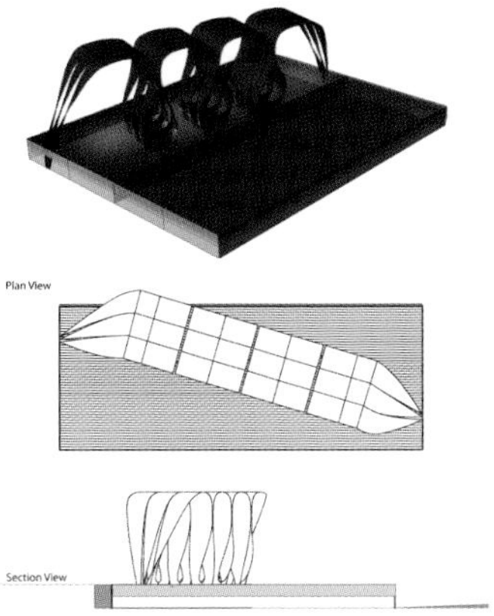

Bench B: Straight

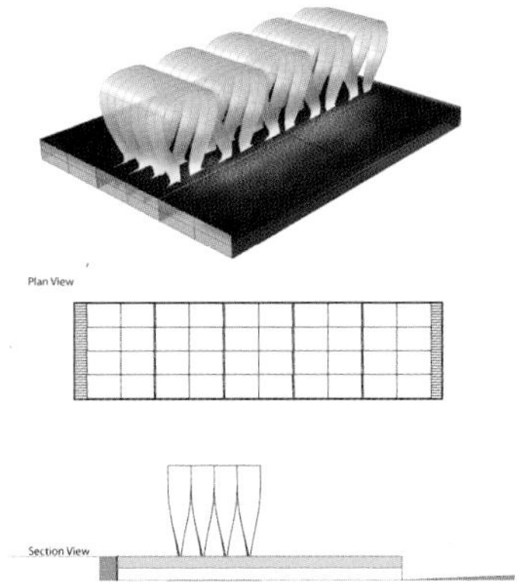

Rall Type 3

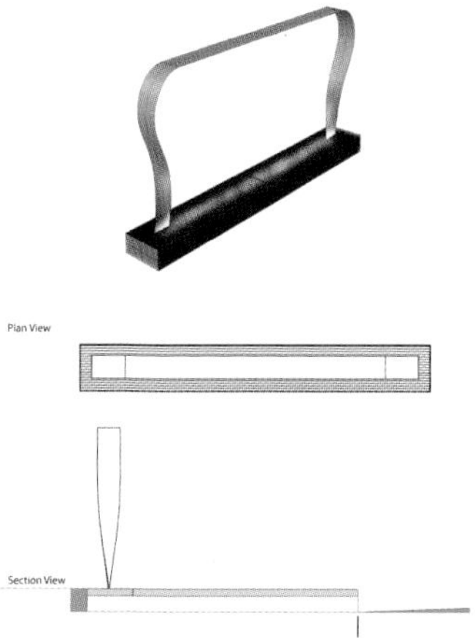

Guardrail

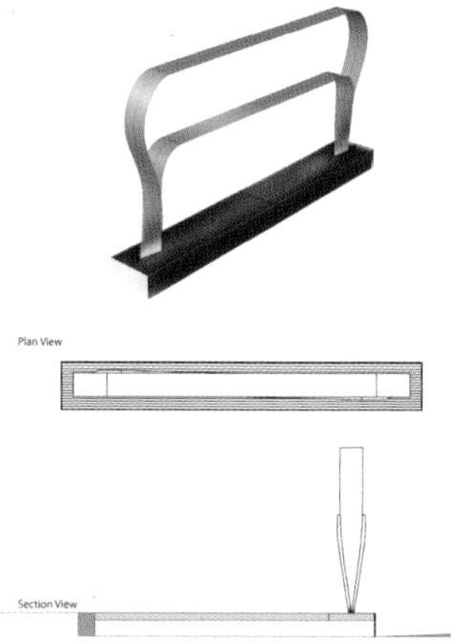

General Design

HONOR AWARD

Tudela-Culip (Club Med) Restoration Project in 'Cap de Creus' Cape

EMF Landscape Architecture and Ardévols Associates Consultants

Location _ Cadaqués, Catalonia, Spain
Client _ Ministry of Environment of Spain, Environmental Department of Generalitat Catalunya, Cap de Creus Natural Park, Gestora de Runes de la Construcció S.A.
Photograph _ Martí Franch, Pau Ardèvol, Esteve Bosch

본 프로젝트는 경관 중심의 자연 복원 프로젝트들에 있어서 훌륭한 귀감이라 할 수 있다. 딱히 많은 비용이 들지 않는 방법들이 동원됐음에도, 디자인에 반영된 적절한 파괴와 건설의 조합을 통해 해당 지역이 지닌 자연적 특성 및 문화적 독창성 모두를 충분히 살려낼 수 있었다. 방문객들을 적절히 활용해 하나의 이야기를 만들어냄으로써 자연 속에서 문화가 탄생할 수 있는 배경을 조성한다. 이처럼 혁신적 접근법을 통해 지우고 비우는 것이 채우고 더하는 것만큼이나 가치 있는 일이 될 수 있는지 진지하게 고민해볼 수 있을 것이다.

This project is a showcase for landscape driven nature restoration projects. Through necessarily inexpensive actions, the design skilfully construes and orchestrates the deconstruction as a combination of destruction and construction to celebrate the site's peculiarities, both natural and cultural. It proposes ways to choreograph on-site visitors into a narrative that stimulates the culture in nature in an innovative approach to finally question whether erasing and voiding is just as valid as filling in and adding.

©Martí Franch

이베리아반도의 동쪽 끝자락인 이곳에 클럽 메드가 세워진 것은 1960년대로, 해당 지역은 바람이 많이 불기로 유명한 스페인의 최북단 귀퉁이에 위치한다. 이곳의 클럽 메드는 개별여행자들을 위한 휴양 빌리지로 건립되었으며, 하절기에 약 900명을 동시에 수용할 수 있는 400개의 객실을 보유하고 있었다.
민주주의가 성숙하고, 환경 보존의 필요성이 대두됨에 따라 '캅 데 크레우스'는 국립공원으로 지정되었다. 빼어난 지질학적 · 생물학적 가치 덕분에 클럽 메드 주변을 포함한 이 지역 전체에 대해 최고 수준의 보존이 이뤄지게 되었다. 2003년 여름 클럽 메드가 영구 폐쇄되었고, 2005년 200헥타르 규모의 토지가 스페인 정부 환경부에 수용돼 2005년에서 2007년에 걸쳐 복원 프로젝트가 진행되었다.

In 1960, Club Med was constructed on the eastern tip of the Iberian Peninsula in one of the windiest and most northern exposed corners of the nation. Club Med was constructed as a private holiday village with 400 rooms that accommodated around 900 visitors in summertime.
With the rise of democracy and ecological conservation, Cap de Creus was declared a Natural Park in 3658. The cape, including the Club Med surroundings, was given the highest level of land protection because of its outstanding geological and botanical value. In the summer of 2003 Club Med was permanently closed, and in 2005, the 200 ha of property was acquired by the Spanish Ministry of Environment and a restoration project was active during 2005 and 2007.

자연 환경 교정에서 경관 복원까지

이 프로젝트의 진정한 목표는 경관을 새롭게 만들거나 파괴하는 것이 아니라, 경관을 경험할 수 있는 환경을 조성하는 것이었다. 이를 위해 해당 지역에 대한 심도 있는 조사와 정확한 현장지도 제작이 포함되었다. 14개월의 본 작업 기간을 포함한 5년간의 진행과정을 통해 디자이너들은 200km 이상의 거리를 도보로 이동하며 15,000장 이상의 이미지를 촬영, 연구했으며, 자연 환경 복원과 관련된 각계 전문가 50여 명을 초빙해 구조물 해체, 자연의 역동성 회복, 그리고 사회적 안정화를 이룰 수 있는 최적의 방안을 모색하고자 힘썼다. 건축에 있어서는 미니멀한 접근방법이 채택되었으며, 현장에서 구한 재료와 코르텐강 등으로 자재를 한정하여 경관의 통일성을 확보하고, 해풍에 대한 내구성을 높이고자 했다.

430개동의 건물들에 대해서는 선별적 해체작업이 이뤄졌는데, 혁신적이면서 과도하지 않은 해체기법이 활용되었다. 도로, 빌딩, 산책로, 그리고 목재 구조물 등 클럽 메드에서 제거하게 될 25개의 다양한 구조물 각각에는 그 특성에 맞는 '십계명'을 미리 정해두었다. 이들 가운데 5곳에 대한 파괴실험을 먼저 진행해봄으로써 예측값이 맞는지의 여부를 확인하고, 기준을 정하는 한편 예산을 책정할 수 있도록 했다. 해체의 마지막 단계는 지하 공간, 먼지, 그리고 시멘트 등 모든 흔적을 깨끗이 제거하는 것으로서 '고고학 발굴'의 기준에 맞춰 다양한 기술을 활용해 수작업으로 이루어졌다. 또한 이 지역 고유의 지형을 복원하고 육지와 바다 사이의 물질 이동을 원활히 함으로써 생태적 역동성을 되찾고자 했다. 이를 위해 시냇물을 되살리기 위한 대규모 토양 모델링 작업, 자연스러운 물 흐름을 방해하는 제방도로 제거, 그리고 퇴적물의 이동을 가능하게 해줄 보다 넓은 경간을 지닌 교각의 건설 등이 필요하였다. 한편 식물학자의 조언에 따라 복원 프로젝트를 위한 식재는 거의 고려하지 않았는데, 이는 토착 식물의 종자를 오염시키지 않기 위해서였다. 분사식 씨뿌리기를 활용하였고, 작업을 끝마친 뒤 1년이 지나자 부지 대부분이 토착 1년생 식물로 뒤덮이게 되었다.

경험을 디자인하는 것은 복원 전략을 짜는 것만큼이나 큰 중요성을 지닌다. 이러한 취지로 봤을 때 본 프로젝트의 접근방법은 과학자, 예술가, 어부, 그리고 어린이 등이 경관에 투사하는 내러티브와 해석에 기반을 둔다고 할 수 있다. 따라서 위계질서가 있는 보행로 시스템을 활용하되 기존의 도로 기반시설의 규모를 줄여 재활용하고, 순환도로를 적극 활용하였다. 이러한 보행로 네트워크는 이 지역의 다층적 자연 및 인공 요소들을 탐색할 수 있는 일종의 여행으로 기획되었다.

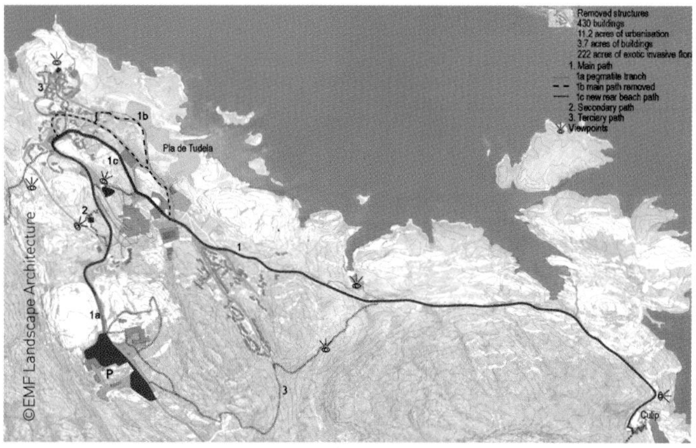

From nature reclamation to landscape restoration

The project´s goal was not to build or un-build, a landscape but to conceive the conditions for its experiencing. To do so, the process involved in-depth site reconnaissance and precise on-site cartography making. During the 5 years process, including the 14 months of work, the designers walked more than 200km on site, took and studied more than 15,000 images, and received up to 50 specialists in different fields related to nature restoration, in search for ways to optimize deconstruction, nature dynamic reclamation, and social valorization. Constructively a minimalist approach was taken, reducing materials to those on site plus Cor-ten steel, for its landscape integration and its resistance to sea exposure, and using only few consistent construction details repeated through the site.

The selective deconstruction of 430 buildings, equivalent of 1.2 ha of edification and 6ha of urbanization with innovative and respectful deconstructive techniques. A specific 'Decalogue' file was prescribed for each of the 25 structures to be removed at Club Med: pavements, buildings, paths, wood structures in various typologies. The end of deconstruction was the final removal of all traces of the basement, dust and cement which was done manually with an 'archeological' standard using mixed techniques.
The ecosystem dynamics revival by remaking the original site's topography and reestablishing runoffs and sediment exchanges between land and sea. This included massive earth modeling actions to re-construe the original creeks, the demolition of road embankments cutting off the natural run off, the recovery of the beach´s original cross section or the reconstruction of a bridge with a larger span to allow for sediment transport.
Following the advice of Botanist, almost no plantings were envisioned for the restoration in order not to pollute the native seeds bank. The stabilization of critical embankments were made with hydro seeding after an on-site seed recollecting campaign. One year after completion the % of ground coverage is close to 100%, mostly with native annuals.

Here the design of the experience is seen as being just as important as the restoration strategy. In that sense, the project's approach is based on the narratives and interpretations put on the landscape by scientists, artists, fishermen, kids. A site responsive hierarchical path system reducing and reusing the existing road infrastructure and promoting circular routes. The network is conceived as a journey to explore the site's layers both natural and humanized. A network of viewpoints to unveil the best panoramas with site responsive designs, mostly on partially deconstructed structures.

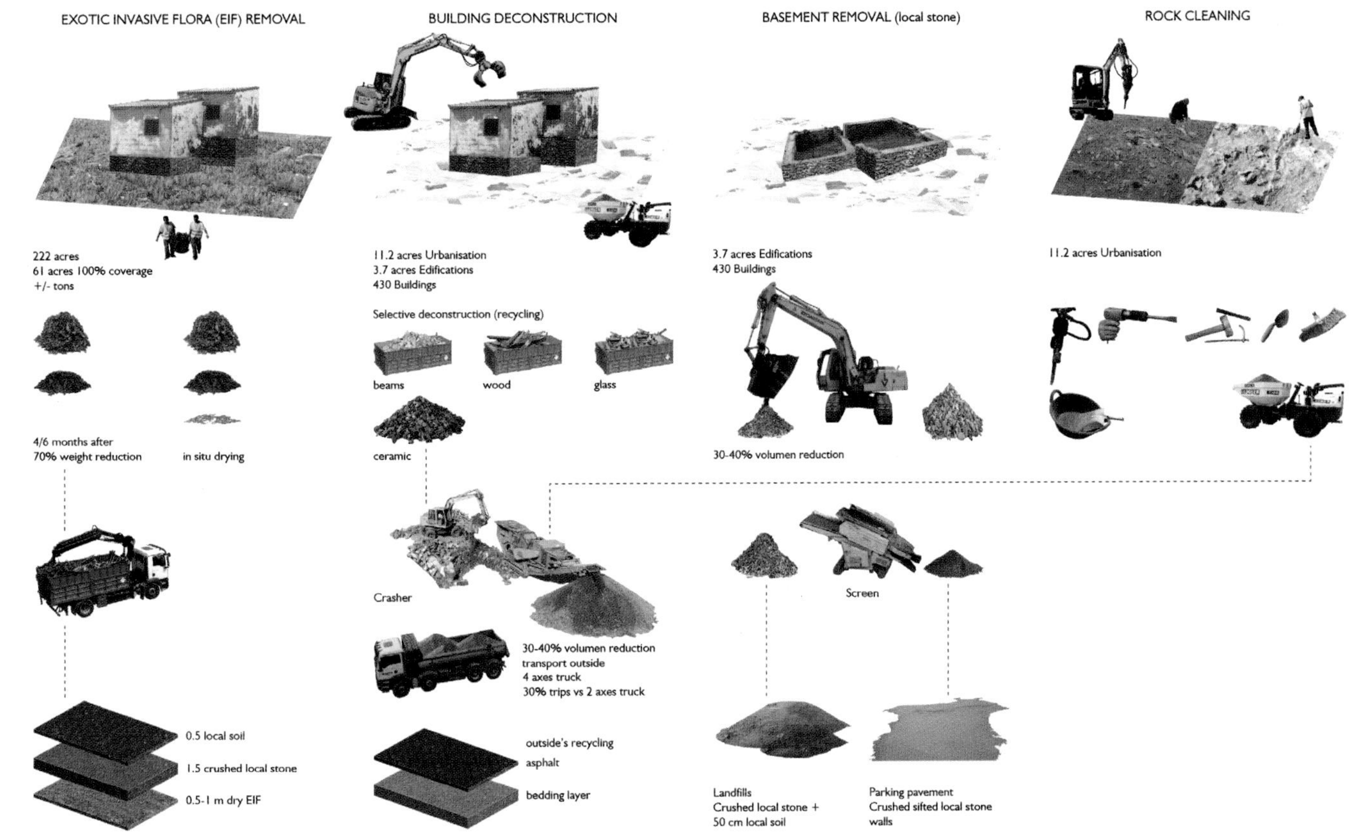

Wall's deconstruction

Cell's basement out of local schist.

Debris management working station.

Rock cleaning by compressor.

Finishes, by brush & compressed air

©Martí Franch, Pau Ardèvol, and Esteve Bosch

©Martí Franch, Pau Ardèvol, and Esteve Bosch

©Martí Franch, Pau Ardèvol

©Martí Franch, Pau Ardèvol

General Design

HONOR AWARD

Shangri La Botanical Garden

Jeffrey Carbo Landscape Architects, Alexandria, Louisiana

©Chipper Hatter

샹그리라 식물원과 자연 센터는 텍사스에서 처음으로 'LEED친환경 인증제도' 플래티넘신규건설 인증을 받은 프로젝트이다. 2008년에 LEED가 처음 도입되었을 당시만 해도 전 세계적으로 플래티넘 인증을 받은 프로젝트는 50개 정도 뿐이었다. 텍사스 남동부에 위치한 252에이커의 부지는 이제 친환경의 중심지이며 지역 경관과 동물 서식지의 교육장이다. 자연경관, 식물원, 혁신적인 환경교육장에서 제공하는 샹그리라 프로그램과 설계는 수많은 지역야생종 삶의 과정들을 볼 수 있게 해준다.

Shangri La Botanical Gardens and Nature Center is the first LEED Platinum-NC project in Texas. When it opened in 2008 it was one of only 50 Platinum projects in the world. The 252-acre site, in southeast, Texas, is now a hub of environmental awareness and education about regional landscapes and animal habitats. Shangri La's design and programming make visible the life processes of many species of wildlife within the context of a native landscape, recreated botanical gardens, and innovative center for environmental education.

조경가와 클라이언트는 샹그리라의 3가지 주요 강점 즉, 식물원, 늪과 같은 강, 그리고 새들이 주는 환경적 이점들을 설명하고 디자인을 통해 이를 더욱 가시화하였으며, 대중들에게도 이 3가지의 생태적 중요성을 각인시켜줄 수 있도록 면밀히 검토하였다.

방문객센터는 소규모 건물들과 주변 조경공간들로 구성되었다. 건물의 형태와 배치가 식물원 쪽으로 열려 있으며, 지속가능한 실천들이 적용되었다. 예를 들어 재활용된 아스팔트 포장이 주차장에 사용되었으며 우수저장장치로 모은 빗물을 건물관리에 필요한 물로 대체 사용하였다. 어린이들이 직접 꾸며보는 정원도 마련되었으며, 자연에 초점을 둔 교육전시는 2.5에이커의 습지와 수질정화 전시도 포함하고 있다. 인공습지에 수중식물들, 소규모 펌프, 도랑을 설치하여 루비호수Luby Lake에서 4일을 주기로 유입되는 물을 거르고 정화시키는 장치로 사용하였다. 마지막으로 철제도랑과 벽돌물탱크에서 물을 정화시켜 돌려보낸다. 샹그리라 방문객센터와 교육장은 자연을 바라보는 스탁 재단의 예술적 비전과 식물에 대한 애정, 환경 자선사업을 강조하는 것이라고 볼 수 있다.

샹그리라는 명칭에서부터 소설에 나올듯한 장소로, 실제로도 조경이 풍부하고 다양하다. 최근 두 차례 일어난 허리케인 재해에도 불구하고, 샹그리라는 자리를 굳건히 하여 자연의 힘을 배려하고 자연의 미를 존경하였다. 샹그리라는 이 지역의 우수한 환경인식을 한 차원 높이는데 크게 기여했으며, 작은 마을 커뮤니티라는 이미지를 바꾸고 환경적 책임과 조경 관리를 통해 경제적으로도 지속성을 고무시키는 긍정적인 효과를 가져다주었다.

Location _ Orange, Texas, USA
Client _ Nelda C. and H. J. Lutcher Stark Foundation
Photograph _ Chipper Hatter, Marc Cramer, Louisiana Helicam

The landscape architects and client rigorously examined Shangri La's three core strengths — its botanical garden, bayou, and birds — to expound on their environmental attributes, to make them visible, and to instill a sense of their importance among the public

The Visitor Center is an enclave of small buildings organized around functional landscape spaces. These buildings form an open foyer to the Botanical Garden and display extensive examples of sustainable practices: recycled asphalt paves the parking lot; pine and cypress trees felled by Hurricane Rita are used as wheel stops, benches and arbors; water collection cisterns serve the building's grey water uses; there is a hands-on children's garden and nature-focused educational exhibits including a 2.5-acre wetland and water cleansing exhibit. This man-made wetland features aquatic plants, small pumps, and runnels that carry, filter, and clean water from Ruby Lake over a four-day period, finally returning the cleansed water through a brick cistern and steel runnel. Shangri La's Visitor Center and its education zones emphasize Stark's vision of art in nature, love of plants, and environmental philanthropy.

This Shangri La, like the fictional place for which it is named, is a rich and complex landscape. Despite two recent catastrophic hurricanes, the project has survived and flourished, teaching us to respect nature's forces and admire its beauty. Shangri La has expanded environmental awareness in this region, changed the image of a small community, and inspired economic endurance through its focus on environmental responsibility and landscape stewardship.

©Marc Cramer

©Chipper Hatter

©Chipper Hatter

©Chipper Hatter

©Chipper Hatter

Shangri La Botanical Garden

Jeffrey Carbo Landscape Architects, Alexandria, Louisiana

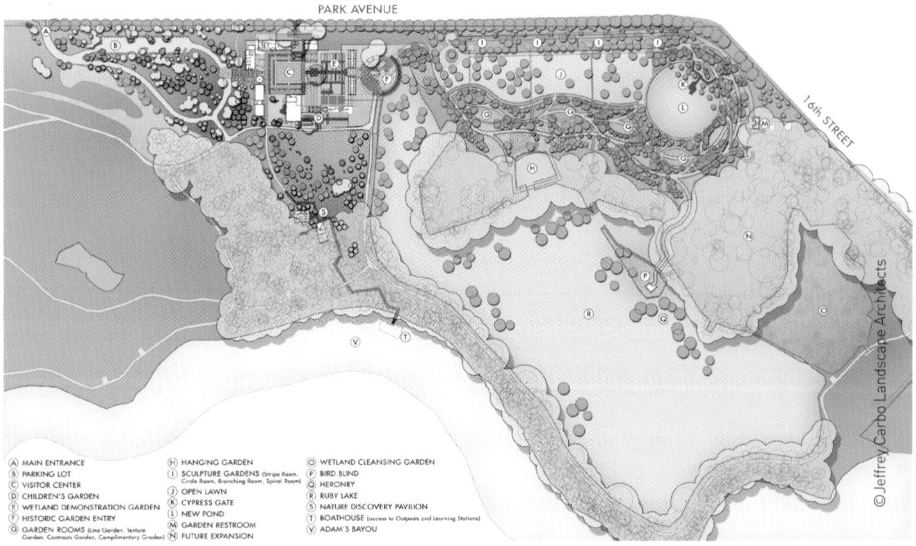

©Jeffrey Carbo Landscape Architects

©Louisiana Helicam

General Design

HONOR AWARD

Winnipeg Skating Shelters

Patkau Architects, Inc. Vancouver, British Columbia, Canada

Location _ Winnipeg, Manitoba, Canada
Client _ The Forks Renewal Corporation
Photograph _ James Dow, Patkau Architects, Inc.

©James Dow

거대한 경관과 함께 얼음판에 6개의 스케이팅 쉘터 묶음이 설치되었다. 쉘터들을 개별적으로 흩어두기보다 옹기종이 모아두는 것이 공동체감을 한층 두텁게 하는듯하다. 트레일 이용자들은 얇은 합판으로 둘러싸인 구조물 안으로 들어와 혹독한 겨울 추위로부터 잠시 쉬어갈 수 있다. 캐나다의 대초원에서 낯선 사람들과 우연한 만남을 갖는 곳이기도 하다.

Six skating shelters huddle together amidst a vast frozen landscape, their intimate grouping serving to both represent and foster a larger sense of community. Wrapped in these thin plywood sheathes, trail-users are offered not only a moment of shelter from the harsh winter elements, but also an opportunity for chance encounter, an opportunity to share in the varying degrees of intimacy that the arrangement affords amidst the ferocious splendor of winter on the Canadian prairies.

6개의 쉘터가 모아져 있어 이용자 수와 이용시간이 자연스럽게 조율된다. 소규모 마을또는 학교, 무리들같이 이용자들은 소수 그룹으로 바람막이 구조물 안에 들어가 옹기종기 모여 잠시 바람을 피하고, 그들만의 이야기를 순간적으로 만들어간다. 그룹으로 모여 있는 6개 쉘터는 입구 위치와 각도를 고려하여 2개씩 짝을 이루어 배치되었다. 각각은 120도의 각도로 짝을 이루고, 2개씩 짝을 맺은 3개의 그룹은 그룹 간에 90도 각도로 배치되었다. 이러한 배열은 각각의 쉘터 사이사이에 내부공간을 만들기도 한다. 개별적 쉘터는 바람막이 기능도 하지만, 2개씩 3개의 묶음배열은 쉘터 간의 그림자 공간을 만든다.

쉘터들은 아주 섬세하고 생동감 있는 구조물이다. 바람이 불때는 약간씩 삐걱거리고 움직이기도 한다. 쉘터는 얼어붙은 강위에서 흔들거리고 눈으로 덮여 있을 때는 바람에 의한 약간의 미동으로 눈을 털어버리기도 한다. 조심스럽고 지탱이 불안해 보이는 쉘터들은 혹독한 캐나다의 겨울의 미를 잘 알게 해주는 사례라고 볼 수 있다. 각각의 쉘터는 얇고 유연한 플라이우드합판로 구부리거나 변형시켜 만들었다. 3/16인치의 2개 층으로 구성된 플라이우드 외피를 접어 삼각형의 베이스로 구성된 나무보강재에 연결하고 중심 스파인과 눈의 하중을 털어버리도록 설계된 선인 리지판에 부착시키도록 설계되었다.

Our proposal consists of a cluster of intimate shelters, each accommodating only a few people at a time. They are grouped in a small 'village' (or 'herd', or 'school', or 'flock', or 'flotilla') to form a collective … of 'something'… irreducible to a single interpretation. They stand with their backs to the wind, seeming to have life and purpose as they huddle together shielding each other from the elements. Grouping the shelters into a cluster begins with the relationship of two, and their juxtaposition to qualify the size and accessibility of their entrance openings. This apparently casual pairing is actually achieved by a precise 120 degree rotation. Three pairs (one with mirror reflection) are then placed in relation to one another through a secondary rotation of 90 degrees to form the cluster and define an intermediate 'interior' space within the larger grouping. Together, the shelters create dynamic solar/wind relationships that shift according to specific orientation, time of day and environmental circumstance.

These are delicate and 'alive' structures. They move gently in the wind, creaking and swaying to and fro at various frequencies, floating precariously on the surface of the frozen river, shaking off any snow that might adhere to their surfaces. Their fragile and tenuous nature makes those sheltered by them supremely aware of the inevitability, ferocity and beauty of winter on the Canadian prairie landscape. Each shelter is formed of thin, flexible plywood which is given both structure and spatial character through bending/deformation. Skins, made of 2 layers of 3/16th inch thick flexible plywood, are attached to a wood armature which consists of a triangular base, and wedge shaped spine and ridge members (the ridge is a line to negate the gravity loads of snow).

©James Dow

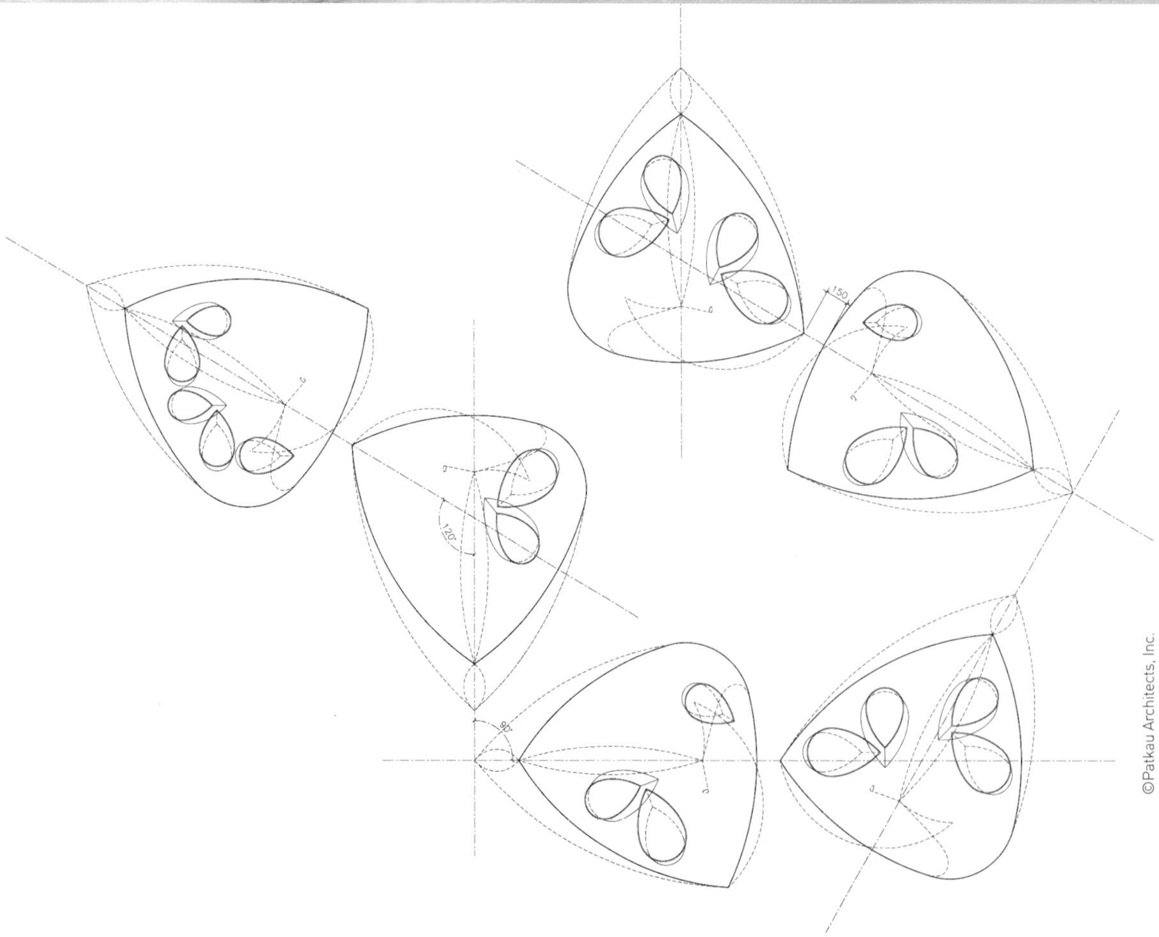

©Patkau Architects, Inc.

Winnipeg Skating Shelters

Patkau Architects, Inc. Vancouver, British Columbia, Canada

©James Dow

Winnipeg Skating Shelters

Patkau Architects, Inc. Vancouver, British Columbia, Canada

©James Dow

General Design

HONOR AWARD

National 9/11 Memorial

PWP Landscape Architecture, Berkeley, California

©PWP Landscape Architecture

메모리얼은 2001년 9월 11일의 세계무역센터와 펜실베이니아주 섕크스빌 펜타곤에 대한 공격 및 1993년 2월 26일의 세계무역센터 공격의 희생자들을 기린다. 트윈 타워가 파괴된 자리에 세워진 분수로 경계가 형성되는 두 개의 보이드와 주변의 오크나무 숲이 뉴욕시의 재건된 세계무역센터의 중심부를 형성하고, 다시 살아난 이 도심에서의 묵상과 추모를 위한 장소를 제공한다.

The Memorial commemorates the victims of the attacks of September 11, 2001, at the World Trade Center, Shanksville, Pennsylvania, the Pentagon, and the World Trade Center attack of February 26, 1993. Two fountain-lined voids, on the locations of the destroyed twin towers, and a surrounding forest of oak trees form the core of the rebuilt World Trade Center in New York City and provide a place for contemplation and remembrance within this revitalized urban center.

설계의 맥락

로어 맨해튼에 있는 이 8에이커의 대상지는 세계에서 가장 인구가 밀집한 도심 주거지와 비즈니스 센터에 위치한다. 7년이 넘는 기간 동안 조경가는 여러 에이전시, 이해당사자와 협업하고 도전적인 과정을 통해 설계하여 방문자들이 복합 구조물을 관통하고, 여러 관할 구역을 지나면서 일관적인 경험을 하도록 했다.

설계와 실행

설계에는 파괴된 트윈 타워 자리 중앙에 위치한 두 개의 거대한 보이드가 특징적으로 나타난다. 보이드의 규모는 2001년 9월 11일의 끔찍한 손실을 연상시키고, 양쪽 보이드의 가장자리에 전시된 이름들은 1993년과 2001년의 공격에 희생된 사람들을 기린다. 보이드를 둘러싸고 있는 플라자는 네 개의 주요 목적을 달성하도록 설계되었다.

· 첫 번째로, 보이드가 절단된 지면에 대해 방문자들이 깊이 있고 폭넓은 인식을 할 수 있도록 한다.
· 두 번째로, 방문자가 메모리얼에서 경험하는 것의 핵심을 이루는 행렬에 물리적, 정서적으로 참여하게 한다.
· 세 번째로, 주변의 도심 가로의 분주한 생활과 메모리얼의 추모적 분위기를 분리한다.
· 네 번째로, 로어 맨해튼에 조용하고, 아름다우며, 인간적인 규모의 공공 오픈 스페이스를 제공한다.

환경적 지속가능성과 디자인적 가치

설계와 건설 과정 내내 플라자의 지속가능성은 재료의 내구성과 경관의 실행 양쪽에서 모두 고려되었다. 플라자의 표면-배수 인프라스트럭처는 자생하는 거대한 물탱크의 기능을 하도록 설계되었다. 빗물과 눈이 녹은 물은 거대한 오수 탱크로 옮겨져, 특수한 drip-and-spray 관수 시스템을 통해 메모리얼의 숲을 유지하는데 다시 사용된다. 재개발된 세계무역센터의 중심부에 있는 숲인 메모리얼의 숲에는 나무가 조밀하게 식재되어 있다. 자라면서 나무들은 그림자가 드리워진 공간을 제공하여 방문자들을 더욱 편안하게 만들 것이고, 플라자의 열 흡수를 감소시킬 것이다. 수많은 나뭇잎의 증산으로 이 구역의 열기가 식을 것이다.

Location _ New York City, USA
Client _ National September 11 Memorial and Museum
Photograph _ PWP Landscape Architecture, Alan Ward

Design Context

Located in Lower Manhattan, this 8-acre site resides in one of the most densely populated urban neighborhoods and business centers in the world. For more than 7 years, the landscape architect coordinated with these multiple agencies and stakeholders and navigated the design through the challenging process to establish a consistent visitor experience that extends over multiple structures and through several jurisdictions.

Design and Execution

The design features two gigantic voids, centered on the locations of the destroyed twin towers. The scale of the voids recalls the terrible losses of September 11, 2001, and names displayed at the perimeter of both voids commemorate the victims of both the 1993 and 2001 attacks. The plaza surrounding the voids is designed to accomplish four main objectives:

· First, to deepen and enlarge the visitor's perception of the level plane into which the voids are cut
· Second, to participate in the procession, both physical and spiritual, that is essential to the visitor's experience of the memorial;
· Third, to separate the reverential mood of the Memorial from the busy life of the surrounding city streets; and
· Fourth, to provide a quiet, beautiful, and human-scaled public open space for Lower Manhattan.

Environmental Sustainability and Design Value

Throughout the design and construction process, sustainability of the plaza was considered in terms of both material endurance and landscape performance. The plaza surface-and-drainage infrastructure is designed to function as a large self-sustaining cistern. Water from rainfall and snow melt is channeled into large holding tanks and re-used to support the Memorial forest via a specialized drip-and-spray irrigation system. The Memorial grove is a dense planting of trees—a forest at the heart of the redeveloped World Trade Center. As they grow the trees will provide shaded space to increase comfort for visitors and reduce heat absorption on the plaza. The transpiration of the many leaves will cool the air throughout the district.

©PWP Landscape Architecture

©PWP Landscape Architecture

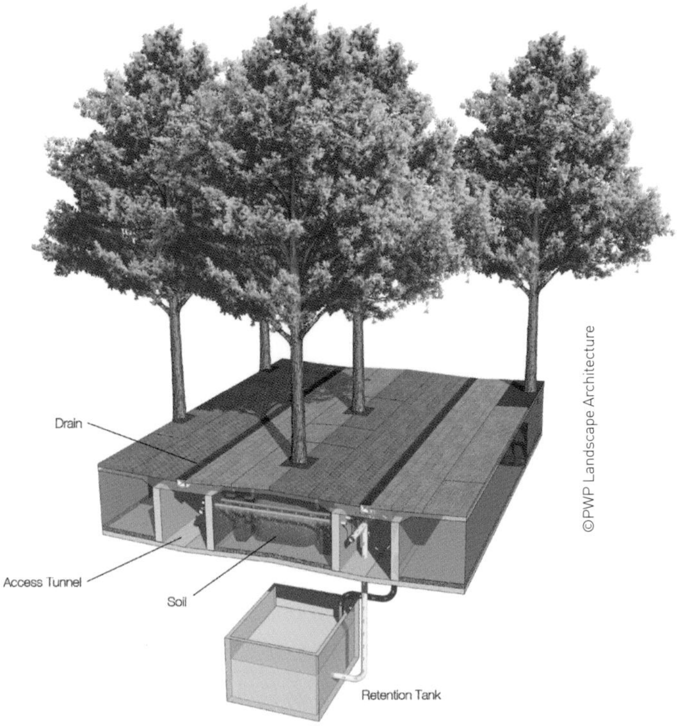
Drain
Access Tunnel
Soil
Retention Tank
©PWP Landscape Architecture

©Alan Ward

©Alan Ward

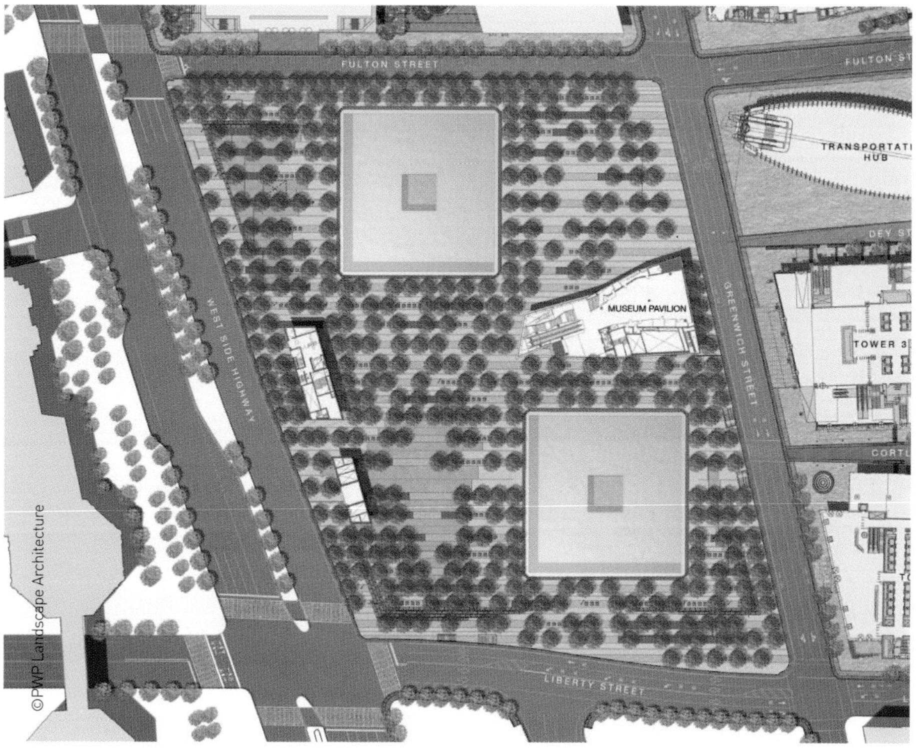
FULTON STREET
TRANSPORTATI
HUB
MUSEUM PAVILION
WEST SIDE HIGHWAY
GREENWICH STREET
TOWER 3
LIBERTY STREET
©PWP Landscape Architecture

General Design

HONOR AWARD

Sunnylands Center & Gardens

The Office of James Burnett, Solana Beach, California

©Dillon Diers

써니랜드 센터 & 가든은 새로운 15에이커의 사막식물 정원을 통해 역사적 사유지인 그곳의 문화적 유산을 기념하는 자료관이다. 조경가는 소노란 사막의 특성을 존중하고, 건조한 남서부의 경관을 위한 새로운 생태적 미학을 드러내는 살아있는 경관을 창조했다.

The Sunnylands Center and Gardens is an interpretive center that celebrates the cultural legacy of the historic estate through a new 15 acre desert botanical garden. The landscape architect created a living landscape that respects the character of the Sonoran Desert and demonstrates a new ecological aesthetic for landscapes in the arid southwest.

캘리포니아 란초 미라지에 있는 써니랜드 센터 & 가든은 월터 애넌버그와 리어노어 애넌버그가 소유한 200에이커의 조용한 사막에 증축된 건물이다. 애넌버그 부부는 1963년에 캘리포니아의 모더니즘 건축가 A. 퀸시 존스에게 사막에 있는 그들의 사유지를 설계해달라는 주문을 했다. 2006년, 애넌버그 재단은 조경가에게 자료관을 위한 정원을 개발해달라는 주문을 했다.

지역에 적합한 식물을 선정하는데 더해, 프로젝트는 사막 서식지의 복원과 고효율의 모세관 관수 체계, 토양 수분 모니터링, 100% 현장 우수 보유, 지열 관정, 중요한 광발전 집합체, 녹색 폐기물 현장 재활용 프로그램이 포함되었다. 프로젝트는 친환경건물인증LEED의 골드 등급 인증을 획득했고, 사용하는 물 중 약 20%는 코첼라 밸리 워터 디스트릭트에서 온 것이다. 프로젝트는 또한 란초 미라지시의 광역 주도권이 이행되기 5년 전부터 이미 앞서 재생수의 사용의 사양과 요건도 충족시켰다.

조경가는 소유주와 밀접하게 작업하며, 센터와 인접한 곳은 정연하고 기하학적인 구성으로 시작해서 사막 초원으로 갈수록 점점 더 자유롭게 흘러가는 계획을 발전시켰다. 또한 15에이커의 대상지에서 땅을 조각하고 그림을 그리듯 식물을 사용했다. 충분한 그늘을 드리우도록 대상지 전체에 걸쳐 나무들을 주의 깊게 식재하였고, 하층 식재의 시각적 구성에도 주의를 크게 기울였다. 거대한 양묘장에서 경험하는 것과 아주 비슷하도록 식재는 "덩어리로" 설계되었다. 이에 따라 수많은 알로에와 아가베, 원통선인장이 광범위한 색채와 질감 표현에 이용되었다.

조경가는 디자인 팀과의 밀접한 협업 속에서 소노란 사막의 섬세한 생명의 균형에 계속 민감한 정원을 창조하면서도 애넌버그의 유산을 기념했다. 많은 물의 사용과 화학 비료, 이국적인 식물에 의존하는 전통적인 팜 스프링의 조경에 대한 대안을 창조하면서, 현재 상태에 도전하고 이 위태로운 생태계의 생태적 문제에 대한 의식을 높이는 정원을 창조했다.

Location _ Rancho Mirage, California, USA
Client _ The Annenberg Foundation Trust at Sunnylands
Photograph _ Dillon Diers, The Office of James Burnett

Sunnylands Center & Gardens in Rancho Mirage, California is an extension of the 200-acre desert retreat of Walter and Leonore Annenberg. The Annenbergs commissioned the California modernist architect A. Quincy Jones to design their estate in the desert in 1963. In 2006, the Annenberg Foundation commissioned the landscape architect to develop a garden for the interpretive center.

In addition to the selection of regionally-appropriate plants, the project features restored desert habitat, high-efficiency capillary irrigation system, soil moisture monitoring, 100 percent on-site storm water retention, geothermal wells, a significant photovoltaic array and an on-site green waste recycling program. The project has received LEED Gold Certification and uses approximately 20 percent of its water allocation from the Coachella Valley Water District. The project also proactively meets the specifications and requirements for the use of reclaimed water five years ahead of the implementation of Rancho Mirage's citywide initiative.

Working closely with owner, the landscape architect developed a scheme that begins as an orderly, geometric composition adjacent to the Center and becomes progressively more free flowing as it moves to the desert meadows. The landscape architect sculpted the earth and used plants in a painterly fashion across the 15 acre site. Trees were carefully positioned throughout the site to ensure that ample shade was provided and great care was given to the visual composition of understory plantings. Plantings were designed "in mass" much like one experiences a large nursery. Therefore, dozens of aloe, agave and barrel cactus were used to great large sweeps of color and texture.

Developed in close collaboration with the design team the landscape architect created a garden that celebrates the legacy of the Annenbergs while remaining sensitive to the delicate balance of life in the Sonoran desert. By creating an alternative to the traditional Palm Springs landscape that relies on heavy water use, chemical fertilizers and exotic plants, the landscape architect has created a garden that challenges the status quo and raises awareness of ecological issues in this imperiled ecosystem.

©Dillon Diers

©Dillon Diers

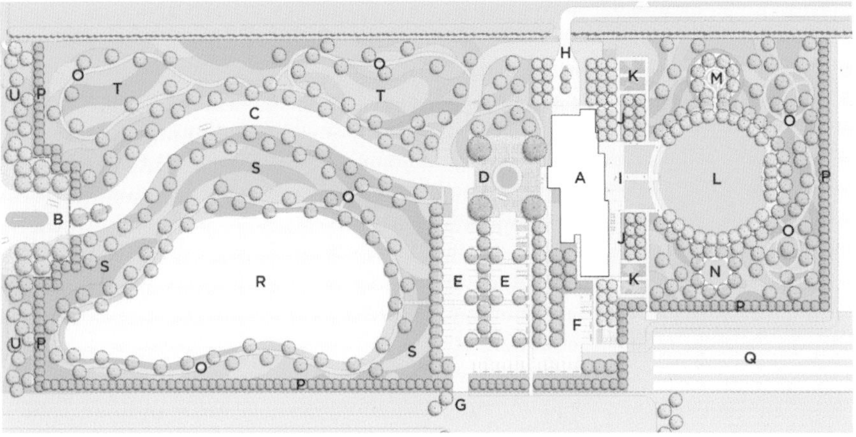

©The Office of James Burnett

A. Sunnylands Center
B. Entry
C. Entry Drive
D. Entry Court
E. Parking
F. Staff Parking
G. Overflow Parking
H. Shuttle Entry
I. Terrace
J. Reflecting Pools
K. Specimen Gardens
L. Great Lawn
M. Labyrinth
N. Performance Circle
O. Botanic Walk
P. Texas Ebony Hedge
Q. Solar Field
R. Wildflower Meadow
S. Berm Garden
T. Stormwater Retention Basin
U. Bob Hope Drive Streetscape

©Dillon Diers

©The Office of James Burnett

©The Office of James Burnett

Residential Design

AWARD OF EXCELLENCE

Drs. Julian and Raye Richardson Apartments

Andrea Cochran Landscape Architecture, San Francisco

줄리안 리차드슨과 라예 리차드슨 박사 부부의 아파트는 일찍이 집 없는 사람들을 위한 멋진 거주지로 잘 알려져 있다. 조경디자인은 가로경관과 중정, 옥상을 아우르고 있으며 모두 이용자 맞춤형 가구가 도입되었다. 지역 고유의 재료를 이용한 이 프로젝트는 자갈을 이용한 침투시스템, 레인가든, 옥상정원 등과 같은 다각적인 빗물관리를 보여준다.

The Drs. Julian and Raye Richardson Apartments provide a dignified home for formerly homeless residents. The landscape design encompasses a streetscape, a central courtyard, and a roof deck – all fully-accessible with custom furnishings. The project uses local materials and offers a multi-faceted stormwater management with permeable paving over a gravel infiltration system, rain gardens, and a green roof.

Location _ San Francisco, USA
Client _ Community Housing Partnership and Mercy Housing
Photograph _ Andrea Cochran Landscape Architecture, Bruce Damonte

회복의 정원

푸르게 우거진 중정은 건물의 중심부를 형성하고 있다. 안마당 위로 서있는 5층짜리 건물과 그 옥상은 휴식 공간, 다육식물정원, 채소가 심어진 밭, 세덤으로 뒤덮인 녹색 지붕으로 거주민에게 힐링 공간을 제공하고 있다. 이러한 실외 정원에서의 경험은 거주민과 스태프들의 일상생활을 풍요롭게 만들어 주고 있다.

빗물 관리

중정 내부의 공간은 폭우가 하부의 자갈 구조물로 침투하도록 디자인되어 있다. 폭우에 영향을 받는 다른 공간은 야자나무와 양치식물이 심긴 레인가든으로 흘러들어가게 되어 있다. 주변의 배수관은 물이 건물에서 빠져나와 자갈 시스템으로 흘러들어가도록 설계되어 있다. 녹색 지붕은 장식적이면서 식용 가능하도록 되어있으며, 도시의 우수처리시스템으로 흘러들어갈 물을 저장하는 역할을 한다.

Restorative Gardens

A lush, central courtyard forms the heart of the building. Five stories above the courtyard, a roof deck offers another healing space for residents with seating areas, succulent gardens, raised beds for vegetable gardening, and a green roof with sedums. The experience of these outdoor gardens permeates the daily life of the residents and staff through various layers of transparency.

Stormwater Management

Within the courtyard, spacers are installed between standard unit pavers to allow stormwater to permeate into the gravel retention basin below. Overflow and other paving areas are sloped into rain gardens, planted with palm trees and ferns. A perimeter drain also routes water away from the building and into the gravel retention system. On the roof, green roofs and planters, both ornamental and edible, also help to capture water that would otherwise enter the city storm system.

©Andrea Cochran Landscape Architecture

©Bruce Damonte

©Bruce Damonte

Residential Design

HONOR AWARD

Quaker Smith Point Residence

H. Keith Wagner Partnership, Burlington, Vermont

Location _ Shelburne, Vermont, USA
Photograph _ H. Keith Wagner Partnership

대상지가 가진 본연의 아름다움, 현대적인 디자인을 모티브로 하고, 독특한 역사를 존중한 조경디자인은 이 새로운 주택을 농업적 풍광과 교묘히 접목시키고 있다. 현대적으로 지어진 건물은 여러 가지 생각과 시적인 발상으로 어우러져서 성공적으로 19세기의 농업적 유산을 현대적으로 재해석하고 있다.

Motivated by the site's raw beauty, a modern design aesthetic and a respect for the unique history of the site, the landscape architecture artfully integrates a new residence within the agrarian landscape. The modern built form successfully transitions into its context through thoughtful and poetic interventions - a modern re-interpretation of the 19th century agricultural estate.

쉘번 농가는 1886년 윌리암 시워드와 릴라 반더빌트 웹에 의해서 지어졌으며 농업적 유산의 모델로 창조되었다. 건축가 로버트 로버슨과 조경가 프레데릭 로 옴스테드의 도움으로 농가는 혁신적인 농촌의 토지 사용의 실례를 보여주며 가공할 만한 3,800에이커의 땅으로 성장하게 되었다. 기존의 집은 40년 전에 지어졌으며, 챔플레인 호수와 애디론댁 산맥을 배경으로 하고 있었다.

긴 수평선을 그리는 지붕 위의 빗물은 코르텐강으로 된 수반과 챔플레인 호수에서 채취한 자갈이 채워진 수로로 떨어진다. 양치식물이 심긴 수로는 건물 파사드를 따라 북쪽으로 흐른다. 연속적인 코르텐강과 돌로 구성된 둑과 폭포는 이 물을 서쪽의 호수로 흘러가도록 한다. 조그만 폭포는 인접한 객실에 명상적 고요함은 물론 욕실에서의 시각적 아름다움을 선사한다.

쉘번 농가의 거대한 19세기형 구조물은 지역에서 구하기 쉬운 재료, 슬레이트, 돌과 지역에서 채집된 나무들로 지어졌다. 설계자는 코르텐강을 사용하면서 지역의 재료를 사용하는 전통을 계속 이어나가려 했다. 지역 도처에 두루 퍼져 있는 농업 장비에서 비롯된 이 재료는 농장의 농업적인 과거, 현재, 미래의 재료에 대한 오마주가 되고 있다.

Shelburne Farms was originally built in 1886 by William Seward and Lila Vanderbilt Webb and was created as a model agricultural estate. With the help of architect Robert H. Robertson and landscape architect Frederick Law Olmsted, the Farm grew to a formidable 3,800 acres demonstrating innovative agricultural and land use practices. The existing house built over 40 years ago, its back on the dramatic views to Lake Champlain and the Adirondack Mountains.

Rainwater falls off of the long horizontal roof of the house into a Corten steel basin & runnel filled with pebbles from Lake Champlain. Native fern planting provides a field for the runnel as it flows north along the façade. A series of Corten steel & stone weirs / falls guide the water as it turns west toward the lake. The falls create a meditative calm for the adjacent master & guest suites, visible from the bathrooms.

The grand 19th century structures of Shelburne Farms were built with locally available materials, slate, stone and locally harvested wood, out of necessity. We wanted to continue the tradition of using local materials while introducing Corten steel. This material eludes to the farm equipment relics that are peppered throughout the site, a homage in material to the agricultural past, present and future of the Farms.

©H. Keith Wagner Partnership

©H. Keith Wagner Partnership

Residential Design

HONOR AWARD

Quattro by Sansiri

TROP Company Limited, Ladprao, Thailand

사람들로 북적이는 방콕의 한 가운데에 세워질 새 콘도를 위해 세 개의 정원을 디자인했다. 주 아이디어는 '실제 거주자 격인 커다란 레인트리*Leguminosae Mimosoideae*, 미모사과와 작은 다람쥐, 새들을 보호하고 새로운 거주지를 만들어 주어 자연 속에서 살게 도와주자'는 취지에서 얻었다. 레인트리는 디자인 컨셉의 중심에 있으며 정원의 다른 모든 요소들은 이 나무들을 보완하기 위해 설계되었다.

Three gardens designed for a new Condominium in the middle of over-crowded Bangkok. The main idea is to respect the existing "Residents", which are old giant Rain trees(Leguminosae Mimosoideae) and their small inhabitants (squirrels and birds) and to encourage the new residents to live with Nature. The Rain Trees become the heart of our design, while all other garden elements are created to complement those trees.

Location _ Bangkok, Thailand
Client _ Sansiri PLC
Photograph _ Wison Tungthunya

콰트로는 방콕의 최대 규모의 지역에 있는 고급 주거 프로젝트이다. 현재 방콕의 모습을 보자. 콘크리트와 아스팔트로 구성된 도시 전체에서 흙은 거의 찾을 수 없을 것이다. 과거에 우리는, 도시외곽의 작은 집에서 작은 정원을 갖고 살면서 도시로 통근이 가능했다. 하지만 더 이상은 그렇지 않다. 태국의 젊은 세대들에게 있어 고향을 떠나 고층건물에서 사는 것은 정상적인 일일지도 모른다. 현재의 급변하는 생활 스타일에 맞추려면, 수평적 보다는 수직적인 주택을 생각해야 할 때이다. 기본적으로 우리는 쌓여있는 '상자' 안에 살고 있다. 아파트와 같은 획일화된 주택을 표현하고 있다-편집자주 30㎡의 큰 규모까지도 그것들은 여전히 '상자'에 불과하다. 그 콘크리트 상자가 흙 대신 서로의 상단부에 부착되어 있다. 이 모든 상황은 모두가 꿈꾸는 '집'의 개념과는 거리가 멀다. 아이들에게 이상적인 '집'에 대해 물어본다면 아마도 아이들은 모두 비슷한 모양을 대답할 것이다. 일부 공간에 정원이 있고 물고기가 사는 연못이 있는 집을 이야기했다면 좋았을 것이다. 이러한 현상은 옳지 않다고 판단되었고 이를 변화시키고자 했다.

Quattro is a High-end Residential Project in the up-scale area of Bangkok. Look at Bangkok now. You can hardly find soil in the city full of concrete and asphalt. In the past, we may prefer to live in a small house, with small garden, outside the city areas, and commute in and out the city daily. Not anymore. To fit the present time's fast life style, It is quite normal these days that younger generation of Thais are moving in town and choose to live in high-rise buildings, instead of their out of town homes. Horizontal Living is out. Vertical one is the thing to do. Basically now we live in a box. Stacked boxes, to be precise. Ranging from 30 sqm to larger ones, they are still boxes. Concrete boxes that are put on top of each other, instead of soil. This is far from the ideal "Home" that everyone has in his/her mind. If you ask kids to draw their ideal "Home", you would surely see similarities between each drawing. It may have a house, a garden of some sort, a fish pond, etc. Compare that to the condominium boxes we are living in, we may still have a house, but a garden and a pond are gone. Well, that is not good, and we would like to change that.

©Wison Tungthunya

©Wison Tungthunya

©Wison Tungthunya

©Wison Tungthunya

Residential Design

HONOR AWARD

New Century Garden: A Garden of Water and Light

Location _ Palm Springs, California, USA
Photograph _ Steve Martinoa

Steve Martino and Associates, Phoenix

팜 스프링스Palm Springs는 중세시대의 현대적 건축과 역사에 대한 사랑과 감동으로 잘 알려져 있는 도시이다. 이 프로젝트는 현대적인 재료 · 기술 · 방식을 총 동원하여, 팜 스프링스의 디자인과 사회적인 역사를 조명하는 새롭고 독특한 사막 경험을 할 수 있게 하며 동시에 그 험악한 사막 지역도 새 시대에서는 디자인 모델로 사용할 수 있다는 기대를 표현하며 '새 시대의 정원'이 되고자 하는 데에 주안점을 두고 있다.

Palm Springs is a city known for its love and appreciation of its "Mid-century" modern architecture and history. The project strives to be the "New-Century Garden" by utilizing contemporary materials, technologies and attitudes to create a bold new and unique desert experience that reflects the design and social history of Palm Springs while showing a desire to celebrate its rugged desert region as a model for design in this new century.

이 사막 집과 정원의 두 가지 테마는 물과 빛이다. 야외 공간은 샌 재신토 산맥San Jacinto Mountains을 배경으로 인상적인 경관을 제공하고 있다. 이 구역은 미닫이 유리문을 통해 실내와 자연스럽게 연결된다. 이 집의 모든 방은 인접한 정원으로 연결되어 있고, 정원은 집에 있는 모든 공간의 중심점이 된다. 어떤 방에서 보는가에 따라서 정원의 경관은 그 느낌이 달라진다.

이 프로젝트는 사막 식물의 장엄한 아름다움을 나타낼 수 있는 시범적인 정원이 되었다. 이 정원은 마을에 있는 일반적인 자연 정원은 아니지만 인상적인 사막 정원이다. 이곳은 사막 식물을 사용해 재미있는 경관을 연출해보고자 한 조경가의 소망을 담아 놓았다. 설계자는 인상적인 형상을 이용하여 관심을 유도하기 위해 일반적인 사막 식물을 보여주었다.

This desert house and garden's two themes are water and light. The main outdoor space has dramatic views of the San Jacinto Mountains as its backdrop. Space seamlessly flows from one area to the next and the pocketed sliding glass doors reinforce the indoor-outdoor connection. Every room in the house opens to an adjacent garden. The gardens set a dramatic focal point from all spaces in the house. Depending on the room, the garden view changes from intimate to dramatic.

This project became a demonstration garden to showcase the spectacular beauty of desert plants. It is not a naturalistic garden but rather a dramatic and theatrical desert garden that was unlike any other garden in town. It was the landscape architect's hope to create a buzz and interest in using desert plants as a 'sought-after' landscape look. The designer showcased ordinary desert plants by creating scenes to draw attention to their dramatic form.

Residential Design

HONOR AWARD

말리날코 개인저택 주변의 탁 트인 지역은 변화무쌍한 정원과 테라스들, 아웃도어룸들의 연속이며, 공간에 대한 풍부한 경험을 제공하고 있다. 향토식물과 길 따라 존재하는 수로의 조화로 자아내는 독특한 분위기는 경관에 대한 감탄을 불러일으키고, 명상을 하기에 좋은 상태를 유지하고 있다.

The surrounding open areas in this Malinalco private residence are a sequence of transitional gardens, terraces and outdoor rooms that allow a diversity of rich experiences of settings and places. The different ambiences combined with the endemic vegetation and the presence of running water along the paths, provoke a reflection state and the landscape contemplation.

Malinalco Private Residence

Location _ Malinalco, Mexico

Photograph _ Hector Velasco, Francisco Gómez Sosa

Grupo De Diseño Urbano, S. C., Mexico City

마을의 대규모 도시 계획에 따른 이 프로젝트의 최고 관심사는 물의 재수집과 재사용이었다. 고대 관개수로의 형태를 딴 기존의 수로들을 따라 새로 조성된 작은 저수지, 수로와 캐스케이드를 포함하여 정원의 컨셉을 이끌어 냈다. 호수 너머에는 공사 중에 발생한 흙을 쌓아놓은 지역이 있는데, 저지대 정글의 느낌을 자아내고 있다. 이곳은 집에서 가장 먼 지점으로, 한 무리의 용설란과 바위들로 가득하고, 오렌지색 빛들이 지속적으로 나비들을 유혹한다. 감귤류 과수원과 또 하나의 채소밭이 그 지대의 한쪽에 배치되어 있는데, 기존의 나무에 더해져서 더욱더 풍성한 정원을 만들고 있다.

새로운 게스트하우스와 테라스가 새 호수의 가장자리에 세워졌는데 마치 일본식 다도실 같다. 단아한 선, 투명한 벽, 탁 트인 베란다의 건축은 생물 형태의 유기체적인 정원의 느낌과 강한 대조를 이룬다. 기존의 수영장 풀 테라스는 증축되었으며, 정원과 호수에 연결이 되도록 하였다. 말리날코 저택은 변화하는 정원, 테라스, 아웃도어룸들의 프로젝트이며, 공간에 대한 무제한적인 경험을 제공하고 있다.

Following the large scale urban planning of the town, one of the project's prime motivations was the recollection and re-use of water. The pre-existing channels, which took the form of ancient "apantles", directed the concept of the garden with the inclusion of a small new reservoir, water channel and cascades. Beyond the lake there is an elevated area (set upon soil excavated during the construction) which recreates the feeling of a lowland jungle; this is the furthest point from the house, and features collections of orange lanterns that constantly attract butterflies, groups of agave plants and rocks. A citrus orchard and a vegetable garden have been placed to one side of the lot, making the most of a number of trees that were already there. The new guesthouse and terrace, was set on the edge of the new lake, not unlike a Japanese tea pavilion. The architecture of clean lines, transparent walls and open veranda establish a strong contrast with the biomorphic and loose organic feeling of the garden. The pre-existing swimming pool terrace was expanded and connected to the garden and lake. The Malinalco residence is a project of transitional gardens, terraces, and outdoor rooms, establishing limitless experiences of settings and place.

Residential Design

HONOR AWARD

Maple Hill Residence

Stephen Stimson Associates Landscape Architects, Cambridge, Massachusetts

Location _ Westwood, Massachusetts, USA
Photograph _ Charles Mayer Photography, Rosemary Fletcher Photography, Stephen Stimson Associates

메이플 힐 저택은 새로 지은 집과 창고, 수영장, 그 밖의 부속 건축물들로 이루어져 있는 5에이커의 저택 경관이다. 경관 프로그램 개발을 위해 주택을 땅의 한 쪽에다가 건설하였고, 대부분의 땅이 열린공간이 되도록 디자인하였다. 이 집에 대한 프로젝트는 건축가, 조경가와 클라이언트 사이의 긴밀한 공조체계로 다양한 대화 등의 상호작용을 통해, 이곳에 거주하게 될 가족들이 갖고 있는 경관에 대한 생각과 프로그램을 반영하는 집을 만들 수 있었다.

The Maple Hill Residence is a five acre residential landscape comprised of a new house, barn, pool and outbuildings. The design sets the residence to one side of the property leaving the majority of the site open for the development of the landscape program. Close collaboration between the Architect, Landscape Architect and Client created a home that blends the programmatic needs of the family with an interactive and resourceful mind-set about the landscape they inhabit.

Maple Hill Residence
Stephen Stimson Associates Landscape Architects,
Cambridge, Massachusetts

조경디자인은 가족의 문화적 요구와 지형적 조건을 보존하고자하는 환경적 윤리를 반영하여 창조되었다. 땅의 공간적 조합은 지정학적, 물, 식물의 경관적인 패턴과 프로그램의 필요성에 대한 세심한 고려와 분석으로 만들어졌다. 벽의 평행한 기하학에 대조되는 것이 물의 축이다. 조심스럽게 위치한 이 수로는 북에서 남으로 흐르고 있으며, 다소간의 각도의 변화가 이루어져 수로의 위쪽에서 아래의 빗물정원으로 침투되도록 설계되어 있다. 다양한 조경공간이 야생동물 서식지의 운반, 세척, 창출을 통해 생태학적 기능을 갖는 이러한 요소에 의해 연결되어 있다. 수문의 패턴과 경계에 위치해 있는 습지시스템은 식재를 위한 기반과 구조를 마련해준다. 주 건물과 근접한 곳에 줄지어 설치된 긴 막대와 정원 공간들, 식재형태는 해당지역의 구조를 보강해준다.

The landscape design was conceived as a complete integration between the cultural needs of the family and a strong environmental ethic that respected the existing site conditions. Spatial organization of the property was derived from the careful analysis and consideration of programmatic needs, combined with the landscape patterns of geology, water and vegetation. Contrasting this parallel geometry of the walls is the water axis. This carefully sited watercourse runs north-south, negotiating grade change and collecting site runoff from the upper areas of the site to infiltration at a stormwater garden below. Multiple landscape spaces are linked by this element which functions ecologically through conveyance, cleansing and the creation of wildlife habitat. Patterns of hydrology and a bordering wetland system create the framework and organization for the site planting. Expressed in long, linear bars and garden rooms adjacent to the main house, planted form reinforces the site structures.

Residential Design

HONOR AWARD

Reordering Old Quarry

Reed Hilderbrand LLC, Watertown, Massachusetts

Location _ Guilford, Connecticut, USA

Photograph _ Millicent Harvey, Charles Mayer

©Millicent Harvey

1950년대의 한 때, 대부분의 주택 소유자들은 그 장소의 역사를 평범한 잔디밭 한 층 밑에 있는 채석장으로 묻어 놓았었다. 그러나 이번 프로젝트는 발견된 해안의 조건을 기념하며 남아있는 돌 부스러기들을 정제하고 편집하고 재정렬하며 신생 삼림의 거친 특성을 받아들이고 있다. 목표를 정해서 이루어지는 적절한 조절은 지반면의 역동적인 질을 높여주며 이 해안 지역의 높이에서 미묘한 변화의 효과를 증폭시킬 것이다.

In this 1950s subdivision, most homeowners have buried the site's history as a working quarry under a layer of suburban lawn. By contrast, this project celebrates the found coastal conditions, refining, editing, and rearranging the remnant tailings and embracing the rough character of the emergent woodland. Targeted and modest interventions enhance the dynamic quality of the groundplane and accentuate the effect of subtle variations in elevation on this coastal site.

이번 프로젝트는 먼저 그 지대에서 발견된 버려진 돌들을 활용하고 있다. 돌 부스러기를 통해 진입할 수 있도록 화강암을 평평하고 완만한 길로 만들 정도로 충분히 가공하였다. 남아있는 토사 채취장 잔여물들이 제거되었으며 몇몇 가장자리는 그 깊이를 강조하기 위해서 분명해 졌다. 토사 채취장의 바닥에서 광맥이 드러나 있으며 그곳에서 몇 줌의 흙이 천연잔디를 지탱해 주고 있다. 매달마다 만조 때에는 물이 토사 채취장에서 솟아 나와서 고체와 액체 사이의 경계를 허물어버리곤 한다. 그곳으로 더 들어가면 한 무더기의 돌 부스러기가 대지의 기준점에서 솟아 나와서 자작나무와 사시나무만 볼 수 있는 건조한 환경을 만들고 있다.

This project primarily utilizes refuse stone found on site. To provide access through the rubble, the granite has been turned and worked just enough to create level, steady paths. The remnant borrow pit was cleared of invasives and some of its edges clarified to accentuate its depth. At the bottom of the pit, ledge is revealed and there are pockets of soil that support native grasses. During monthly high tides, water rises within the pit, muddying the distinction between solid and fluid. Further into the site, a tailings pile rises from the datum of the ground creating an almost xeric condition where only birch and aspen can gain purchase.

Residential Design

HONOR AWARD

©Bionic

Urban Spring

Bionic, San Francisco

샌프란시스코의 샘과 개울은 한때는 보편적이고 잘 보였으며 언덕에서부터 용솟음쳐 내려와서 만으로 빠져나갔다. 오늘날에는 대부분이 파이프와 도시의 하수구를 거쳐서 간다. 디자인은 정확한 구조, 장치, 세부를 그 지대의 미묘한 차이가 있는 조건에 적용하며 기능적인 공간, 미기후, 도시의 야생동물 서식지의 우아한 조합을 창출해내고 있다.

San Francisco's springs and streams were once common and visible, emerging from hills and ultimately draining to the Bay. Today most are routed through pipes and city sewers. The design applies precise structures, devices and details to the nuanced conditions of the site, creating an elegant composition of functional spaces, microclimates, and urban wildlife habitat.

©Bionic

©Bionic

Location _ San Francisco, USA
Client _ Marcel and Jennifer Wilson
Photograph _ Bionic

현존하는 장소

이 프로젝트는 가파른 북향 언덕 위에 있는 25'x100' 부지를 대상으로 하고 있다. 집은 1930년에 지어졌다. 도시의 건물들은 양옆이 다 맞닿아 있어서 그 안으로 진입하는 유일한 방법은 현관문을 통해서이다.

구조 – 명확한 표현

계단, 벽, 층들은 정원의 다양한 층과 순환을 명확하게 표현하고 있다. 보전된 강철로 지어진 두 개의 계단은 그 장소의 가장 가파른 지역을 타고 가며 정원으로 이어졌다.

물 – 장치물

샘물은 후면 외관에서 8피트 떨어진 땅에 있는 얇은 진흙층을 통해서 솟구쳐 나온다. 아래의 수로는 그 장소의 가장 낮은 곳에서 붓꽃이 가득한 습지로 이어져 있으며 샘물을 검은색 멕시코 자갈이 깔린 강철 프레임으로 떨어뜨려 놓는다. 프레임과 자갈돌은 샘물의 흐름을 분산시키며 샘물이 대지로 침투되도록 허용한다.

Existing Site

This project is situated in a typical 25'x100' lot on a steep north facing hillside. The home was built in 1930. In this part of the city the buildings touch on both sides, so the only access to the property is through the front door.

Structures - Articulation

Stairs, walls, and decks articulate the various levels and circulation of the garden. Two staircases built with salvaged steel span the steepest section of the site and extend into the garden.

Water - Devices

The spring emerges through a shallow clay layer in the soil eight feet off the back façade. The lower runnel extends to a wetland of irises at the lowest elevation of the site and drops the spring flow into a steel frame lined with black Mexican pebble. The frame and pebbles dissipate the flows and allow them to infiltrate back into the ground.

Analysis and Planning

AWARD OF EXCELLENCE

The One Ohio State Framework Plan

Sasaki Associates, Inc., Watertown, Massachusetts

Location _ Columbus, Ohio, USA

Client _ The Ohio State University

Photograph _ Sasaki Associates, Inc.

미국에서 규모가 큰 대학 중 한 곳에서 '오하이오 주 협력체제 계획The One Ohio State Framework Plan'을 통해 계획안의 역할이 재정립되었다. 지속가능성에 대한 요구, 예산 감축, 미적 측면만 강조되는 점 등 점점 복잡해지는 문제에 대응하기 위해, 유일한 통합원칙과 시나리오, 혁신적인 소프트웨어 툴을 제공한다. 이는 변화하는 환경에 대학이 캠퍼스와 커뮤니티의 장기적인 비전으로서 유동적으로 적응할 수 있도록 한다.

The One Ohio State Framework Plan redefines the role of planning at one of the largest universities in the country. In response to increasingly complex challenges - sustainability imperative, reduced access to capital, and a driving vision centered on increased collaboration - it provides a unique combination of principles, scenarios and innovative software tools that allow the university to agilely adapt to changing circumstances while always moving towards a long-term vision of campus and community.

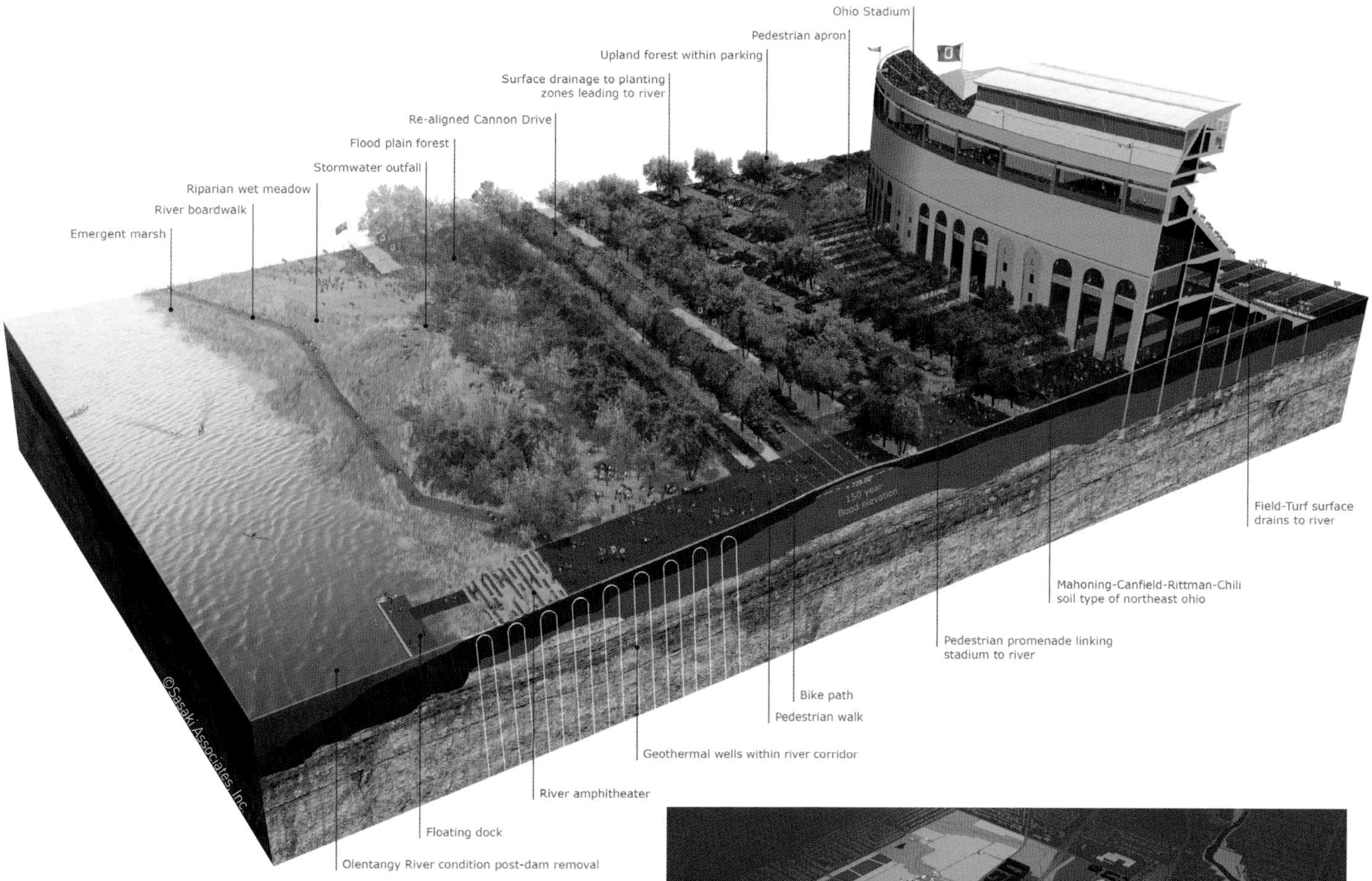

Analysis and Planning

HONOR AWARD

Governors Island Park and Public Space Master Plan

West 8 Urban Design & Landscape Architecture, P. C., New York City

Location _ New York City, New York, USA
Client _ The Trust for Governors Island
Photograph _ West 8

Wusong Riverfront: Landscape Infrastructure Pilot Project

SWA Group, Sausalito, California

Location _ Kunshan City, Jiangsu Province, China
Client _ Huaqiao Economical Development Zone Programme Building Bureau
Photograph _ Hui-Li Lee, Chih-Wei Chang, and Mandana Parvinian

©Hui-Li Lee, Chih-Wei Chang, and Mandana Parvinian

Core Area of Lotus Lake National Wetland Park Landscape Planning

Beijing Tsinghua Urban Planning & Design Institute, Beijing, China

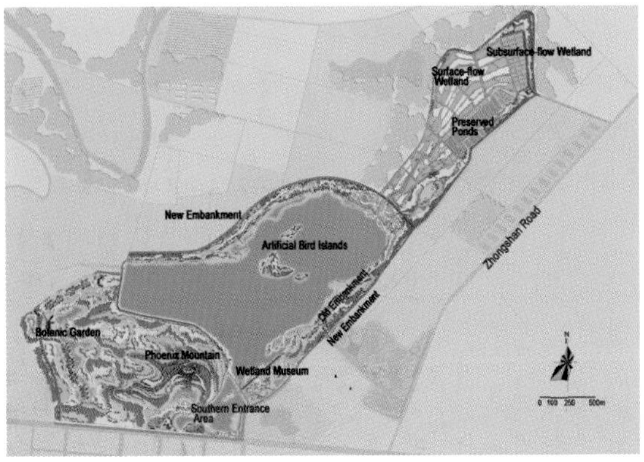

©Beijing Tsinghua Urban Planning & Design Institute

Location _Tieling City, Liaoning Province, China
Client _ Tieling City Planning Bureau
Photograph _ Beijing Tsinghua Urban Planning & Design Institute

Coastal Roulette: Planning Resilient Communities for Galveston Bay

SWA Group, Houston

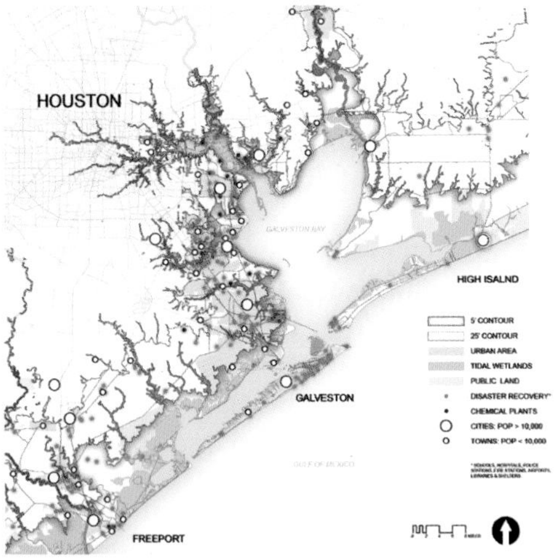

©SWA Group

Location _Galveston Bay, Texas, USA
Client _ The SSPEED Center at Rice University
Photograph _ SWA Group

Nanhu: Farm Town in the Big City

SWA Group, San Francisco

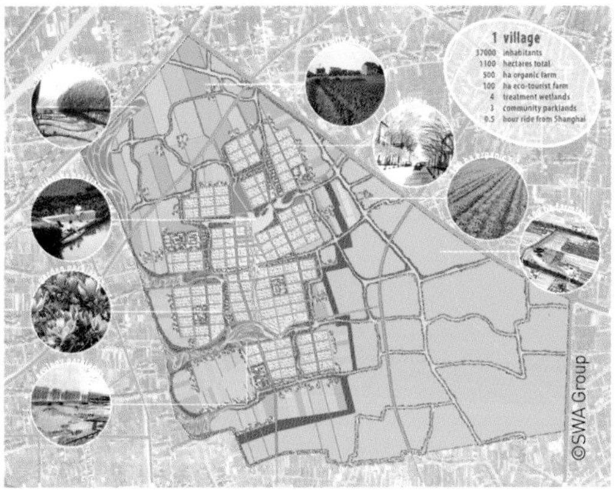

Location _Jiaxing, China
Client _ Jiaxing Alliance Development Corporation
Photograph _ SWA Group

A Strategic Master Plan for the Dead Sea

Saskai Associates Inc., Watertown, Massachusetts

Location _Dead Sea, Jordan
Client _ Jordan Development Zones Commission
Photograph _ Sasaki Associates

SW Montgomery Green Street: Connecting the West Hills to the Willamette River

Nevue Ngan Associates, Portland, Oregon

Location _ Portland, Oregon
Client _ City of Portland Environmental Services, Portland Development Commission, and Portland State University
Photograph _ Nevue Ngan Associates

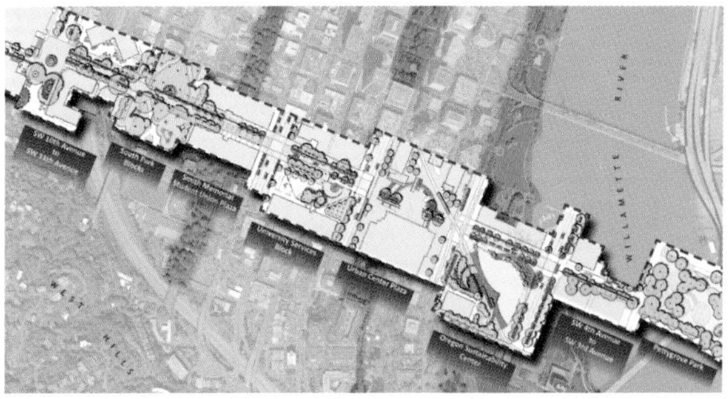

Red Mountain / Green Ribbon - The Master Plan for Red Mountain Park

WRT, Philadelphia

Location _ Birmingham, Alabama
Client _ Red Mountain Greenway and Recreational Area Commission
Photograph _ Wallace Roberts & Todd, LLC

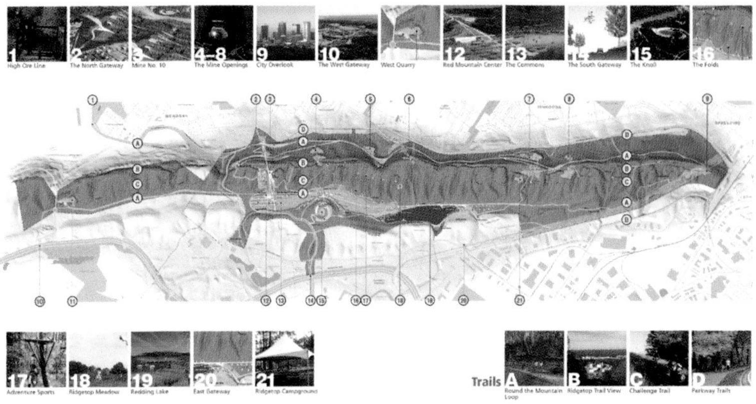

Communications

AWARD OF EXCELLENCE

Digital Drawing for Landscape Architecture: Contemporary Techniques and Tools for Digital Representation in Site Design

Bradley Cantrell and Wes Michaels

Publisher _ John Wiley & Sons, Inc.
Photograph _ Bradley Cantrell, Wes Michaels

©Bradley Cantrell, ASLA and Wes Michaels, ASLA

Communications

HONOR AWARD

Asphalt to Ecosystems: Design Ideas for Schoolyard Transformation

Sharon Gamson Danks, Bay Tree Design, Inc.

©2010 by Sharon Gamson Danks, Asphalt to Ecosystems

Publisher _ New Village Press
Photograph _ 2010 by Sharon Gamson Danks, Asphalt to Ecosystems: Design Ideas for Schoolyard Transformation

Landscape Infrastructure: Case Studies by SWA

SWA Group, Los Angeles

©SWA Group

Publisher _ Birkhauser
Photograph _ SWA Group

Landscape Urbanism Website and Journal

Sarah Peck

©Landscape Urbanism

Photograph _ Landscape Urbanism

What's Out There

The Cultural Landscape Foundation

©The Cultural Landscape Foundation

Photograph _ The Cultural Landscape Foundation

Research

HONOR AWARD

Arizona Department of Transportation Ironwood Tree Salvage and Saguaro Transplant Survivability Studies

Logan Simpson Design Inc. and Arizona Department of Transportation

Client _ Arizona Department of Transportation
Photograph _ Logan Simpson Design Inc.

Productive Neighborhoods: A Case Study Based Exploration of Seattle Urban Agriculture Projects

Berger Partnership, Seattle

Photograph _ Berger Partnership

Landmark Award

AWARD OF EXCELLENCE

Village of Yorkville Park

Ken Smith Landscape Architect, Landscape Architect of Record: Schwartz Smith Meyer Landscape Architects, Inc.

Location _ Toronto, Canada
Client _ City of Toronto, Department of Parks, Forestry, and Recreation
Photograph _ Peter Mauss/Esto

index

Works of Landscape Architecture

/ park

Music Park in Seville

Location _ Barrio de la Música, Seville, Spain
Size _ 32.487m^2
Landscape Design _ Costa Fierros Arquitectos
Completion _ 2011
Consult _ ela no.293

08

Almere Mandelapark

Location _ Former Mandela Park, Almere, The Netherlands
Size _ 3.3 hectares
Landscape Design _ Karres en Brands
Completion _ 2011
Consult _ ela no.292

20

South Pointe Park

Location _ Miami Beach, Florida, USA
Size _ 89,000m^2
Landscape Design _ Hargreaves Associates, Inc.
Completion _ 2011
Consult _ ela no.291

32

46

Railroad Park

Location _ Birmingham, Alabama, U.S.A.
Size _ 76,890m^2
Landscape Design _ Tom Leader Studio
Completion _ 2010
Consult _ ela no.288

62

The CityDeck

Location _ Green Bay, Wisconsin, U.S.A.
Size _ 2.5 acres
Landscape Design _ Stoss Landscape Urbanism
Completion _ 2011
Consult _ ela no.285

72

Park am Gleisdreieck

Location _ Berlin, Germany
Landscape Design _ Atelier LOIDL
Completion _ 2011
Consult _ ela no.284

Toronto Central Waterfront

Location _ Toronto, Canada
Size _ 3.5km length
Landscape Design _ West 8 urban design & landscape architecture
Completion _ 2011
Consult _ ela no.277

83

Lincoln Park

Location _ Miami Beach, U.S.A.
Size _ 10,000m^2
Landscape Design _ West 8 urban design & landscape architecture
Completion _ 2011
Consult _ ela no.276

92

Uptown Normal Circle

Location _ Normal, Illinois, U.S.A.
Landscape Design _ Hoerr Schaudt Landscape Architects
Completion _ 2010
Consult _ ela no.275

100

112

Gardens by the Bay

Location _ Singapore
Size _ 54 Hectares
Landscape Design _ Grant Associates
Completion _ 2012
Consult _ ela no.293

124

Side Effect

Location _ Bat Yam, Israel
Size _ 2,000m^2
Landscape Design _ Amir Lotan
Completion _ 2010
Consult _ ela no.287

136

Sensational Garden

Location _ Frosinone, Italy
Landscape Design _ Nabito Architects and Partners
Completion _ 2011
Consult _ ela no.285

index

Urban Redevelopment of the Plaza del Milenio

Location _ Valladolid, Spain

Size _ 2.5 Hectares

Landscape Design _ EXP ARCHITECTES and DAD ARQUITECTURA

Completion _ 2011

Consult _ ela no.286

148

Erie Street Plaza

Location _ Milwaukee, Wisconsin, USA

Size _ 13,000sf (0.25 acres)

Landscape Design _ Stoss Landscape Urbanism

Completion _ 2010

Consult _ ela no.285

160

168

MediaCityUK Exterior Spaces

Location _ Salford, England

Landscape Design _ Gillespies

Completion _ 2011

Consult _ ela no.281

178

Plaza Ricard Viñes

Location _ Lleida, Spain

Size _ 9,200m2

Landscape Design _ Benedetta Tagliabue

Completion _ 2010

Consult _ ela no.276

/ public space

Burbank Water and Power Magnolia Power Plant Campus

Location _ Burbank, California, U.S.A.

Size _ 2.8 acres

Landscape Design _ AHBE Landscape Architects

Completion _ 2011

Consult _ ela no.290

188

Gubei Pedestrian Promenade

Location _ Shanghai, China

Size _ 34 square kilometers

Landscape Design _ SWA Los Angeles Office

Completion _ 2010

Consult _ ela no.282

202

214

D-Cube City

Location _ Seoul, Korea

Size _ 25,756m^2

Landscape Design _ Oikosdesign landscape + architecture

Completion _ 2011

Consult _ ela no.292

230

Marina Bay Sands Integrated Resort

Location _ Singapore

Size _ 40 acres

Landscape Design _ PWP Landscape Architecture

Completion _ 2011

Consult _ ela no.287

2012 ASLA Professional Awards

Qunli Stormwater Park

Location _ Haerbin City, Heilongjiang Province, China
Landscape Design _ Turenscape and Peking University
Awards _ 2012 ASLA Professional Awards (General Design-AWARD OF EXCELLENCE)
Consult _ ela no.294

Canada's Sugar Beach

Location _Montreal, Toronto, Canada
Landscape Design _ Claude Cormier + Associés Inc.
Awards _ 2012 ASLA Professional Awards (General Design-HONOR AWARD)
Consult _ ela no.294

Lafayette Greens

Location _ Detroit, Michigan, U.S.A.
Landscape Design _ Kenneth Weikal Landscape Architecture
Awards _ 2012 ASLA Professional Awards(General Design-HONOR AWARD)
Consult _ ela no.294

Quarry Garden in Shanghai Botanical Garden

Location _ Shanghai, China
Landscape Design _ THUPDI and Tsinghua University
Awards _ 2012 ASLA Professional Awards (General Design-HONOR AWARD)
Consult _ ela no.294

Arizona State University Polytechnic Campusn

Location _ Mesa, Arizona, U.S.A.
Landscape Design _ Ten Eyck Landscape Architects, Inc.
Awards _ 2012 ASLA Professional Awards(General Design-HONOR AWARD)
Consult _ ela no.294

200 5th Avenue

Location _ New York City, U.S.A.
Landscape Design _ Landworks Studio, Inc.
Awards _ 2012 ASLA Professional Awards(General Design-HONOR AWARD)
Consult _ ela no.294

index

/ general design

Powell Street Promenade

Location _ San Francisco, California, U.S.A.
Landscape Design _ Hood Design
Awards _ 2012 ASLA Professional Awards(General Design-HONOR AWARD)
Consult _ ela no.294

Tudela-Culip (Club Med) Restoration Project

Location _ Cadaqués, Catalonia, Spain
Landscape Design _ EMF Landscape Architecture and Ardévols Associates Consultants
Awards _ 2012 ASLA Professional Awards(General Design-HONOR AWARD)
Consult _ ela no.294

Shangri La Botanical Garden

Location _ Orange, Texas, U.S.A.
Landscape Design _ Jeffrey Carbo Landscape Architects
Awards _ 2012 ASLA Professional Awards(General Design-HONOR AWARD)
Consult _ ela no.294

Winnipeg Skating Shelters

Location _ Winnipeg, Manitoba, Canada
Landscape Design _ Patkau Architects, Inc.
Awards _ 2012 ASLA Professional Awards(General Design-HONOR AWARD)
Consult _ ela no.294

National 9/11 Memorial

Location _ New York City, U.S.A.
Landscape Design _ PWP Landscape Architecture
Awards _ 2012 ASLA Professional Awards(General Design-HONOR AWARD)
Consult _ ela no.294

Sunnylands Center & Gardens

Location _ Rancho Mirage, California, U.S.A
Landscape Design _ The Office of James Burnett
Awards _ 2012 ASLA Professional Awards(General Design-HONOR AWARD)
Consult _ ela no.294

2012 ASLA Professional Awards

/ residential design

Drs. Julian and Raye Richardson Apartments

Location _ San Francisco, U.S.A.
Landscape Design _ Andrea Cochran Landscape Architecture
Awards _ 2012 ASLA Professional Awards(Residential Design-AWARD OF EXCELLENCE)
Consult _ ela no.294

Quaker Smith Point Residence

Location _ Shelburne, Vermont, U.S.A
Landscape Design _ H. Keith Wagner Partnership
Awards _ 2012 ASLA Professional Awards(Residential Design-HONOR AWARD)
Consult _ ela no.294

Quattro by Sansiri

Location _ Bangkok, Thailand
Landscape Design _ TROP Company Limited
Awards _ 2012 ASLA Professional Awards(Residential Design-HONOR AWARD)
Consult _ ela no.294

New Century Garden: A Garden of Water and Light

Location _ Palm Springs, California, U.S.A.
Landscape Design _ Steve Martino and Associates
Awards _ 2012 ASLA Professional Awards(Residential Design-HONOR AWARD)
Consult _ ela no.294

index

Malinalco Private Residence

Location _Malinalco, Mexico
Landscape Design _ Grupo De Diseño Urbano
Awards _ 2012 ASLA Professional Awards(Residential Design-HONOR AWARD)
Consult _ ela no.294

Maple Hill Residence

Location _ Westwood, Massachusetts, U.S.A.
Landscape Design _ Stephen Stimson Associates Landscape Architects
Awards _ 2012 ASLA Professional Awards(Residential Design-HONOR AWARD)
Consult _ ela no.294

Reordering Old Quarry

Location _ Guilford, Connecticut, U.S.A
Landscape Design _ Reed Hilderbrand LLC
Awards _ 2012 ASLA Professional Awards(Residential Design-HONOR AWARD)
Consult _ ela no.294

Urban Spring

Location _ San Francisco, U.S.A
Landscape Design _ Bionic
Awards _ 2012 ASLA Professional Awards(Residential Design-HONOR AWARD)
Consult _ ela no.294

What would she like to watch?

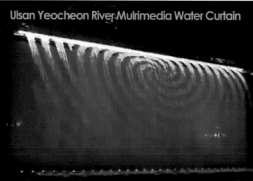

2012 YEOSU EXPO Big-O Fountain

[The-O] Fountain

Size : Diameter 35m, Height 47m

Type : Moving Water Jet, Water Screen, Mist (3kinds)

Number of Nozzles : 752pieces

Ordering : The Organizing Committee for EXPO
2012 YEOSU Korea

Design Creation·Production : ECA2

Construction Design·Manufactures·Construction·Water Performance : Plus Fountain Co., Ltd.

[Sea Fountain]

Size : Length 120m, 3line

Type : Mini-shooter, Hyper-shooter, Explosion, Mist, Fan Oarsman (5kinds)

Ordering : The Organizing Committee for EXPO
2012 YEOSU Korea

Manufactures : Hyundai Engineering & Construction (WET)

Construction Design·Construction : Plus Fountain Co., Ltd.

[Process of Works]

- ·2011.5 Design work started.
- ·2011.9 Construction work started.
- ·2012.2 Construction work completed.
- ·Total labor : 6,750 persons per year.

(Just for onsite workers for fountain construction work excluding The-O structure, floating platform and other works)

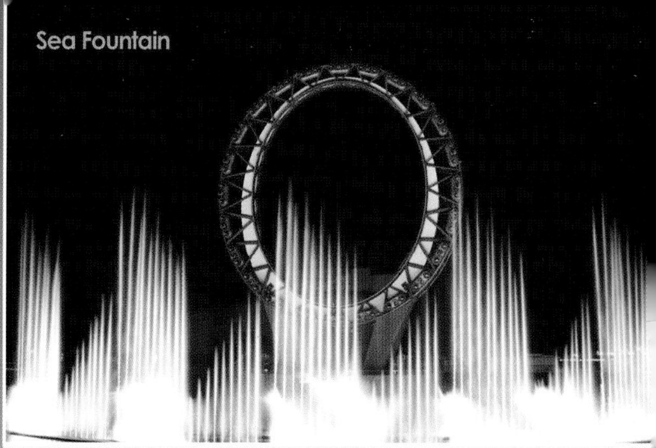

Sea Fountain

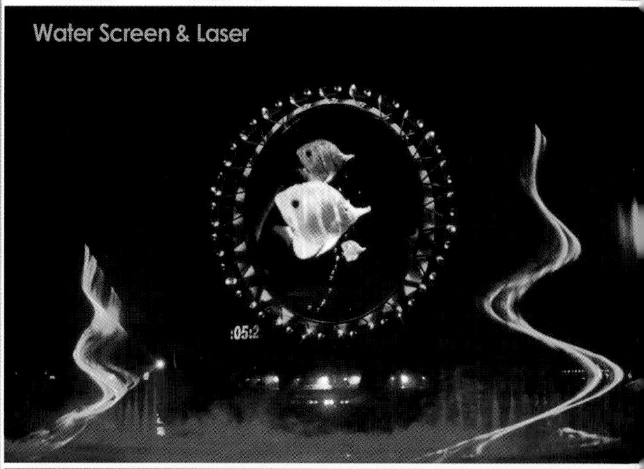

Water Screen & Laser

Mist

Multi Vector Jet 1

Multi Vector Jet 2

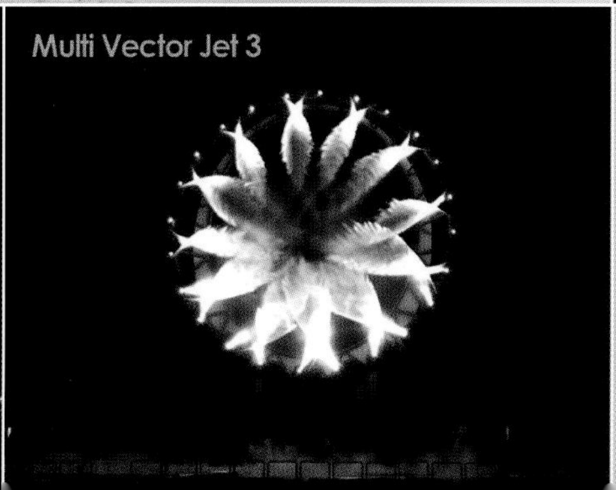

Multi Vector Jet 3

plus fountain design & construction
PLUS FOUNTAIN CO.,LTD

Music Fountain, Floor Fountain, Water Drop, Water Curtain, Artificial Waterfall
Landscaping Plan · Design · Manufacture · Construction

Head Office | Dea-Ryong BLD, 3~6F 84-12 Seocho-Gu Seoul, Korea
T.+82-02-529-1801 F.+82-02-529-1809

R&D Center | Siheung Industrial Material Distribution Center 23-211, Siheung-Dong, Geumcheon-Gu Seoul, Korea

E-mail : plusf@chol.com | http://www.plusf.com

30

ela

Environment & Landscape Architecture
30th Anniversary